# THE LOGIC OF AUTONOMY

Autonomy is the central idea of modern practical philosophy. Understood as self-legislation, autonomy seems to require that the validity of norms depends on recognition, namely, that their addressees, being autonomous agents, recognise these norms to be valid. But how can one be bound by norms whose validity depends on their being recognised as valid by their addressees? The questions of how autonomous morality and, on this basis, the authoritative character of law can be understood, present persistent puzzles that have been widely discussed, but still await a satisfactory solution.

This book presents an analysis of the idea of autonomy as self-legislation and its consequences for law and morality. It links the idea of autonomy with the idea of the balancing of normative arguments, develops a notion of normative arguments as distinct from normative judgements and statements and explains claims to correctness and objectivity that are found in normative discourse. Thus, a 'logic of autonomy' emerges, and it is pervasive in normative reasoning. It connects theses regarding the logic of norms, the structure of balancing, human and fundamental rights, legal validity, legal interpretation, and the relations among legal systems, offering a theory of central elements of normative argumentation, a theory that is undergirded by the mutual relations that exist between and among its parts as well as through the relations that it bears to other theories. Moreover, it offers an alternative to Kantian notions of autonomy and provides solutions to problems that other theories have failed to master.

**Volume 5 in the series Law and Practical Reason**

**Volume 5 in the series Law and Practical Reason**

The intention of this series is that it should encompass monographs and collections of essays that address the fundamental issues in legal philosophy. The foci are conceptual and normative in character, not empirical. Studies addressing the idea of law as a species of practical reason are especially welcome. Recognising that there is no occasion sharply to distinguish analytic and systematic work in the field from historico-critical research, the editors also welcome studies in the history of legal philosophy. Contributions to the series, inevitably crossing disciplinary lines, will be of interest to students and professionals in moral, political, and legal philosophy.



**Volume 1**: The Normative Claim of Law
*Stefano Bertea*

**Volume 2**: Community and Collective Rights: A Theoretical Framework for Rights held by Groups
*Dwight Newman*

**Volume 3**: New Essays on the Normativity of Law
*Edited by Stefano Bertea and George Pavlakos*

**Volume 4**: Hannah Arendt and the Law
*Edited by Marco Goldoni and Christopher McCorkindale*

# The Logic of Autonomy

## Law, Morality and Autonomous Reasoning

Jan-R Sieckmann

·HART·
PUBLISHING

OXFORD AND PORTLAND, OREGON
2012

Published in the United Kingdom by Hart Publishing Ltd
16C Worcester Place, Oxford, OX1 2JW
Telephone: +44 (0)1865 517530
Fax: +44 (0)1865 510710
E-mail: mail@hartpub.co.uk
Website: http://www.hartpub.co.uk

Published in North America (US and Canada) by
Hart Publishing
c/o International Specialized Book Services
920 NE 58th Avenue, Suite 300
Portland, OR 97213-3786
USA
Tel: +1 503 287 3093 or toll-free: (1) 800 944 6190
Fax: +1 503 280 8832
E-mail: orders@isbs.com
Website: http://www.isbs.com



British Library Cataloguing in Publication Data
Data Available

ISBN: 978-1-84946-346-1

Typeset by Hope Services Ltd, Abingdon
Printed and bound in Great Britain by
Lightning Source UK Ltd

To Julia and Lisandro

# *Preface*

The core idea of this book is to link the notion of autonomy with both norm theory and the method of balancing. In this respect the book is, I believe, distinct from other accounts of autonomy in the literature. It draws on ideas that have been developed quite apart from the notion of autonomy, but stem from an analysis of the logical distinction between rules and principles and of the method of balancing.

The distinction between rules and principles, introduced by Ronald Dworkin, has been given a great deal of attention but precious little support. Indeed, the terminology of rules and principles bears no clear relation to the issue at stake, namely, that the norms figuring as arguments in the course of balancing conflicting norms must have logical properties that differ from those of the norms that result from this balancing. This point, however, is crucial. It is made here by distinguishing normative arguments, judgements and statements, where normative arguments are understood not as statements of norms or – more precisely – of their validity but as requirements to the effect that a particular norm be recognised as definitively valid.

The second element is the analysis of the balancing of normative arguments. In this respect, a main line of enquiry is whether and to what extent balancing presents a method of rational justification. Authors who take up balancing usually try to show how it can provide objectively correct results or to show at the very least that balancing offers the best approach to normative justification. What happens, however, if one focuses on the other side of balancing, its indeterminacy? Recognising the indeterminacy of balancing carries with it the implication that the judgement resulting from balancing cannot be derived from pre-established premises, but includes an element of individual choice.

From the logical structure of normative arguments and the indeterminacy of balancing there emerges the notion of autonomy in the true sense of self-legislation: the normative judgement resulting from balancing is free in the sense that one might just as well have chosen another result, but the logical structure of the prevailing argument, being a requirement of the validity of the resulting norm, means that one must always present one's judgement as obligatory, for it is required by what one deems to be the stronger argument.

This notion of autonomy is analysed here with an eye to its philosophical foundations as well as to its application in various fields of legal philosophy and legal theory, in particular, the theory of rights, legal validity, legal interpretation, and the relations that hold between and among legal systems. Thus, a coherent account of law within the framework of autonomous morality emerges, and this lends support, in turn, to the distinctions between normative arguments, judgements, and statements on which the notion of autonomy rests.

The ideas presented in this book have been developed in various contexts and on various occasions, and I am indebted to a number of colleagues who have helped me to refine my ideas. I extend special thanks to Georgios Pavlakos, who not only accepted this book for publication in his series 'Law and Practical Reason' but also made substantive comments on its content. Stanley L Paulson undertook the task of monitoring my English, and he also offered important substantive suggestions. I profited, too, on various occasions, from the criticism of Robert Alexy, Jaap Hage, Nils Jansen, Daniel Oliver Lalana and Peng-Hsiang Wang, and from discussions in Robert Alexy's seminar for doctoral students at the University of Kiel, as well as from Eugenio Bulygin's Seminar for Logic and Philosophy of Law at the University of Buenos Aires.

Jan-R Sieckmann
Buenos Aires, January 2012

# *Contents*

# 1

# *The Idea of Autonomy*

AUTONOMY IS THE central idea of modern practical philosophy. Taken literally, it means self-legislation,[1] that is, establishing the validity of a norm by the addressees' own normative decisions. Thus, autonomous agents determine for themselves which norm is valid for them. Nevertheless, the idea of autonomy as self-legislation encounters serious problems.

First, autonomy seems to have a paradoxical structure.[2] Autonomy as self-legislation seems to require that the validity of norms depends on recognition, namely, that their addressees, being autonomous agents, recognise these norms to be valid. On the other hand, norms are meant to be binding on their addressees. But how can one be bound by norms whose validity depends on their being recognised as valid by their addressees? If, by contrast, norms are valid independently of individual judgement, how can one claim that individuals are autonomous? If they do not determine which norms are valid, they are not self-legislating.

A second problem is the relation of autonomy to authority, in particular, the authority of law. If the validity of norms depends on their being recognised as valid by their addressees and, thus, on consent, how is an authoritative determination possible? The tension between autonomy and authority casts into doubt the idea of law as a binding normative system. If everyone decides on his or her own as to which norm is valid, there is no room left for the idea of binding norms.[3]

These problems are well known but no satisfactory solution to them has been found. We still await an adequate conception of autonomy along with a sufficient understanding of the structure of autonomous reasoning as well as the rudiments of law and morality that follow from this structure. In this chapter, I will first present the problems of autonomy and authority, and then outline the solution to these problems that I pursue further in the following chapters.

[1] On the interpretation of autonomy as self-legislation, see Bittner (1983: 120); Reath (2006: 92 ff ). On autonomy in general, see Kaufmann (1996); Schneewind (1998).

[2] See Wood (2008: 109 f); Reath (2006: 93); Baumann (2001: 11); Bittner (1983: 118 ff); Wolff (1973: 180 f).

[3] One might try to find a solution to this problem in the idea of political autonomy, that is, autonomy that is exercised collectively in order to establish commonly binding norms. This means to introduce procedures whose result does not depend on each individual's consent. Thus, however, a conflict arises between individual and collective autonomy, and a justification is required why autonomous individuals may be subject to collective decisions.

## 1.1 THE PARADOX OF AUTONOMY

The dilemma posed by the idea of autonomy is this. Self-legislation implies that the validity[4] of a norm depends on the choice of the party addresseed by the norm in rendering it valid. This choice must, of course, be reasonable. That is, it must comply with requirements of rational decision-making.[5] But it cannot follow from already existing norms, as determined by morality or practical reason. If, however, a norm is valid only owing to the choice of its addressee, one might well say that it cannot be binding on him and hence cannot be valid in a normative sense. The paradox of autonomy stems, then, from the requirement that, on the one hand, autonomous decision must be self-determined and therefore cannot follow from already existing norms but, on the other hand, is meant to establish a valid norm and must therefore presuppose that there are normative reasons as to why the norm in question ought to be regarded as valid and, hence, be binding on its addressees. Thus, autonomous decisions cannot be completely free; they must be normatively bound. The first requirement makes validity depend on individual acceptance, whilst the second requirement implies that the validity of norms is in some sense independent of the acceptance of their addressees. How can one escape from the horns of this dilemma?

It seems that philosophical discussion has not yet found a plausible solution[6] and is concerned, rather, with other phenomena that are related to but distinct from autonomy as self-legislation.

A common interpretation of autonomy defines it as the capability to recognise the moral law and to act according to it, a conception attributed to Kant.[7] Thus,

[4] Validity here means that a norm ought actually to be applied and followed, that is, normative validity, not formal or empirical validity in the sense that certain criteria for membership in a system of norms are met.

[5] Thus, reasonableness is understood here as composed of autonomy and rationality. Autonomy consists in making choices bound but not determined by normative arguments. Rationality consists in complying with requirements necessary to pursue a certain end. Practical rationality means, accordingly, to comply with the necessary requirements of the justification of norms or normative decisions. Reasonableness consists in the combination of autonomous choice and practical rationality. This interpretation of reasonableness and rationality contrasts, for example, with that of Rawls (1993: 48). In particular, Rawls defines reasonableness as a virtue of persons, and attributes a moral content to it, defining it as the readiness to propose principles or standards as fair terms of cooperation, and the willingness to abide to them. Rationality is understood as means-end rationality. By contrast, reasonableness and rationality are regarded here, in the first place, as properties of actions, which does not exclude defining corresponding personal virtues of those who perform such actions. Although rationality is understood here as means-end rationality, an essential feature of practical rationality is the end of justifying norms, normative statements or normative decisions. Thus, it is not limited to empirical arguments. Reasonableness does not have a specific moral content but, as the combination of autonomous choice and practical rationality, has a formal character. For another interpretation of reasonableness and rationality, see Aarnio (1987). However, a closer analysis of these conceptions is beyond the scope of the present study.

[6] In spite of various suggestions to resolve this problem, see, eg, Paton (1958: 182 f); Beck (1960: 123).

[7] See Kant (1996a: 4:428, 431, 432, 440, 461); (1996b: 5:31). See also Wildt (1982: 173); Baumann (2001: 154).

one retains the idea of the objective validity of moral norms.[8] This, however, does not conform to the idea of autonomy as self-legislation, for it presupposes the existence of a moral law that is valid independently of and prior to its being recognised or accepted by autonomous agents. If one endorses the notion that norms are valid not because individuals accept them as valid but because some predetermined criterion is at work, one ends up with a theory that undermines individual autonomy.

One might see autonomy in the fact that, although the rational will necessarily adopts the moral law, one must understand oneself as a rational being in order to be subject to the moral law.[9] Thus, norms do not exist in a mind-independent world, but validity is attributed to norms. The problem remains, however, how one can understand oneself to be bound by norms that count as valid only as a consequence of one's own decision. In any case, this conception of 'autonomy without choice', with the moral law as the only option to choose, presents at most a borderline case, which cannot cope with the fact that large parts of morality are concerned with reasonable choice, that is, free decision based on normative arguments and constrained by the demands of rationality.

If, by contrast, one tries to preserve autonomy by granting that the moral law or other principles binding on autonomous agents are of a formal character only and leave room for individual decision, the problem arises as to how one could regard as normatively bound such a decision. If, in particular, agents choose maxims subject to the constraint of the Categorical Imperative,[10] various maxims may pass this test. But then this criterion does not offer a reason to believe that the maxim an agent chooses is binding on him. He might just as well have chosen another maxim.

A procedural interpretation of the categorical imperative, understood as a deliberative process rather than a static criterion of validity,[11] will not resolve this problem either. Whether the deliberative process can have more than one result or is uniquely determined remains a problem. If different results are possible, it seems that none of them can be regarded as binding. If only one result is possible, there can be no autonomous choice.

Another suggestion is that an agent is free when he first chooses a maxim but is afterwards bound by this maxim.[12] This, however, would mean that further deliberation is excluded and that the first decision is authoritative. Consequently, bindingness follows from authority and not from autonomous reasoning. Moreover, according to this interpretation one would lose one's autonomy by making use of it, which is hardly credible. Nothing can prevent an autonomous agent from questioning his former decisions and making a new choice. The former decision has, as such, no bearing on the present decision.

[8] See Wood (2008: 112); Kain (2004: 257 ff).
[9] See Kant (1996a: 4:450).
[10] See Paton (1958: 183).
[11] Reath (2006: 104).
[12] Brandom (1994: 50 ff).

Since practical philosophy has not found a satisfactory answer to the paradox of autonomy, some authors have suggested that the idea of individual autonomy is a mere metaphor[13] and that the notion of autonomy makes sense only if understood as political autonomy.[14] Accordingly, the discussion of autonomy is often not concerned with self-legislation[15] but with self-determination,[16] with personal autonomy,[17] with commanding oneself to do what one thinks it would be a good idea to do,[18] the capability to opt out of membership in the moral community or to forbear from following the moral law,[19] or, finally, with the problem of free will. These accounts do not, however, offer us an understanding of the idea of self-legislation. Rather, they must be distinguished from it.

The possibility and existence of free will is a central issue in philosophical discussions of autonomy. The issue is whether individual decisions can be free of causal or empirical determinations.[20] However, this approach does not offer a conception of individual self-legislation, but is concerned with a rather different problem, namely, that of how to relate the existence of individual decisions to empirical conceptions of the world, whether or not they are causal, and to investigations of cognitive psychology that offer empirical explanations of how the human mind works.[21]

The notion of self-legislation must also be distinguished from self-determination and from personal and from private autonomy. Self-determination may be understood negatively, as the opposite of heteronomy,[22] that is, the right to decide on one's own, and not subject to the influence of others, or positively, in the sense of personal autonomy, including, on the one hand, the capability and on the other, the right to lead a self-determined life. This includes the decision for or against being moral, but not the determination as to which norms are morally valid. Private autonomy means the competence to regulate one's own legal affairs. None of these approaches implies that the validity of norms is established by the addressees themselves; all of these approaches are at least compatible with the idea of pre-existing norms, which are valid independently of individual judgement, or, if they include choice, cannot show why the norm chosen should be regarded as binding. Therefore, these notions cannot explain the idea of autonomy as self-legislation.

By contrast, the notion of public autonomy includes self-legislation, for it concerns the determination of publicly binding norms. It faces, however, the problem of how self-legislation is possible. Without a conception of individual self-legislation, it is not clear how collective self-legislation can work. If the point of public auto-

[13] Patzig (1994: 174 ff).
[14] Baumann (2001: 11).
[15] Recent exceptions are Wood (2008: 106 ff); Reath (2006: 92 ff); Kain (2004: 257 ff). See also Nino (1991: 137 f); Nagl-Docetal (2003).
[16] Hurley (1989: 314 ff); Mele (1995).
[17] Raz (1986); Spector (1994); Mele (1995).
[18] Korsgaard (1996: 107).
[19] Tugendhat (1993: 89).
[20] See Patzig (1994: 176); Schneewind (1998: 515, 520).
[21] See also Korsgaard (1996: 96 f).
[22] See Schneewind (1998: 4).

nomy is that individuals might be subject to majority decisions or the decision of political organs, this assumption, again, needs a justification that refers to individual judgement.

A conception of normative reasoning that respects individual judgement and, indeed, presupposes individual autonomy is offered by discourse theory, which suggests that norms are valid if and only if they could find consent as the result of an ideal discourse.[23] The criterion of consensus respects individual autonomy. However, discourse theory does not present an account of how autonomous agents are bound by normative arguments within a discourse and how they can be bound by a consensus based on discourse, for nothing prevents autonomous agents from withdrawing their consent.

Moreover, the possibility of consent, that is, the fact that a norm is discursively possible,[24] is insufficient to establish normative validity in the sense that a norm actually ought to be applied and followed, for various norms might well find consent in a discourse that turn out to be incompatible. Since valid norms must include obligations to obey and incompatible obligatory norms cannot be valid at the same time, the criterion of possible consent is not an appropriate criterion of normative validity.[25]

If, on the other hand, one suggests that certain norms must necessarily find consent in an ideal discourse, one replaces individual autonomy by criteria of validity that are independent of individual normative judgement. For example, transcendental-pragmatic arguments attempt to point to necessary presuppositions of communicative practice,[26] which everyone inevitably accepts by taking part in communication, and these arguments would have us to believe that some presuppositions among them point to rights that must necessarily be recognised. As far as such rights enhance autonomous reasoning, they conform to the idea of autonomy and might be justified as presuppositions of this idea or, less ambitiously, as instruments of autonomous reasoning. However, transcendental-pragmatic arguments are incompatible with autonomous reasoning if they purport to introduce substantive restrictions on what autonomous agents can claim or accept as valid norms. An autonomous individual need not accept the rules of a communicative practice if he can suggest an alternative. Therefore, the existence of a communicative practice and its presuppositions are irrelevant to autonomous reasoning.

[23] See Habermas (1996; 1998).

[24] On this notion, see Alexy (1989a: 17, 135).

[25] In response to this problem, Alexy distinguishes between discursive correctness, which means that a norm could be the result of a procedure that conforms with the rules of discourse (1991: 399), and an absolute procedural notion of correctness, which allows for only one correct solution and which the participants of a discourse will use as a regulative idea in their arguments (1991: 412 f). This distinction does not resolve the problem, however. On the one hand, it turns out that participants cannot use the discourse-theoretical notion of correctness in their arguments. On the other hand, presupposing absolute correctness as a regulative idea is not sufficient to justify particular normative claims that participants make in their arguments.

[26] See Apel (1973); Habermas (1991); Alexy (1995).

Hence, none of the conceptions discussed above offers an adequate account of individual autonomy. By contrast, I will suggest a conception of autonomous reasoning that defines autonomy as a structure of decision-making, according to which a normative judgement is formed on the basis of the balancing of normative arguments. A central thesis of this analysis is that the structure of the balancing of normative arguments offers a solution to the outlined paradox of autonomy.

## 1.2 AUTONOMY AND AUTHORITY

The idea of autonomy presents a problem not only in itself, but also in its relation to the idea of legal authority. Authority is an essential feature of law.[27] Law is a normative order meant to be binding on its addressees, and this requires that legal norms be authoritatively established, applied and enforced. However, authoritative law restricts individual autonomy, and consequently a central issue of the philosophy of law as well as of political philosophy is the relation between the idea of autonomy and the authoritative character of law.[28]

This relation is of primary importance for the legitimacy of law, the justification of its enforcement, and the obligation to obey the law. Conceptions of law presupposing its authoritative character without justifying it in accordance with requirements of autonomous morality do not, in these respects, present a satisfactory account. At least for the officials of a legal system, in particular its courts and judges, qualifying a norm as valid law is not normatively neutral but is meant to determine that this norm be applied and followed, or at least that it would be justified to apply and follow this norm. Thus, a normative conception of law is needed, which answers questions of what is legitimate, justified or obligatory.

Such a conception cannot start with the idea of authority, but must be based on the idea of autonomy. If by the validity of a norm in the normative sense one understands that this norm ought to be applied and followed, validity can only be established according to the criterion of whether autonomous individuals must or may reasonably[29] accept this norm as valid.[30] There are no criteria of normative validity that are independent of their reasonable acceptance by autonomous

[27] Raz (1979: 30; 1986: 70 ff; 1994: 210 ff).

[28] See, eg, Raz (1979: 3). See also Iosa (2011: 31).

[29] 'Reasonable' means, in this context, in accordance with standards of practical rationality that everyone must respect in his reasoning about norms or normative statements, for example, requirements of logic, empirical correctness, and certain rules of argumentation, especially those of correct balancing. Reasonable agents are those who are able to present and consider arguments in accordance with requirements of formal rationality. It is important to note that reasonableness does not include requirements as to the content of arguments. On reasonableness as the composition of autonomy and rationality, see above 1.1.

[30] More precisely, one must distinguish two criteria, the necessity that reasonable agents accept a norm as valid, and the possibility of such an acceptance. The second criterion is one of legitimacy, not of the normative validity of a norm in the full sense that the norm ought actually to be applied and followed. Nevertheless, a legitimate acceptance of a norm by autonomous agents constitutes a form of normative validity.

beings.[31] Normative validity can be established only by some form of consent or acceptance of autonomous agents. This also holds for legal norms.

Accordingly, a basic thesis of this enquiry is that the conception of the authority of law must form part of a normative theory based on the idea of individual autonomy. A second thesis is that a normative concept of law is needed, that is, a concept according to which the legal validity of a norm implies that judges ought to or, at least, may apply and follow it. Two arguments support this thesis.

First, law as a normative system must include a claim that its norms be applied and followed. This is an internal claim of law, relative to the legal system itself. Nevertheless, it cannot be a merely system-relative claim (system S requires that A be done) but must include a non-relativised normative claim (one actually ought to do A, given certain conditions determined by system S). One might call this an absolute 'ought', by contrast to an 'ought' that merely holds according to the content of a particular system of norms.[32] In fact, the qualification as 'absolute' is superfluous, because it expresses nothing more than normativity simpliciter, as this is understood in a valid norm. By contrast, system-relative statements are not really normative, but merely state normative claims within the system to which they refer.

Secondly, a normative concept of law is needed because judges, according to their official duties, are bound to apply the valid law but also are morally responsible individuals, and an obligation to apply and follow the law must therefore at least be compatible with the moral requirements applying to them. Since judges also are autonomous individuals, these moral requirements must be developed in accordance with a theory of moral autonomy. Consequently, what is required is a concept of law based on and compatible with a theory of moral autonomy, which includes as a basic tenet that judges ought to apply the law, or at the least that they would be justified in doing so.

By contrast, positivist theories of law claim that the concept of law is not connected with an obligation to obey the law or with any other moral criteria.[33] This

[31] This thesis contradicts accounts of 'moral realism', which claim the moral validity of substantive norms independently of individual consent. If such a theory were to succeed, this would restrict the range of autonomous reasoning and hence be in conflict with the idea of individual autonomy. However, it is not clear how anyone who understands himself as an autonomous agent could accept such a theory. This is not to deny that moral realism is widely discussed and supported by quite a number of authors (see, eg, Parfit (2011); Wedgwood (2007); Moore (2004); Shafer-Landau (2003); McDowell (1998); Putnam (1995); Brink (1989)). A crucial problem of realist accounts is, however, that they interpret normative discourse as statements of existing norms, but autonomous agents cannot enter into normative discourse with such statements, because the determination of which norms are valid depends not only on their judgement but on those of other autonomous agents as well. Although realist theories might find application with regard to established moral norms, they cannot offer a complete theory of morality. Since they do not offer a solution to the problem of autonomous morality, their discussion lies beyond the scope of this analysis.

[32] See Sieckmann (1990: 100 f, 247). It could also be described as 'non-perspectival' or 'obligation simpliciter', see Stavropoulos (2009: 345). One should note, however, that an absolute 'ought', or absolute normativity, defined in this sense might hold relative to certain facts, including the existence of a legal system or of particular legislative acts. It need not be abstract, like the normativity 'simpliciter' to which Pavlakos (2010) refers.

[33] As suggested, in particular, by Hart (1958: 593; 1994: 203). This version of positivism must be distinguished from one that connects a positivist definition of law with an obligation to obey the law, see,

is the core of the 'separation thesis', stating that there is no conceptually necessary connection between law and morality.[34] However, also legal positivism – if it should prove to be relevant for law as a normative practice[35] – faces the problem of how to justify legal judgments and their enforcement against autonomous individuals, that is, taking the perspective of the norm addressee, whether there is an obligation to obey the law.[36] The author who has discussed this problem most extensively within a positivist conceptual framework is Joseph Raz. His account comes close to a normative theory of law, for he accepts the idea that law necessarily claims legitimate authority and asks what conditions are necessary to justify this claim. However, by assuming that law is authoritative by nature, not only as a system but also with regard to each legal norm, he curtails law in a way that makes it impossible to develop an adequate account of the normative claim of law. A short analysis of his theory will show why an alternative conception of law is required, one that develops a theory of law based on the idea of individual autonomy.

Raz's theory includes the social fact thesis, which states that what law is, is a matter of social fact (1979: 37), the pre-emption thesis, stating that legal norms constitute exclusionary or pre-emptive reasons (1979: 30; 1986: 59; 1999: 143, 171), and the thesis that law necessarily claims legitimate authority (1979: 33). Raz holds, however, that this claim cannot be generally justified, neither by means of what he calls the 'normal justification thesis' nor by means of additional arguments (1986: 70).

The social fact thesis forms the basis of Raz's legal positivism. Raz endorses a 'strong social thesis', also called the 'sources thesis', stating that 'a jurisprudential theory is acceptable only if its tests for identifying the content of the law and determining its existence depend exclusively on facts of human behaviour capable of being described in value-neutral terms, and applied without resort to moral argument' (1979: 39 *et seq*). The pre-emption thesis states that legal norms, being exclusionary reasons, exclude both the consideration of conflicting non-legal reasons in legal decisions (1999: 143, 171) and those first-order reasons that authoritative decisions should depend upon (1986: 59).[37] The pre-emption thesis is closely

eg, Radbruch (2001: 85), and can be called 'normative positivism'. Radbruch, however, changed his position after the Second World War (2006), for normative positivism appeared to be unsustainable with regard to the extreme injustice of the NS system. As to this change, see Paulson (2006).

[34] However, there may be conceptual connections between law and morality that do not refer to the criteria of legal validity and the obligation to obey the law. See Sieckmann (2009a: 225 ff). For example, one might hold that law necessarily needs moral justification, but that criteria of legal validity must be positive, and that there is no general moral obligation to obey the positive law.

[35] By contrast, legal positivism might claim to offer merely empirical and analytical accounts of law, without effect as to which legal judgments or decisions one should make. Such a position is of no interest to the present analysis.

[36] Although there is not a strict equivalence between these questions, in a coherent legal system the justification of applying and enforcing the law must go together with an obligation to follow the law.

[37] More cautiously Raz (1994: 214), defining the pre-emption thesis as stating that authoritative decision is a reason for performing an action that is not added to the other reasons for action but should replace at least some of them.

related to the concept of authority. Raz characterises authority as the ability to change reasons for action (1979: 16, 21), and normative or authoritative power as the ability to change a special type of reason, namely, protected reasons, which combine a reason for action with an exclusionary reason (1979: 18 *et seq*). Since, according to the third thesis, legal decisions claim to have justified authority, they constitute exclusionary reasons.

Raz denies, however, that the claim of legitimate authority made by law can be justified as a general proposition. First, he assumes that autonomy and authority are compatible because autonomous agents need not deny the existence of exclusionary reasons constituting authority (1979: 27). Hence, the ultimate criterion of justification is acceptance by autonomous agents. Secondly, the normal justification of authority is that the authoritative decision, based on the balancing of first-order reasons that apply to the addressees of this decision, is more likely to lead to a correct result than acting on the basis of one's own judgement respecting the balance of first-order reasons (1986: 53; 1994: 214: the 'normal justification thesis'). Thirdly, there is no general obligation to obey the law even if it is reasonably just (1986: 70). The normal justification of authority falls short of the claim to authority that law makes for itself (1986: 77, 80), and justification by consent is possible but applies only to those who consent to the authority in question (1986: 99).

In sum, Raz suggests that the criteria of legal validity are empirical, that law claims to exclude other sorts of reasons and is, therefore, authoritative in nature, but that this claim cannot in general be justified. Given the premises, the result is certainly correct. Starting from the social fact thesis, the conflict between individual autonomy and the claim to authority of law can only be resolved by denying a general obligation to apply and follow the law.

From the point of view of someone who accepts the obligation to apply and follow the law, however, the result is not satisfactory. Since one knows that positive law might sometimes be extremely unjust, it would not be reasonable to claim that one is always justified in applying and following the positive law. And since the primary duty of a judge is to apply and follow the law, it appears to be impossible that an autonomous agent could reasonably accept the duties of a judge if the law were only positive law qua social fact. Hence, judges either have to pretend that they accept the authority of law although in fact they do not, and they will not apply the law where it appears to be too unjust. Or they will have to be ready to resign if it should prove to be the case that they must reject the application of an unjust law for moral reasons. However, the second option confronts the problem that it would be immoral to leave a position where it is possible, retaining the position, to speak to and correct an unjust state of affairs. Thus, according to a positivist conception of law, judges either have to be insincere with regard to their readiness to apply the law or they are compelled to act in a morally irresponsible way by resigning where they could have done something that morality or justice requires. A positivist conception of law is in no way acceptable if one assumes that judges are to be morally responsible, just, and reasonable.

## 1.3 THE LOGIC OF AUTONOMY

The central issue of the following analysis is the justification of norms based on the idea of autonomy. Such a justification requires autonomous reasoning, that is, a reasoning by autonomous agents that results in determinations as to which norm is definitively valid and, hence, binding on these agents. Autonomous reasoning starts with agents making interest-based normative claims and forming normative judgements as to which norm ought to be accepted as valid regarding these claims. It recognises the right of each autonomous agent to present normative claims and judgements, but acknowledges also that no one can determine that this or that norm is definitively binding on other agents by means of his individual normative judgement.[38] Definitively binding norms can only be determined by normative statements that take into account the diverse judgements of autonomous agents (interdependence thesis), which requires a process of intersubjective reflection directed to the norm that ought to be regarded as binding, in particular in cases of reasonable disagreement among autonomous agents. Thus, normative statements must be based on more than individual normative judgements. On the other hand, autonomous reasoning implies that no norm can regarded as definitively valid independently of the normative claims or judgements of autonomous agents.

For example, in the case of offensive speech, interests in the protection of personal honour and interests in making such speech compete. Agents will make normative claims based on these interests, such as the claim that offensive speech be forbidden, or that any speech, even offensive speech, be permitted. The conflict between such claims requires balancing, on the basis of which agents will form normative judgements. These judgements will give priority to one of the competing claims, although it is often to be understood conditionally, for example, that every form of speech, even insulting forms, be permitted as long as it has a legitimate cause and does not merely aim at humiliating someone. However, different agents may offer differing normative judgements, and none of them can claim to determine the normative situation on his or her own. Thus, a second-order balancing is required, including an intersubjective reflection on the question of which norm ought to be accepted as definitively valid in the field of competing normative claims and judgements. Such intersubjective reflection might yield a common acceptance of a particular norm as definitively valid. If it does, one can claim this norm to be objectively justified and, in the event that a commonly binding norm is required, as objectively binding on its addressees.

The starting point of autonomous reasoning is interest-based claims, which constitute normative arguments requiring that a certain norm be accepted as

[38] One might say that, at this stage of autonomous reasoning, statements of definitive validity must be agent-relative. Individual agents cannot make a non-relative statement of definitive validity based on their judgement alone, but can only state validity according to their individual normative view. See 2.2.4, 4.3.2, 6.2.

definitively valid. Its core consists in the balancing of normative arguments,[39] a process that results in individual normative judgements and eventually, if a process of intersubjective reflection yields such a result, in normative statements of definitively binding norms. The peculiar structure of normative arguments and of their balancing by autonomous agents determines the structure of autonomous reasoning or, in short, the 'logic of autonomy'.[40] It makes it possible to understand the concept of autonomy as self-legislation.

### 1.3.1 How Not to Understand Autonomy

In order to develop this idea, one must put aside certain well-known philosophical discussions. The problem with the idea of autonomy as self-legislation is how one can be bound by a norm whose validity depends on one's own judgement. If one is in a position to decide[41] which norm is valid, this norm obviously cannot be binding on one's decision. And since one is free to change one's normative view, one also cannot be bound by a previous decision to regard a certain norm as valid. The dichotomy of choice or bindingness seems to be inescapable as long as we think of the validity of norms as something like the objective existence of these norms. Either a norm exists objectively, that is, independently of its recognition by the norm's addressees, in which case there is no autonomy, or it does not, in which case it cannot be binding on those whom it addresses. Is there any alternative to this dichotomy?

If we are going to be in a position to find such an alternative, certain current assumptions must be avoided.

(1) We must not presuppose that substantive moral norms exist independently of their recognition by autonomous agents. Accordingly, we must avoid a commitment to moral realism at the level of normative argumentation.[42]

Autonomous reasoning grants the validity of norms independently of individual consent only in so far as they constitute a framework for moral reasoning. This includes, formally, demands of practical rationality. Such requirements are, for

[39] This corresponds to the idea of the balancing of principles, to be found, in particular, in Dworkin (1978: 22 ff) and Alexy (2002a: 47 ff). See Sieckmann (1990: 52 ff). However, the distinction between rules and principles on which it is based seems to be artificial with regard to the diverse uses and connotations of these terms, and without any clear relation to the characteristics of normative arguments that figure as reasons in balancing. See also Sieckmann (2010a). The following analysis will distinguish between normative arguments, judgements and statements, leaving aside the discussion of rules and principles.

[40] Logic is used here in a wide sense, including structural analysis of arguments and formal structures of argumentative procedures. Developing a formal logic for normative argumentation is a different issue. The purpose of this investigation is the analysis of formal structures of normative argumentation.

[41] The terms 'autonomous judgement' and 'autonomous decision' are used synonymously here. Autonomous judgement includes an element of choice or decision because it is not determined by given criteria, and autonomous decision includes an element of judgement because it is a decision as to which norm is justified as morally valid.

[42] This does not exclude realism in the sense that socially or institutionally established norms exist as social facts. See Searle (1995). But this form of realism has no direct relevance for normative argumentation.

example, to provide a justification for normative claims, to treat like cases alike, or to strive for the fulfilment of normative requirements to as great an extent as possible. And this includes, substantively, normative arguments based on legitimate claims of autonomous agents. Such arguments are already valid and hence binding on other agents, though only as an argument, for an autonomous agent has made this claim. Other agents must accept such a claim as a valid argument, which must be balanced against competing arguments.

Beyond requirements of rationality and normative argument, definitive norms may be claimed to be binding if, as the result of collective autonomous reasoning, the claim in question is backed by a reasonable convergence of autonomous agents, and in addition, a commonly binding norm is required.[43] However, the validity of such norms depends on the acceptance of autonomous agents, and this contradicts moral realism.

(2) We must reject the idea that normative arguments for a particular norm imply claims respecting the moral correctness of this norm in a cognitive sense.

Autonomous agents must put forward normative arguments as to which norm ought to be regarded as valid, but they cannot individually establish norms that are binding on other agents. Therefore, they cannot claim, on their own, to know what is morally right.[44] On the other hand, they need not justify their interest-based claims and corresponding normative arguments on cognitive grounds. Rather, autonomy includes the normative competence to put forward such arguments, thus creating the obligation of other agents to give due respect to these arguments in their reasoning.

(3) We must avoid a descriptive as well as a prescriptive interpretation of norm-sentences used as normative arguments.[45]

According to a descriptive interpretation, norm-sentences express normative statements or propositions. If such statements are truely normative, and not merely statements of empirical facts regarding a particular norm,[46] they include a description of a norm (N) and an ascription of validity to this norm, claiming that

[43] Sieckmann (2007a). See 4.3.3, 6.4.

[44] 'Morally right' in an objective sense of what every reasonable agent must recognise. Therefore, autonomous reasoning does not, at the level of arguments, allow for claims of correctness as they are included in assertions, which, by contrast, Robert Alexy regards as necessary. On the correction thesis, see Alexy (1989b: 214 ff); (1998b: 209 ff). See also my critique (2007b: 189 ff) of his position and Alexy's reply (2007b: 347 ff). The relation between cognitive claims and procedural justification is also discussed in Nino (1996: 115), who stresses the incompatibility of cognitive claims and procedural justification, but uses this as an argument against discourse theory. Rawls (1985: 223), suggests a principle of epistemic abstinence, but only for political theory. Against this principle Raz (1994: 61 ff).

[45] Norm theories are usually divided into descriptive and prescriptive conceptions of norms. See Stuhlmann-Laeisz (1983: 23); Alchourrón and Bulygin (1971: 121); v. Wright (1963: 132). This distinction is also made in terms of constatutive and regulative speech, see Kamp (2001: 19).

[46] The descriptive conception of norm-sentences is ambiguous. One interpretation, which is at stake here, refers to norm-sentences that describe normatively valid norms. Other interpretations would have us understand normative propositions as descriptive statements to the effect that a norm has been promulgated (see von Wright 1963: 132) or as statements that convey information about norms or their implications (see Alchourrón and Bulygin 1971: 121). These are descriptive statements of empirical facts, not norms. Descriptive statements about norms are of no concern in the present analysis of normative reasoning.

its normative content actually ought to be applied and followed. In this sense, normative statements imply the claim that the stated norm exists. However, autonomous agents cannot reasonably make such a claim in their arguments, for they cannot presuppose the existence of a norm apart from the normative views of other autonomous agents. In their arguments, they can only make claims as to which norm *ought to be accepted* as valid.[47]

On the other hand, we must also avoid a prescriptive interpretation of norm-sentences used as normative arguments, because autonomous agents are not in a position to set prescriptions addressed to other autonomous agents.[48] They can make normative claims or demands on other agents. However, the extent to which such claims are to be accepted as definitively valid norms, that is, ought actually to be applied and followed, depends not on the judgement of one agent alone but can only be determined on the basis of the normative judgements of all autonomous agents involved.

In short, the first step in analysing autonomous reasoning is to put aside the usual discussions of moral realism, cognitivism and the descriptive or prescriptive character of normative sentences. These discussions make little sense without a sufficient understanding of the structure of normative justification. What is required, instead, is an analysis of what happens when autonomous agents introduce normative arguments in an attempt to establish norms as valid and binding.[49]

### 1.3.2 Structure of Autonomous Reasoning

The core of autonomous reasoning consists in the balancing of normative arguments based on the claims of autonomous agents.[50] Normative arguments require a particular result from this balancing, a result presented by a normative judgement stating that a certain norm ought to be recognised as definitively valid and therefore ought actually to be applied and followed. Definitive validity means that a norm is the result of a balancing of all relevant arguments and information.

[47] Accordingly, the concept of normative arguments differs from the usual understanding of arguments as sets of premises from which a certain result is inferred. Normative arguments are practical in that they demand a certain action, in particular, the acceptance of a particular norm as definitively valid. The reason for this acceptance is that the action is required. This conception seems to be particularly adequate for a procedural conception of argumentation, where argumentation is conceived of as a type of activity and results do not follow from logical inferences but are established by acts of argumentation.

[48] On a prescriptive interpretation norms are imperatives, but imperatives do not have a proper structure to figure as arguments in a rational justification of norms, for they prescribe what is to be done and do not allow for argumentation. Again, one must note that the term 'prescriptive' is ambiguous. It is sometimes used not only for prescriptions but also for recommendations or other sorts of normative expressions. This wider sense might include normative claims or demands. However, in order to avoid confusion, it seems advisable not to use terminology that is based on an idea that conflicts with that of autonomy.

[49] One should note, however, that not every instance of normative reasoning is autonomous reasoning in this sense, for normative reasoning might include a case in which established norms are applied in a deductive manner without discussion of their validity.

[50] See Sieckmann (1992: 296; 2004: 66; 2007a: 149).

That is, it marks the transition from argumentation to the statement of an immediate action-guiding norm.[51]

The example sketched above of the conflict of offensive speech with personal honour displays four characteristics of autonomous balancing.

(1) The result of the balancing cannot be inferred from already existing norms, but must be established by autonomous judgement.

If the case were to be decided according to pre-established norms, no room would be left for autonomy. One might object that conflicts can be resolved by established rules. For example, courts might have established a rule that the right of free speech has priority over conflicting rights if the speech is an adequate contribution to the discussion of public affairs, and then the argument might be about what counts as 'adequate' in this context. However, the answer to this question has not been established by the mentioned rule, and even if it had, the rule might be questioned in a new case. Therefore, the problem remains one of balancing. Thus, autonomous reasoning is opposed to interpretive reasoning, in so far as the aim of interpretation is the determination of the existing meaning of a given norm.[52] It is also opposed to conceptions that regard the balancing of arguments as some form of calculation. If sufficient information were available to perform such a calculation, no room would be left, again, for autonomous choice. Autonomous reasoning is compatible with rules of correct balancing, but it presupposes that such rules do not determine the result of the balancing.[53] Thus, it is important to distinguish autonomous reasoning from both interpretation and calculation.

(2) Normative arguments are the result of claims that autonomous agents make based on their interests.

The scheme of such claims is that one wants a norm to be valid and therefore claims that it ought to be valid. Interest-based normative claims are legitimate and constitute normative arguments. They constitute valid normative arguments simply because an autonomous agent has made this claim. No further justification is required.[54] Validity as a normative argument implies that all other agents are obligated to give due consideration to this argument in their reasoning.[55] There are limits, however, to the validity of such arguments. Normative arguments can require only those results of the balancing that are possible. Since the results

[51] More precisely, the normative judgement stemming from the balancing includes two elements: first, that a particular norm *ought to be* definitively valid and, secondly, that the norm *is* definitively valid. The second will be called a normative statement. Such a statement complies with the demand included in the normative judgement. A problem to be discussed below is that an unqualified normative statement is not already justified on the basis of an individual normative judgement. See 4.3.2, 6.2.

[52] Autonomous reasoning does not exclude conceptions that regard interpretation as the attribution of meaning to sentences or to other linguistic entities. Such an attribution of meaning may be the result of a balancing of normative arguments. See 10.1.

[53] As to rules of correct balancing, see 5.3.

[54] Contrary to Nino (1996: 165), one need not justify one's interests in order to adduce valid normative arguments.

[55] Accordingly, autonomous reasoning implies a normative power in a Hohfeldian sense, enabling autonomous agents to create argumentative obligations for other agents. See Hohfeld (1923: 23 ff).

depend on the judgements of autonomous agents, only those results are possible that are reasonably acceptable to all other agents. Thus, a criterion of universalisability applies. In general, one cannot deny the relevance to an argument of the interests of the other autonomous agents and cannot transform an interest into a normative argument if this by virtue of its very content is directed at an unjustified interference with the interests of the other agents. For example, interests in murder, rape or robbery cannot constitute valid normative arguments that other agents have to consider in their deliberation. Thus, interest-based claims of autonomous agents constitute normative arguments only if they can count as being legitimate.

(3) Normative arguments include requirements for validity, that is, they demand that a particular norm be accepted as definitively valid.

The issue of autonomous reasoning can be understood as the question of which norm ought to be accepted as the result of the argument. Accordingly, normative arguments include requirements to the effect that a particular norm be accepted as the result of the argumentation. Thus, they include requirements that a particular norm be definitively valid. Using 'O' for the deontic operator 'ought to', '$VAL_{DEF}$' as predicate for '. . . is definitively valid', and '$N_i$' as a variable for norm individuals,[56] normative arguments include the following structure:

$$O\ VAL_{DEF}\ N_i$$

It is important that such requirements for validity not be interpreted as normative statements or propositions. For in order to count as an argument within the balancing of conflicting arguments, a normative argument must allow for the validity of conflicting arguments while retaining its argumentative force in a situation of conflict. That is, normative arguments must not only be objects of the balancing, but must also figure as reasons within the balancing.[57] This would not be possible if normative arguments had the character of statements or propositions. For normative statements demand compliance with the stated norm and, therefore, preclude the consideration of competing normative requirements.[58] A statement and the proposition included in it purport to denote a fact. If, however, it is a fact that one ought to comply with a norm, no competing norm can be recognised as valid at the same time. By contrast, requirements for validity retain their validity as arguments for a particular result even in a situation of conflict with other normative arguments.

[56] 'Norm individuals' are the objects to which the predicate of validity is applied.

[57] Therefore, normative arguments must clearly be kept apart from optimisation requirements as well as from requirements to be optimised in the sense of Alexy (2002a: 47 f and 2003: 294 ff), but also from prima facie norms, pro tanto norms, or defeasible norms. See Sieckmann (2011).

[58] This holds for direct normative statements that one ought to do something. By contrast, also indirect or meta-statements about norms can be called 'normative statements', such as, for example, that one ought to do something according to the norms of a certain system, or that a norm is valid in a certain sense. Normative statements in indirect form or of meta-character might hold true for incompatible norms, but cannot be used as normative arguments, for they do not have the normative force that normative arguments must have in order to figure as reasons precisely in those situations presenting a conflict with competing arguments. See chapter 3.

(4) The structure of requirements for validity implies that normative judgements include a claim to the normative necessity of the established result.

Accordingly, autonomous agents must make a *claim to the normative necessity* of their judgements:

> (NN) Whichever norm, stemming from a balancing of competing normative arguments, the agent states as definitively valid, he must claim that the validity of this norm is required by the stronger argument.

This claim to normative necessity is crucial to the structure of autonomy. Autonomy is defined as a structure of normative decision-making, that of forming normative judgements based on the balancing of normative arguments. The structure of this balancing can explain both aspects of autonomous judgement: to choose freely a norm and at the same time being bound in one's decision. Therefore, this judgement can be understood as an act of self-legislation.

On the one hand, an essential feature of the balancing of normative arguments is that the priority of one argument over the others cannot be deduced from objective criteria but requires normative judgement. Therefore, the agent could have taken a different decision. His judgement is free in this sense.

On the other hand, a norm is established as valid by this balancing. In this sense, balancing presents a form of legislation. A legislative act requires, first, attributing validity to a norm, which, secondly, must count as normative validity in the sense that the norm is to be applied and followed. Thirdly, the act must imply that the norm addressees ought to accept this norm as valid. These features of legislation follow, for a legislator cannot say that he establishes a norm as valid although anyone is free to follow it or not, and a legislator cannot claim that one ought to follow this norm although there is no reason why one ought to accept it as valid. Such expressions would fly in the face of the very purpose of legislation. Accordingly, the mark of a legislative act is the attribution of normative validity to a norm together with the claim that the norm addressees ought to accept it as valid.

Judgements based on the balancing of normative arguments include these features. They attribute definitive validity to a norm, thus claiming that one ought to accept this norm as valid and that it is to be applied and followed. The second feature follows from the pragmatic, action-guiding function of normative statements. The first feature follows from the structure of normative arguments qua requirements for validity of a certain norm. Any judgement resulting from the balancing of normative arguments, albeit free and not determined by pre-established criteria, must reflect the claim that it is required by the prevailing normative argument. Thus, whatever the judgement may be, it is bound by normative arguments requiring that this result of the balancing be chosen. Owing to this structure, autonomous judgement is not an arbitrary decision, like the choice between tea and coffee. Rather, whatever the judgement may be, it is required by the prevailing normative argument and hence must be understood as a decision required by normative reasons.

For example, if one decides that offensive speech be permitted, this is not simply because someone wants it. Rather, it follows from the principle of free speech, which is regarded the stronger argument in the balancing.

This renders the logical structure of normative arguments, being requirements for validity of a certain norm, crucial to the structure of autonomy. The structure of normatively bound decision-making is precisely what characterises the structure of autonomous morality. The conceptual requirement that a moral choice is both free and also bound by moral standards is fulfilled by the structure of balancing normative arguments. Thus, the balancing of normative arguments appears to be the essence of moral autonomy. Still, this structure is not specific to morality. Rather, it holds for all kinds of balancing normative arguments; legal judgments, too, that are based on this sort of justification are autonomous judgements, such as, for example, judicial decisions based on the balancing of legal principles, administrative decisions exercising discretion bound by legal principles, and legislation bound by constitutional principles. All these types of decision display a common structure in that they are not mere decisions, but rather judgements based on the balancing of normative arguments.

### 1.3.3 Definitions of Autonomy

We can now define the concept of autonomy more precisely. The general idea of autonomy as self-legislation can be stated as follows:

$DF_A$ 'Autonomy' means establishing the definitive validity of norms by means of the normative judgements of the norm-addressees themselves.

This idea includes individual as well as collective autonomy. On the one hand, autonomy includes the idea that autonomous agents can judge on their own what is obligatory, prohibited or permitted. On the other hand, a collective of autonomous agents can form judgements in order to establish commonly binding norms.

Individual autonomy can be defined as follows:

$DF_{AI}$ 'Individual autonomy' means establishing the definitive validity of a norm by one's own individual normative judgement.

This conception of individual autonomy faces a problem, however. Since autonomous agents cannot establish by their individual judgement alone definitive norms binding on other autonomous agents, binding norms can only be established by means of an argumentation in which all of these agents can participate, and where the interests and arguments of all are given due consideration. Nevertheless, autonomous agents can form individual normative judgements based on a balancing of all relevant arguments. Such judgements are definitively valid in the sense that they are judgements all-things-considered. No arguments remain that could, according to the view of the agent, alter the balance. Autonomy includes the idea that one is able to make such individual normative judgements.

Accordingly, one can distinguish between procedural definitive validity and substantive definitive validity. The former means that all arguments have been considered, so that autonomous agents can form individual normative judgements as to which norm they hold to be definitively valid. The latter means that a norm is definitively valid in the sense that it is actually binding on its addressees. This can be established only by means of an intersubjective, discursive process.[59]

Consequently, individual autonomy in the sense defined above must be understood as establishing the definitive validity of a norm in the procedural sense, connected with the claim that the norm should be accepted, applied and followed as the result of this procedure. This normative claim confronts, however, the autonomy of other agents. Therefore, on the issue of bindingness, individual autonomous judgements can only determine which norms the agent regards as binding on himself. This, however, should not be interpreted as saying that an autonomous agent establishes norms only for himself. Normative judgements claim to establish a norm that ought to be applied and followed by all its addressees. Limiting autonomy to establishing a norm only for oneself would not conform to the general or universal character of normative justification. If such a justification is to be valid, it cannot refer to particular individuals. A restriction of the validity of autonomously established norms can only be brought about by way of the autonomy of the other agents. Respect for their autonomy requires that the claim to bindingness made for the norms one holds to be definitively valid be limited. With respect to other agents, such a claim can be made only as holding in principle, that is to say, as a normative argument that others have to take into account.

Accordingly, if it should prove to be possible to establish definitive validity of a norm in a full or substantive sense, this can only be done by a community of autonomous agents. A norm is valid for such a community if its members regard the respective norm to be definitively valid for them. This collective dimension of autonomy may also be called 'political autonomy'.[60] One can define political autonomy as follows:

> DF$_{AP}$ 'Political autonomy' means establishing norms to be definitively valid and binding by the normative judgements of the norm-addressees themselves.

[59] The element of intersubjectivity is also emphasised by Darwall (2006), who attempts to develop morality from the 'second-person standpoint'. A similar feature of his approach is the idea that agents make claims against each other. 'A second-personal reason is one whose validity depends on presupposed authority and accountability relations between persons and, therefore, on the possibility of the reason's being addressed person-to-person' (2006: 8). However, Darwall does not distinguish between normative arguments, judgements and statements. In addition, he interprets morality in terms of conclusive reasons (2006: 26), or at least as purporting to be supremely authoritative (2006: 29). Thus, the structure of autonomous reasoning as the balancing of normative arguments is missed. Also the emphasis on the relational character of these demands obscures the fact that they are made against everyone.

[60] The correlate to 'political autonomy' seems to be 'private autonomy'. Still, private autonomy has the connotation that its object is merely the normative situation of a particular individual. By contrast, individual autonomy is concerned with collectively binding norms, not only with norms for an individual itself. Therefore, I prefer the term 'individual autonomy'.

Political autonomy in the sense defined above aims, accordingly, at establishing commonly binding norms by means of the normative judgements of the respective norm-addressees. One might conclude that autonomy as self-legislation can only be defined at the collective level. This, however, would go too far. Individual autonomy is essential for any account of autonomy, for only individual agents can put forward normative arguments and make normative judgements. The crucial problem is how to connect the individual and the collective level. The following analysis tries to provide a solution to this problem. It purports to reconstruct political autonomy on the basis of individual autonomous judgements.

An important point of this analysis is that autonomy is regarded as a feature of normative judgement or decision-making. A normative judgement establishes, as a result of the balancing of normative arguments, that a norm is definitively valid. Accordingly, an agent has autonomy if he is in a position to take a normative decision that is based on the balancing of normative arguments. Such a decision is bound by arguments, but not determined in its result by pre-established criteria. As a borderline case, there might only be a single relevant argument, so that the result is determined, but a decision is nevertheless required to transform the normative claim of the argument into a normative judgement. One can define the autonomy of an agent as follows:

> $DF_{AA}$ An agent has autonomy if he is in a position to take a normative decision that is bound by normative arguments.

Autonomy can also be defined as a specific *structure of decision-making*. By contrast to autonomy as a feature of an agent, it is not a property of someone, but a characteristic of a situation in which a normative decision is to be taken. This seems to be the most elementary sense of autonomy, abstracting from the agents involved and focussing merely on the structure of argument. This structure is characterised by the balancing of normative arguments:[61]

> $DF_{AB}$ Autonomy exists if a normative decision is to be taken by means of the balancing of normative arguments.

Again, as a borderline case, it might be the case that a single relevant argument applies. This seems, however, to be a merely theoretical possibility. In fact, practical reasoning is always concerned with competing arguments. Therefore, one can define autonomy as the balancing of normative arguments.

The notion of autonomy as the balancing of normative arguments is a formal conception of autonomy, which must be clearly distinguished from the value of

[61] This definition of autonomy does not require that normative arguments be based on individual interests. The crucial point is the balancing of normative arguments. However, if the normative arguments to be balanced are not established by interest-based claims, the conception of autonomous reasoning remains incomplete, for autonomous agents must have the right to form normative arguments based on their interests and to reject interference that is not backed by such arguments.

autonomy.[62] It must also be distinguished from autonomy in the sense of a capacity and in the sense of a right to decide autonomously.

Autonomy as a *capacity* requires that an agent be able to take autonomous decisions, that is, that he be aware that he must establish priorities among conflicting normative claims and be in a position to balance these arguments correctly. Correctness here depends on formal requirements of rationality with respect to the balancing of normative arguments, such as, for example, consistency, conclusiveness, coherence, empirical correctness, universalisability, and intersubjective reflection.[63] Accordingly, an autonomous agent is one who is able to make normative judgements that are based on the balancing of normative arguments according to formal requirements of rationality.

The *right* to autonomous decision-making includes several aspects.[64] First of all, it includes the right to form normative arguments and judgements. What is of special interest here is, however, that this right implies an obligation on the part of all autonomous agents to consider in their reasoning the normative arguments and judgements put forward by all other autonomous agents. Consequently, definitively valid norms cannot be established without regard to the normative arguments and judgements of each and every autonomous agent. Since the individual agents themselves have to decide how to comply with this demand, no autonomous agent is subject to the normative judgements of the other agents, and all have equal standing. The right not to be subject to the normative judgements of other agents casts doubt, however, on whether binding norms can be established by means of autonomous reasoning.

## 1.4 CENTRAL ISSUES IN A THEORY OF AUTONOMOUS REASONING

The idea of autonomy needs to be developed within the framework of the normative argumentation of autonomous agents, in short, autonomous reasoning. A central thesis of the following analysis is that autonomous reasoning requires a conception of argumentation that is not based exclusively on propositions and logical inferences. In this respect, it is opposed to common conceptions of argument that regard arguments as sets of premises and conclusions. Such conceptions are not adequate for autonomous reasoning. For they require presuppositions that autonomous agents must reject, in particular, premises with the structure of propositions that are used to state that certain norms exist without reference to their acceptance by other autonomous agents. This means disrespecting the autonomy of other agents and hence must be excluded in autonomous reasoning.

[62] By contrast, Hurley (1989: 328), considers autonomy a value that might conflict with other values. Although one may regard autonomy as a value, this is clearly distinct from the formal conception of autonomy as a structure of normative decision-making.

[63] As to requirements of rationality for normative justification in general, see Buchwald (1990: 250 ff ).

[64] See 4.2.3, 8.2.

In addition, propositional reasoning is not capable of adequately representing conflicts arising between normative arguments. Since propositional arguments carry a claim to truth or correctness that is incompatible with a similar claim of a conflicting argument, the conflicting argument cannot be regarded as valid if the arguments are to be presented in the form of propositions.

Autonomous reasoning deals with arguments offered by autonomous agents. Such arguments may conflict and, moreover, must be regarded as valid precisely in the situation of conflict with other arguments. The resolution of such conflicts requires the balancing of normative arguments. Autonomous reasoning requires therefore, first of all, a normative language that is capable of representing such a balancing as a method of rational justification. The central elements of this reasoning are the normative arguments put forward as reasons for particular results of the balancing, as well as the normative judgements and statements resulting from balancing. The logical structure of normative arguments determines the structure of normative justification. As a consequence, the claim to correctness made on behalf of judgements based on balancing is interpreted as a normative claim, which is only in part a cognitive claim. Another issue is the question of in which sense and in which respects normative judgements or statements can claim to be objectively valid.[65]

Applying the conception of autonomous reasoning to law and morality, the conception of rights and, in particular, of autonomy rights is of interest, supporting the idea of universal human rights and a conception of fundamental rights that provides not only procedural but also substantive restrictions on authoritative decision-making. Moreover, the conception of autonomous reasoning has consequences for the theory of the legal system in general, in particular for the theory of legal validity, legal interpretation, and the relations between legal systems.

Thus, the logic of autonomous balancing pervades normative reasoning in general. It connects theses regarding the idea of moral autonomy, the logic of norms, the structure of balancing, theories of individual rights, legal validity, legal methodology, and the theory of legal systems. All this serves as an argument of coherence in favour of the suggested conception of autonomous reasoning. It offers an analysis of central elements of normative argument that is consistent and is supported by mutual relations between and among its parts as well as through its relations to other theories. Moreover, it provides solutions to problems that other theories are not able to cope with. The elaboration of these claims is the purpose of the following chapters.

[65] Later on, the criterion of 'reasonable convergence' will be introduced in order to establish the objective validity or bindingness of norms. See 4.3.3, 6.4.

# 2

# *Normative Language*

A CENTRAL THESIS of the present analysis is that the usual interpretations of normative language do not provide for an understanding of the idea of autonomy. The two main lines in interpreting normative language are represented by the descriptive and prescriptive conceptions of norm-sentences.[1] On a descriptive interpretation, norm-sentences are taken to express existing norms. A normative expression 'Thou shall not kill' is therefore understood as a statement to the effect that there is a norm prohibiting killing. This norm is stated as valid, implying that it actually ought to be applied and followed. Since this statement is understood as descriptive in nature, the norm expressed in it is claimed to exist independently of any statement of it. However, the assumption of pre-existing norms does not provide for an autonomous construction of norms, for there is no room for autonomous choice. On a prescriptive interpretation, normative expressions are interpreted as acts of prescription, most clearly in the case of imperatives. Autonomous agents, however, are not in a position that would make it possible for them to perform acts of prescription directed to other autonomous agents, for this would fail to respect their autonomy. One should note that, once norms or competences to create norms have been established as valid and are not placed in doubt, a descriptive or prescriptive use of normative language will be possible. Still, they are not adequate for autonomous reasoning. Autonomous reasoning aims at constructing norms. In order to do this, autonomous agents must argue. They cannot, however, adduce a normative argument by making a statement designating which norm ought actually to be applied and followed or by prescribing to other autonomous agents what they ought to do. Therefore, neither descriptive nor prescriptive accounts provide a linguistic framework for autonomous reasoning.

One might then suggest that statements of norms need not be descriptive, but might instead express certain mental states or be included in performative acts, such as 'We hereby state that everyone ought to do A'. Thus, they do not state a norm that exists independently of and previous to the statement in question. Leaving aside the problems of such conceptions of non-descriptive statements,[2] however, it is not

[1] See 1.3.1.

[2] On the problems of expressivism as a semantic theory, see, eg, Schroeder (2008). The conception suggested here is not, however, semantic expressivism, for it does not regard attitudes or mental states as the meaning of normative arguments. Normative arguments include claims or demands. Making such a demand is connected with some mental state, but the meaning of the normative argument is not to

clear how such conceptions could provide a notion of a normative argument. As long as they claim that arguments have the form of statements, the point remains that adducing an argument in the form of a normative statement designating what is definitively valid would fail to respect the autonomy of other agents. To make a statement is to claim a fact. Autonomous agents cannot present their normative views as facts, for the views of other agents count as well in determining which norm is to be definitively valid. On the other hand, they must be capable of introducing normative arguments and expressing their normative views without claiming for them definitive validity. Therefore, they need a linguistic form distinct from that of statements, in order to commence a normative argument.

## 2.1 A FRAMEWORK FOR AUTONOMOUS REASONING

Consequently, a normative language is needed that is capable of giving expression to autonomous reasoning. Autonomous agents cannot adduce an argument by stating existing norms or by prescribing behaviour to other agents. What they can do is make claims as to what should be accepted as a definitively valid norm. Someone claiming a right to free speech can legitimately make this claim owing to his autonomy, thus obligating other autonomous agents to take into account this claim. On the other hand, such a claim cannot determine what is definitively required or permitted. First, the legitimate claims of other autonomous agents count as well, possibly requiring a balancing of competing claims. Secondly, the individual normative judgement that stems from this balancing cannot determine the normative situation, for the views of other autonomous agents deserve equal respect and might suggest a contrary result. Accordingly, an autonomous agent may legitimately make normative claims and form normative judgements based on the balancing of such claims, but he cannot make a definitive normative statement on his own. Statements of definitively valid norms are possible only after such norms have been established by means of an argument in which claims and judgements of all autonomous agents receive due consideration.

The idea of autonomy suggests that practical argumentation comprises normative arguments resulting from claims of autonomous agents, the balancing of competing arguments against each other, normative judgements resulting from such a balancing, and a second-order balancing – all of this yielding, then, intersubjectively reflected normative judgements. Being all-things-considered judgements, they can claim definitive validity in a procedural sense.[3] If, in addition, it turns out that certain norms actually are definitively valid and hence binding on their addressees, normative statements must be possible that are objectively valid and not merely individual judgements.

express such a state, but to express a normative content, which abstracts from any mental state involved in adducing a normative argument.

[3] See 1.3.3.

> Normative arguments are, for example, the demand of free speech or that of personal honour. In the case of offensive speech, the demands of free speech claim that such speech be permitted, and the demands to protect personal honour require that such speech be forbidden. Such demands constitute arguments that are neither imperatives nor statements of definitively valid norms. They include normative claims, that is, they require a certain result stemming from the balancing. The issue of normative argumentation is, then, first, how to get from normative arguments to a normative judgement as to which norm is definitively valid with regard to all relevant arguments. This step requires the balancing of the conflicting normative arguments, which leaves space for autonomous reasoning. Secondly, in case the first-order balancing leads to competing normative views of autonomous agents, a second-order balancing is required on the question of which norm is to be definitively valid for all agents, seen from the standpoint of their competing normative views, although still in the form of an individual normative judgement. Finally, if it turns out that reasonable agents must accept a certain norm as the result of the argument, a normative statement as to the substantive definitive validity and bindingness of this norm can be made.

Normative language must make it possible for one to express the arguments, judgements and statements that occur in autonomous reasoning. Obviously, normative arguments that are to be balanced against each other and normative judgements expressing the results of such balancing follow different logical rules. Whereas normative arguments may include incompatible requirements, at the level both of normative judgements and of normative statements, norm conflicts must be resolved if the reasoning is to be correct. This follows from the conclusive character of normative judgements and statements. They claim to conclude the argument, presenting an all-things-considered judgement or a directly action-guiding device. This does not exclude the possibility of error or of criticism of such judgements or statements. They cannot preclude the continuation of the argumentation. Their point, however, is to state something that needs no further discussion but can count as the result of an argumentation. Thus, they are, according to their content, meant to terminate the argument, and this is possible only if all conflicts of arguments have been resolved.

The applicability of different logical rules suggests, moreover, that normative arguments, on the one hand, and normative judgements and statements, on the other, differ where their logical structure is concerned. The explication of this difference requires a closer analysis of normative sentences, of different types of their use, and of the corresponding meaning of normative expressions.

## 2.2 NORMS, NORMATIVE ARGUMENTS, JUDGEMENTS AND STATEMENTS

Normative arguments, judgements and statements attribute different types of validity to certain norms. Two distinctions are implied here: first, that between norms in a semantic sense and normative expressions that attribute validity to these norms[4] and, secondly, that between the types of validity attributed by normative arguments, judgements and statements.[5]

### 2.2.1 Semantic Conception of Norms

Normative speech-acts claim that a norm is valid in some sense. For example, if someone makes a normative statement 'It is forbidden to smoke here', this does not merely formulate a norm but expresses that such a norm is actually valid. This attribution of validity again includes two elements: first, the statement of the validity of the norm in question, regarded as a semantic entity; such a statement does not follow from the norm-sentence as such, for this sentence does not state anything as to the validity of the norm; and, secondly, the claim to validity implied in using a norm-sentence to state the validity of a norm,[6] as distinct from merely mentioning it. Therefore, it is necessary to distinguish between mere norm-formulations and sentences stating the validity of norms and, in addition, between normative sentences and the speech-acts in which such sentences are used. These distinctions form the basis of the 'semantic conception of norms'.

The 'semantic conception of norms' is the view that norms are the meaning of normative sentences.[7] Normative sentences are sentences that are or can be formulated using deontic terms such as 'ought to', 'obligatory', 'forbidden', 'permitted', or by using other kinds of normative expression related to deontic sentences, such as 'has a right to', 'has the competence to'. Such sentences may be mere norm-formulations or sentences used to state the validity of a norm.

The distinction between norms in a merely semantic sense[8] and sentences ascribing validity to norms is important in two respects. First, it makes it possible for one to distinguish various types of validity, in particular, the validity of a normative argument, which may also be called 'validity in principle', and the definitive validity of the norms stemming from balancing. Thus, one needs an object to which one can attribute these types of validity. This object is the norm in the semantic sense. Secondly, the distinction above makes clear that using norm-sentences includes the ascription of validity. Norms in a merely semantic sense are of no interest to normative discourse. Normative discourse includes ascriptions of validity, and these form part of the speech-acts and the normative statements expressing their content.

What are the characteristics of normative expressions that attribute validity to a particular norm? Autonomous reasoning includes, first of all, normative

[4] See Alexy (2002a: 21 ff); Sieckmann (1990: 25 ff) on the distinction between norms and normative statements.

[5] See Sieckmann (2009a: 104 ff).

[6] This refers to the Fregean distinction between merely formulating a thought and stating that it is true. See Frege (1891: 35).

[7] See Alexy (2002a: 22); Sieckmann (1990: 25).

[8] See Sieckmann (1990: 26) as to the notion of a purely semantic conception of norms, which will be used here.

arguments to be balanced against each other, and normative judgements and statements, which state the results of such balancing. Normative judgements are speech-acts, or the content of such speech-acts, as to what ought to be the case or ought to be done. They present a direct use of a norm-sentence and attribute validity to a norm only implicitly.[9] Normative statements are explicit or implicit statements of validity of a norm. Thus, normative judgements are a type of normative statement, which attributes validity only implicitly. Since such a statement refers, according to its linguistic form, directly to a norm-sentence and does not explicitly state the validity of a norm, it can be called a direct normative statement.[10]

Accordingly, one can distinguish four types of normative speech-act relevant to autonomous reasoning:[11]

(1) normative judgements or direct normative statements, including a conclusive normative use and presenting the result of an argument;
(2) statements of the definitive validity of a norm, making explicit, for example, the attribution of validity included in normative judgements;[12]
(3) normative arguments, using norm-sentences as an argument, that is, they are meant to commence or continue an argument, which may include a balancing with counter-arguments;
(4) normative statements of validity as an argument, making explicit the claim to validity included in normative arguments. The normative claim connected with them is that the argument be taken into account in a balancing with competing arguments.

### 2.2.2 Normative Statements

Normative statements express, either directly or by implication, that a certain norm is valid. Hence, they are statements of the validity of a norm. Examples of such statements are:

(1) 'One ought not to harm anyone'.
(2) 'It is valid that one ought not to harm anyone'.
(3) 'It is a valid norm that one ought not to harm anyone'.
(4) '"One ought not to harm anybody" is a valid norm'.
(5) 'It is a fact that one ought not to harm anyone'.
(6) 'It is true that one ought not to harm anyone'.

[9] Normative judgements that present the result of a balancing are a special kind of normative judgement, requiring that a norm ought to be recognised as definitively valid. They will be called 'autonomous judgements'.

[10] See Raz (1983: 49) for a similar notion of direct normative statement.

[11] See Sieckmann (2005).

[12] More precisely, one must distinguish between statements of definitive validity in a procedural sense and in a substantive sense. See 1.3.3 and 4.3.2.3, as to the distinction between procedural and substantive definitive validity.

The first statement is a direct expression of a norm that, as it is actually used, implies the assertion of the validity of the norm expressed.[13] The direct use of a norm-sentence may be called 'direct normative statement' or 'normative judgement'.[14] It implies the claim to the validity of the norm expressed.

By contrast, the other statements explicitly attribute some kind of validity to a norm. They may be called 'statements of validity'. The difference between a direct normative statement and the statement of the validity of the norm in question is, accordingly, that the former attributes validity implicitly and the latter explicitly. Both are normative statements as well as statements of validity.

Statement (2) ascribes validity to a norm 'one ought not to harm anyone', or to a normative proposition 'that one ought not to harm anyone'.[15] Statement (3) has the same structure, but makes clear that what is meant is the validity of a norm, and not some other concept of validity. Statement (4) also has the structure of ascribing validity to a norm, but this time to a norm-sentence, not to the meaning of a norm-sentence. Although statements of the structure (2)–(4) appear to be artificial, they do not seem to cause problems.

Statements (5) and (6) seem to be less artificial, but their adequacy is controversial. Statement (5) qualifies a norm as a fact, which contradicts positions that facts must form part of the real, empirical world. Statement (6) predicates the truth of a norm, but it is controversial whether norms can be said to be true.[16] Both statements seem to be correct semantically, that is, they do not appear to be nonsense. Nevertheless, according to the semantic conception of norms one must distinguish between the norm and its validity. The norm itself is merely a meaning-content without any indication of whether the norm is valid. It would then not make sense to say that a norm is a fact, or is true. What can be said to be a fact is the validity of a norm, and what can be said to be true is the statement of the validity of a norm. If one wants to call norms a fact, or treat them as either true or false, the term 'norm' must then be understood as the fact of the validity of the respective

[13] One might object that direct normative statements in fact are imperatives or, more generally, prescriptive speech-acts, and do not have the structure of a statement. This objection is mistaken, however. First, normative statements do not have the typical structure of an imperative, which would be 'Do not harm anybody else!' or 'We hereby order that one shall not harm anybody else'. Secondly, acknowledging the prescriptive character of a statement is compatible with the logical structure of a statement. The term 'prescriptive' is ambiguous. It can refer to the action-guiding character of norms, or to the act of prescribing something. In the first sense, each definitively valid norm is prescriptive because definitive validity implies a demand to apply and follow this norm. Accordingly, statements of the definitive validity of a norm are prescriptive in this sense. This way, it would be a mistake to contrast prescriptive speech-acts and normative statements. In the second sense, a normative statement cannot be qualified as a prescription because it claims to express an existing norm and not to create one. However, this does not alter the fact that normative statements are prescriptive in the first sense, that is, because of the content of the norm stated in it as definitively valid.

[14] Abstracting from the pragmatic element of the speech-act, also the content of this act may be called a normative judgement or statement. Since the distinctive pragmatic character of speech-acts must or at least can be presented in their content, it will often be convenient to refer to the content, leaving aside the pragmatic element.

[15] A 'proposition' is what is expressed by a sentence of the structure 'that p'. No assumptions are made as to the possible reference of p.

[16] On this issue, see, eg, Holländer (1993).

norm or as a proposition that a norm (understood in the semantic sense) is valid. Such statements, semantically, are statements of facts, capable of being true or false. Still another question is whether such statements can be justified, which again depends on the concept of validity being employed.

Direct normative statements and explicit statements of the validity of the proposed norm are interchangeable and therefore pragmatically equivalent. This 'equivalence thesis' requires, however, some elaboration. It holds as far as validity is attributed without qualification or reservation, as in direct normative statements. Not every statement of validity, however, implies a direct normative statement. There are diverse notions of validity, such as, for example, definitive validity, validity as a principle or normative argument, prima facie-validity, pro tanto-validity, or validity as the membership in a normative system. Not all of them have the normative implications included in direct normative statements.

More systematically, one might understand the notion of validity in a wide sense as a device to distinguish relevant from irrelevant information, that is, information that must be taken into consideration from that which must not. In this sense, one may regard the membership of a norm in a legal system as a type of validity, without implying a claim that one ought to apply and follow this norm. By contrast, a notion of validity that is specific to norms characterises validity by the implication that the norm in question ought actually to be applied and followed. This is the characteristic of normative validity.

One must further distinguish various types of normative validity. First, normative validity in an absolute or full sense must be kept apart from restricted or relativised forms of validity. The former claims the validity of the norm in each instance to which it is applicable. The norm is stated as valid in the full range of its applicability. The latter claims validity only from a certain perspective or under certain conditions and admits that the proposed norm may prove to be invalid in some cases to which it is (according to its content) applicable. Examples of restricted or relativised validity are:

(a) pro tanto-validity in the sense that a norm is valid only from the perspective of a certain principle, abstracting from other principles that are applicable to the case, or from the perspective of a certain legal system;[17]
(b) prima facie-validity in the sense that a norm is valid only as the preliminary result of an argument, which may be changed by new information; this is opposed to definitive validity or validity 'all-things-considered';
(c) prima facie-validity in the sense that a norm is valid for normal or typical cases but may prove to be invalid in exceptional cases.

In all of these cases of restricted or relativised validity, a norm qualified as valid may prove to be invalid in some cases to which it is applicable.

[17] By contrast to mere membership in a legal system, legal validity in the sense of pro tanto-validity according to a particular legal system recognises the claim of the legal system that the norm in question is to be applied and followed.

With respect to the absolute or full type of normative validity one must further distinguish a strong and a weak form. The strong form of normative validity demands compliance with the norm precisely as the norm demands. That is to say, the norm is claimed to be immediately action-guiding. This presupposes that the norm is stated 'all-things-considered', and all conflicts with competing arguments have been removed. Therefore, one can treat the norm as designating a normative fact. One might call this 'definitive validity'.[18] The weak form of normative validity requires that the norm is to be balanced with competing arguments. Thus, the norm is regarded as a normative argument, not as an immediately action-guiding device. Still, it is regarded as valid in an absolute or full sense. For the existence of counter-arguments does not affect its validity as a normative argument. Even if the counter-argument prevails in a particular case, the overridden argument does not lose its validity as an argument for this case.

Regarding the diverse notions of validity one might doubt which is the type of validity that direct normative statements attribute. First, one can preclude the restricted or relativised forms of validity. For, since the direct normative statement does not make explicit the form of validity, one cannot determine which type of restriction or relativisation should be meant.[19] Therefore, the standard interpretation of direct normative statements must be that they attribute an absolute or full form of validity.

The most natural interpretation of direct normative statements is that they claim the validity of a norm just as it stands, without qualification or restriction. Accordingly, a statement that one ought not harm anyone implies that one ought to follow this norm whenever it is applicable. This seems to be an immediately action-guiding norm. The type of validity attributed by a direct normative statement is, then, that of strong absolute validity.

This interpretation conflicts, however, with the equal autonomy of agents, which excludes the possibility that an autonomous agent determine by his individual judgement that a norm definitively be applied and followed by other agents. Such a claim can hold only in principle, that is, as a normative claim against other agents. Therefore, normative statements of autonomous agents cannot claim validity in the simple and unqualified sense that the norm stated ought to be applied and followed by other agents. Such statements may claim definitive validity respecting the norm in question, but only validity in principle for the requirement to apply and follow this norm.

Normative statements can correctly state the definitive validity of a norm only in the sense in that its definitive validity is the result of autonomous reasoning. Consequently, they are connected with two claims: first, that the statement

[18] Sill one must distinguish definitive validity in a procedural and in a substantive sense. See 1.3.3, below 2.2 and 4.3.2.3.

[19] Of course it might be possible to interpret a direct normative statement according to its context. The issue here is, however, whether and in which way a direct normative statement can be understood as a precise and complete linguistic expression, that is, one that has a semantic content on its own.

in question is justified according to requirements of autonomous reasoning and, secondly, that the stated norm ought to be applied and followed. The second claim, however, holds only in principle or as a normative argument. Thus, one must distinguish normative statements of the results of autonomous reasoning from statements of the bindingness or objective validity of a norm.[20] A norm is objectively valid if the claim of normative validity holds, not only in principle, but definitively.

### 2.2.3 Normative Arguments

By contrast to normative judgements or statements, normative arguments merely claim that a norm ought to be accepted as definitively valid. They include *requirements of definitive validity* (reiteration thesis). This implies the claim that the norm in question is valid in principle.

> For example, respecting the issue of offensive speech, one might argue that we ought not to offend anyone's personal honour. This argument demands that one ought to accept, as the result of the argument, the conclusion that one ought definitively not to offend anyone in his or her honour and, hence, that one ought not to use offensive speech. The argument itself, however, does not state that this norm is definitively valid. It implies only that it is valid in principle, that it ought to be definitively valid, and that it has to be balanced against counter-arguments.

Accordingly, normative arguments are not directly action-guiding, at least not with respect to actions falling outside a procedure of argumentation. Their definitive normative content is restricted to a procedural demand of a correct balancing of conflicting normative arguments along with the claim that the argument in question is given adequate weight in this procedure.[21]

The definitive content of normative arguments can be made explicit by normative statements, which state, for example, that a norm N is valid in principle, and that it be given due weight in a procedure of balancing. Such statements, however, are descriptions of the content of a normative argument and must be distinguished from the normative argument that is used as a reason in a procedure of balancing. Thus, they are *meta-level normative statements*, either qualifying a norm as a valid normative argument or making explicit the normative implications of its validity. Again, although such statements are implied in putting forward a normative argument, they refer only indirectly to the content of the argument and must be distinguished from using a normative sentence to make an argument.

[20] See 4.3.2.3.

[21] Normative arguments also have implications regarding the action they refer to. For example, an argument that one shall not hurt anyone else includes the definitive claim that in principle one should omit such actions. These implications do not affect the distinction between normative arguments and normative statements.

Despite this difference, there are mutual implications between the direct use of norm-sentences and a meta-level description of its content. The meta-level statement of validity as an argument implies that there is a valid normative argument, and the use of a norm-sentence in putting forward a normative argument implies a meta-level statement of the validity of this norm as an argument. Hence, one cannot accept one without accepting the other.

Accordingly, there are various ways to express normative arguments:

(1) Its direct use, for example, saying 'One ought not to offend anyone in his or her honour'.
(2) The statement that such an argument is valid as an argument.
(3) The explication of the definitive requirements implied in such an argument.

Such implied requirements are, for example, that one ought to balance the respective argument against competing arguments and give due weight to it in this balancing. They may again be expressed by a direct normative statement or by a statement of validity. However, it is important to note that normative arguments have a content that goes beyond what can be expressed by means of normative statements.

### 2.2.4 Structure of Autonomous Judgement

Statements of normative validity put forward an action-guiding demand together with the claim that this demand is valid and hence ought to be applied and followed. However, autonomous judgements can neither refer to existing norms nor command obedience on the part of other autonomous agents. The question, then, is how autonomous judgements are possible, that is, how they can claim to be valid and hence binding on anyone.

One can describe the structure of autonomous justification as follows. Colliding principles $P_1$ and $P_2$ require that particular norms $N_1$ and $N_2$ be accepted as valid. These norms lead, at least in some instances, to incompatible consequences, that is, to the contrary requirements that p ought to be (Op) and that p ought not to be ($O\neg p$). In order to resolve this norm conflict, a priority must be established between the conflicting arguments with regard to the normative consequence in question. The priority will in general not be absolute but conditional, that is, it will hold under a condition C. Together with the conditions of priority, the normative consequence that receives priority form the norm that results from the balancing.

One can illustrate the structure of the balancing of normative arguments, and the role of normative judgements in it, by means of the scheme shown in Figure 2.1.

The symbols and abbreviations used in Figure 2.1 are as follows:

$VAL_{DEF}$: predicate of definitive validity

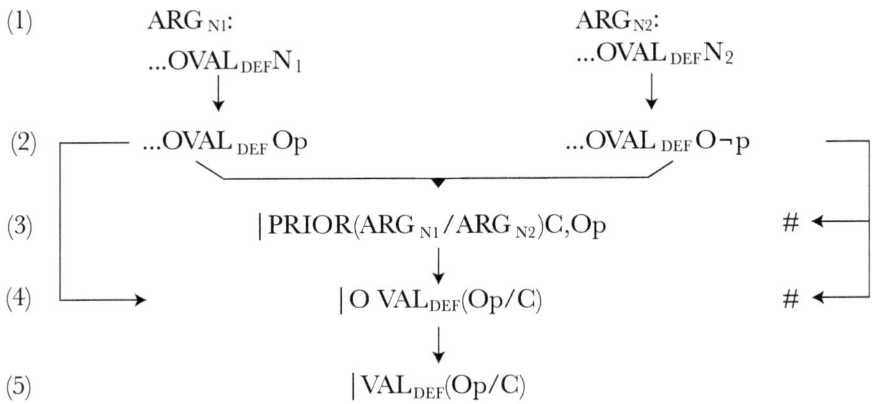


**Figure 2.1: The structure of balancing**

O: deontic operator 'ought to be'

$N_1$, $N_2$: norm individuals

p: state of affairs

¬: negation.

| : assertion-sign,[22] indicating that a sentence is actually used in a judgement or statement;[23]

. . .: argument-sign, indicating the use of a normative sentence as a normative argument.

$ARG_{N1}$: the argument of the principle of free speech.

The content of this argument includes the claim:

. . . $OVAL_{DEF}$ $N_1$: a permission granted to acts of speech ought definitively to be valid.

$ARG_{N2}$: the argument of the principle of personal honour.

[22] Here, Frege's judgement-stroke ('*Urteilsstrich*') is adopted; it expresses not merely a thought but the acceptance of the thought by the speaker as true, see Frege (1879; 1891). Dummett uses the term 'assertion-sign' (1981: 378).

[23] Hage (1997: 132) uses sentences beginning with a capital letter (Sentence) in order to express a state of affairs, and sentences beginning with a lower-case character (sentence) to denote a state of affairs. Since using a descriptive sentence is to express a state of affairs, this is a different way of expressing the distinction between using and formulating merely the content of a sentence. However, introducing a separate symbol has the advantage of making it possible for one to distinguish various types of use of normative sentences, in particular, its use to describe a valid norm and its prescriptive use, and also its use in making a normative statement and a normative argument.

The content of this argument includes the claim:

. . . $OVAL_{DEF}$ $N_2$: a prohibition of offenses to personal honour ought definitively to be valid.

| PRIOR ($ARG_{N1}$/$ARG_{N2}$)C,Op: statement of priority that argument $N_1$ receive priority over argument $N_2$ under condition C with regard to consequent Op.

| $OVAL_{DEF}$ (Op/C): a normative judgement that a norm Op/C (to be read: if C, then Op) ought to be definitively valid.

| $VAL_{DEF}$ (Op/C): a normative statement that a norm Op/C is definitively valid.

The scheme displays the following relations, which, however, are not logical inferences but steps required within a correct procedure for the balancing of normative arguments:

ad (1):

The argument of the principle of free speech, $ARG_{N1}$, includes a requirement of the definitive validity of a norm permitting speech ($OVAL_{DEF}N_1$). This is no more than the explication of the content of the argument. A similar relation holds for $ARG_{N2}$.

From (1) to (2):

The argument $ARG_{N1}$ implies a requirement that the consequent of $N_1$ or any implication of it (represented by Op) be accepted; in the example this is the requirement that a particular speech ought to be permitted.

On the other side, the argument of the principle of personal honour, $ARG_{N2}$, includes a requirement of the definitive validity of a norm prohibiting offences to one's personal honour ($VAL_{DEF}N_2$), implying the contrary solution $O\neg p$ (the requirement that certain speech ought not to be permitted).

From (1) and (2) to (3):

The priority relation PRIOR is established, not by logical inference, but by a procedural act of balancing with respect to the competing arguments. The established priority of Op under condition C is required by the prevailing normative argument $ARG_{N1}$. On the other side, it blocks (#) the claim of the opposite result of the conflicting argument $ARG_{N2}$.

From (3) to (4):

The priority for the $ARG_{N1}$ implies, as a consequence of the content of this argument, a requirement of the definitive validity of norm $N_1$ under condition C (represented as Op/C).

From (1) and (2) to (4):

The claim of the argument $ARG_{N1}$, claiming that $N_1$ ought to be definitively valid, is transformed into a normative judgement that $N_1$ ought to be definitively valid in so far as it receives priority over the competing argument in the balancing. The transformation is not a logical inference, but a result of the judgement of priority (3). However, it is required by the prevailing normative argument, that is, by (1) and (2).

On the other side, the argument $ARG_{N2}$ includes a contrary requirement, which, however, is blocked (this is represented by the symbol '#') by the priority judgement established by the balancing.

From (4) to (5):

> The normative statement that expresses the definitive validity of a norm as the result of the balancing, $|VAL_{DEF}$ (Op/C), is required by a normative judgement $|OVAL_{DEF}$ (Op/C).[24]

The analysis shows that in the balancing of normative argument various relations are involved, but that there is no logical inference from one of the normative arguments to be balanced (. . . $OVAL_{DEF}N_1$, . . . $OVAL_{DEF}N_2$), or from the antecedent of one of these arguments, or from any other criterion, to the resulting statement of priority, normative judgement or normative statement. The result follows from a normative decision of the one making the judgement. The relations between normative arguments, judgements and statements show, however, that whatever norm someone will judge to be prior and definitively valid, it must be claimed that the result of the balancing is required by the normative argument that, according to this judgement, has the greater weight or importance in the particular case. Together with a normative statement of the definitive validity of a norm N, the agent must also accept a normative judgement that this norm ought to be definitively valid, and this judgement is required by the prevailing normative argument. Since the weight one assigns to the competing arguments again depends on an evaluation, this type of reasoning is no more than an explication of the reasons an agent gives for the balancing judgement. Nevertheless, one must present the decision as required by reasons. The justification of the decision is that it complies with the prevailing normative requirement.

This makes it possible for one (from the internal point of view of someone making a normative judgement) to understand one's decision as establishing a norm as valid and since it is, on the one hand, free but, on the other, normatively required, to understand it as an act of autonomy in the sense of self-legislation. Accordingly, one can define autonomous judgements as follows:

> $DF_{AJ}$: Autonomous judgements are normative judgements that result from the balancing of normative arguments.

The question of the normative effects of autonomous judgements for other agents remains.[25] Although such judgements attribute (at least implicitly) normative validity to a norm, implying that this norm is to be applied and followed by its

[24] The 'law of competing principles' as formulated by Alexy (2002a: 54) describes the transition from (3) to (5). This is correct as a description of the content of a rational normative system, but it does not display the justificatory relation between normative arguments, priority relation, normative judgements and statements of definitive validity.

[25] See 4.3.2, 6.2.

addressees, these judgements cannot include a claim to the effect that the norm is to be binding for other agents. This implication is blocked owing to the autonomy of the other agents. What remains is a claim that in principle other agents ought to recognise the validity of the proposed norm and act accordingly. Thus, the autonomous judgement of one agent constitutes a normative argument to be duly considered by the other agents, claiming that a certain norm should be recognised as valid. Hence, the normativity of autonomous judgements includes two aspects: being required by normative arguments, and constituting normative arguments for other agents demanding the recognition of the validity of the proposed norm.

## 2.3 THE NON-PROPOSITIONALITY THESIS

With the conception of normative arguments as reiterated requirements for validity, one is contending that, by contrast to normative statements and judgements, normative arguments do not have the logical form of propositions. A normative argument claiming that certain speech *be* permitted is not a statement that this speech *is* permitted. Of course, one can make statements about normative arguments, for example, that a norm permitting free speech is valid as a normative argument and is to be recognised to as high a degree as possible. They can be called 'indirect normative statements',[26] for they do not refer directly to a deontic modality, for example, that one ought to do something. By contrast, using a normative argument in balancing cannot take the form of a direct normative statement of what one ought to do. Direct normative statements claim immediately to guide action, but incompatible directives cannot be valid at the same time in this sense. One might also say that normative statements purport to state normative facts, and such facts exclude the validity of incompatible facts. Therefore, conflicts between norms must be resolved before one can make a direct normative statement. The same holds for normative judgements. One cannot rationally judge, at the completion of an argumentation, that something ought to be the case and make the same claim for an incompatible norm. At the completion of an argumentation, normative judgements must claim that all relevant aspects have been considered and, consequently, all conflicts have been resolved in this judgement.

The non-propositionality thesis has been criticised, however, in various respects. Alexy agrees that balancing requires an ideal 'ought', as distinct from the real 'ought' that demands actual compliance, but he holds that not only a real but also an ideal 'ought' can be expressed in the form of a normative proposition.[27] He ignores, however, the distinction between direct and indirect normative statements. The possibility of indirect normative statements is not in dispute. The issue is whether direct normative statements can be used to give expression to arguments that are to be balanced against competing arguments. At one point, Alexy

[26] Indirect normative statements include statements of the validity of norms, but also other statements that refer to norms.

[27] Alexy (2009: 28).

indeed makes this claim. He also acknowledges, however, that a contradiction at the level of definitive, that is, directly action-guiding 'ought' is inadmissible in a rational argument. His statements thus seem to be contradictory.

If direct normative statements can be used as arguments in balancing, a statement that one ought to do A must include, not a directly action-guiding requirement, but a mere ideal 'ought'. This can take two forms.

First, an ideal 'ought' might be understood not as a modification of an elementary category of 'ought', but as a category on its own. A statement that one ought to do A then might be interpreted as stating not that one actually ought to do A but that one ideally ought to do A. The problem with this approach is that the 'ought' ceases to be an elementary category, which can be qualified in various ways as to its character of validity, but that the basic category combines an 'ought' with some particular type of validity. The actual 'ought' and the ideal 'ought' would form independent and irreducible categories, and it seems that other types of validity of norms as well would have to be regarded as such categories. This, however, is implausible. It faces the objection that all these different types of norm include a common element, that of the 'ought', which forms a basic category.

Alternatively, one might regard the 'ought' as an elementary category but claim that one must interpret direct normative statements not as an actual 'ought' but as an ideal 'ought'. The problem with this approach is that a natural interpretation of a statement 'One ought to do A' is that one actually ought to do A. If one does not accept this interpretation, the fact that one actually ought to do A requires a special expression. Thus, a statement 'One ought to do A' might be interpreted as saying 'One ideally ought to do A', and an actual 'ought' must be expressed, for example, by saying 'One actually ought to do A'. However, if 'ought' is to be understood as the ideal 'ought', then the statement 'One actually ought to do A' would amount to the statement 'Actually one ideally ought to do A'. Then, however, it would seem to be impossible to express an actual 'ought', for any statement of an actual 'ought' could only refer to an ideal 'ought'.

To conclude, the most natural way of interpreting normative statements is that a direct normative statement 'One ought to do A' means that one actually ought to do A.[28] Since this excludes competing arguments, direct normative statements cannot be used to express normative arguments as they are used in the balancing with competing arguments.

A second criticism is that the conception of normative argument lacks a precise semantic foundation.[29] Indeed, there is no developed semantic theory for normative arguments comparable to that for propositions. Still, this does not by itself constitute an objection to this conception. For the analysis of the balancing of normative arguments and of autonomous reasoning, a propositional framework is

[28] Even if one could interpret direct normative statements as mere arguments, any linguistic framework must provide a form for expressing that something actually ought to be done. The core of the non-propositionality thesis is that this linguistic form cannot be used directly to express normative arguments as reasons for balancing.

[29] Wang (2010: 29 ff).

inadequate. Such a framework would turn normative argument into a discourse about existing norms. Autonomous agents conceive themselves, however, as the authors of norms. In so far as norms exist before and independently of autonomous choice, autonomy does not exist. Therefore, a propositional semantic framework is incompatible with the idea of autonomy. Autonomous reasoning includes propositions only in indirect statements about normative arguments or in statements of rational constraints on the balancing of normative arguments or in statements of the results of such balancing. The structure of autonomous reasoning itself requires a different framework, however, one that allows for the construction of normative arguments in a form different from that of propositions.

The problem of what might count as an adequate semantics for normative arguments remains. Some suggestions have been made in this section, but a semantics for normative arguments still needs to be developed. In any case, the issue here is an analysis of the structure of autonomous reasoning, presupposing that autonomous agents understand sufficiently well the meaning of the arguments they use. A semantic theory as to what this meaning is could promote this understanding if it is adequate. A theory based on the paradigm of propositional reasoning that does not correspond to the structure of autonomous reasoning is, however, inadequate and even detrimental in this respect.

## 2.4 THE LOGIC OF NORMATIVE ARGUMENT

The rejection of the propositional character of normative arguments leads to the problem of the logical relations that hold for normative argumentation. Such relations are usually defined on the basis of propositional logic, which is extended to predicate logic and various forms of modal logic, in particular, deontic logic, and the logic of preferences.[30] If, however, the propositional character of normative arguments is rejected, the foundations of the logic of normative argumentation remain unclear.

The distinction between normative arguments and normative judgements or statements suggests that the application of different 'logics'[31] is needed. This may be called the 'fragmentation thesis'. The distinction between and among normative arguments, judgements and statements demarcates different parts of normative argumentation, in which different inference rules apply. Hence, a fragmentation of deontic logic results. Deontic logic, in a general sense of the logic of norms or normative sentences, must include at least:

(a) a logic of normative arguments, which refers to norms used as arguments in a procedure of weighing and balancing, and

[30] See Hansson (2001).

[31] Logic is understood here in a larger sense of formal relations and inference rules, not necessarily in the technical sense of a system of logic with a formally specified language, a formal semantics, and an inferential apparatus, as explained in Prakken (1997: 10).

(b) a logic of normative judgements and statements referring to normative propositions put forward in such judgements or statements.

### 2.4.1 Inference Rules for Normative Arguments

#### *2.4.1.1 Elementary and Relational Normative Arguments*

A conflict between normative arguments exists if the respective arguments have incompatible implications. That is, one argument demands a solution that a state of affairs p be realised (Op), for example that speech of a certain kind be permitted, another argument demands a solution that non-p be realised ($O\neg p$), for example, that speech of a certain kind should not be permitted. A different type of conflict between normative arguments is that of complete or direct conflicts, where one argument denies the validity of the other. Balancing problems belong to the first type, that of incompatible implications of normative arguments. Therefore, in order to construct normative arguments that figure as reasons in a procedure of balancing, these implications must be included in the analysis of normative arguments.

Accordingly, two types of normative argument must be distinguished, elementary and relational normative arguments. An elementary normative argument is, for example, the principle of free speech, namely, that everyone be permitted to say whatever he or she wishes. An elementary normative argument constitutes the basic premise or the core of a normative argument. In this sense, principles that act as reasons in balancing are elementary normative arguments. A relational normative argument includes an inference relation between an elementary normative argument and a particular result required by this argument, for example, that someone be permitted to say this or that owing to the principle of free speech. A complete normative argument must have a relational structure, the core of which is formed by an elementary normative argument. Statements of elementary arguments have the structure:

$$VAL_{ARG}N_i$$

Relational arguments are represented as:

$$VAL_{ARG}(N_i,R_k)$$

where $R_k$ denotes a possible result of a procedure of balancing.[32]

[32] It seems that relational arguments are what Hage calls principles, which, if their conditions are fulfilled and if the principle in question is not excluded in the relevant case, amount to reasons (1997: 137).

### *2.4.1.2 Implications of Elementary Normative Arguments*

Which inference rules hold for normative arguments? This is the central problem of the logic of normative arguments. The inference rules in question (represented by '->') define the argumentative steps that are required and that must be accepted as correct in a rational argument. Thus, they define pragmatic inferences valid in an argumentative procedure, not necessarily logical inferences in a strict sense.

A basic requirement is that the inference rules for normative arguments must preserve the character of a normative argument, that is, figuring in a procedure of balancing not only as an object of this balancing, but also as an argument for a particular result stemming from it. Many types of inferences are not permitted. Even an inference based on material equivalence (represented as '↔'), as in:

$$VAL_{ARG}(OA) \ \& \ (A \leftrightarrow B) \ \text{->} \ VAL_{ARG}(OB)$$

is not valid, for a state of affairs B may have an undesirable property that precludes accepting a normative argument 'OB'.

For example, establishing a legal system might require the organisation of political communities. This constitutes an argument for the existence of political communities. The existence of political communities is understood to exclude non-citizens from at least some political rights. But it would be wrong to offer the claim that some agents ought to be excluded from political rights as a normative argument. The alleged material equivalence between the existence of political communities and the exclusion of non-citizens from some political rights does not warrant an inference from the argument for the existence of political communities to an argument for the exclusion from political rights.

Only the logical equivalence of the norm contents A and B could preserve the character of normative argument. Logical equivalence of sentences can be defined as the identity of the meaning (represented by the symbol '=') of the respective sentences. Hence, the following inference rule holds:

(IA1) If Ni is valid as a normative argument and $N_i$ is logically equivalent to $N_j$, then $N_j$ is valid as a normative argument.

$$VAL_{ARG}Ni \ \& \ (N_i = N_j) \ \text{->} \ VAL_{ARG}N_j$$

This rule refers to statements of validity and to the relation of identity, not to the norms itself. It follows, therefore, predicate logic with a rule of identity, and norms are used as logical individuals, that is, as objects to which predicates apply. In this respect, a special deontic logic is not required.[33]

[33] As a consequence, the Frege-Geach problem of how the meaning of complex sentences follows from the meaning of its parts (see, eg, Schroeder (2010: 41 ff)) is not a problem of the logic of normative arguments. Statements of validity follow predicate logic, the descriptive parts of normative arguments as well, and the normative claim included in normative arguments does not permit logical inferences beyond the identity of meaning.

### *2.4.1.3 Implications of Relational Normative Arguments*

Relational normative arguments are statements to the effect that there is an argument for a particular conclusion. The logical relations that hold for them are different from those of elementary normative arguments. Relational arguments include a reference to a suggested result R. Hence, additional inference rules may be based on relations between descriptions of such results. They go beyond the requirement of logical equivalence. Nevertheless, it is not clear which inference rules apply.[34]

> For example, a principle for the protection of personal honour is an argument for the legal prohibition of insulting speech ($R_1$). With the further premise that a legal prohibition of insulting speech implies that people are threatened with legal sanctions ($R_2$), one might conclude that this principle is an argument for threatening people with legal sanctions. This, however, would not be correct. Even if $R_2$ is implied as a legal consequence by $R_1$, it does not seem adequate to say that the principle of the protection of personal honour is tantamount to an argument to threaten people with legal sanctions.

Hence, the fact that $R_1$ logically implies $R_2$ does not suffice to establish an inference that a normative argument for $R_1$ also holds for $R_2$. Thus, the logic of relational normative arguments is distinct from that of propositions. Using a propositional framework for normative argumentation will, consequently, lead to mistakes.

On the other hand, it seems that inferences from relational normative arguments may be based on the relation of promotion.[35]

> The protection of personal honour will be promoted if its violation is subject to an obligation to pay damages. Although it does not logically follow from the protection of personal honour that there is an obligation to pay damages, the principle of the protection of personal honour is a valid argument for an obligation to pay damages in the case of a violation, for the latter obligation promotes or contributes to the fulfilment of the principle.

The relation of promotion holds if something contributes to the fulfilment of a principle, but also if it facilitates this or makes it more likely. Accordingly, a normative argument ($N_1$) for a particular result ($R_1$) supports requirements of any means ($R_2$) that promote (PROM) the fulfilment (FM) of what the argument demands ($N_1$). That is, one may correctly infer according to the following rule:

> (IA2) If $N_1$ is valid as a normative argument for $R_1$ and the fulfilment of $R_2$ promotes the fulfilment of $R_2$, then $N_1$ is valid as a normative argument for $R_2$.

$$VAL_{ARG}(N_1,R_1) \ \&\ PROM(R_2,R_1) \text{ -> } VAL_{ARG}(N_1,R_2)$$

[34] The adequacy of the 'bridge concept' of inference ($p \rightarrow Oq$) is denied by Zuleta (2008: 99 ff), who suggests an embedded structure: $O(p \rightarrow q)$. This conforms in part (in so far as the deontic operator is placed in front of any normative expression) to the analysis suggested here. Zuleta does not, however, consider this reasoning with respect to conflicting arguments.

[35] See also Hage (1996: 206; 1997: 137).

A corresponding relation holds with regard to elementary arguments regarding $N_1$.

(IA3) If $N_1$ constitutes a valid argument and a particular result R promotes the fulfilment of $N_1$, then $N_1$ is a valid argument for R.

$$VAL_{ARG}(N_1) \;\&\; PROM(R,N_1) \text{ -> } VAL_{ARG}(N_1,R)$$

A remarkable feature of these inferential structures is that they are opposed to what is usually accepted as valid teleological inference. Teleological inferences usually conclude that necessary means for a required end are required as well.[36] By contrast, the qualification as a valid relational normative argument is transferred to all norms whose fulfilment promotes a required end, whether or not it is a necessary means. In a crude notation, the basic structure of teleological reasoning is:[37]

$$Op,\ p \rightarrow q, \text{ consequently } Oq$$

By contrast, the basic structure of inferences in relational normative arguments is:

$$VAL_{ARG}Op,\ q \rightarrow p, \text{ consequently } VAL_{ARG}Oq$$

In addition, the 'logic of promotion' is distinct from the rules of propositional logic. If a result $R_1$ promotes fulfilment of a requirement $N_1$, one might be tempted to represent this relation as:

$$R_1 \rightarrow FM(N_1)$$

Then, however, according to the 'law of aggregation': $p \rightarrow q$, consequently $p \;\&\; r \rightarrow q$, one should expect:

$$R_1 \;\&\; R_2 \rightarrow FM(N_1)$$

However, the second result, $R_2$, might be detrimental to the fulfilment of $N_1$. Thus, the inference does not hold.[38] On the other hand, a disjunctive extension of the antecedent is also not possible. If $R_1$ promotes fulfilment of $N_1$, it does not follow that the same holds for the disjunction '$R_1$ or $R_2$'. The disjunction can be fulfilled by $R_2$ alone; this, however, might not promote fulfilment of $N_1$.

[36] See also the critique of this assumption in Bratman (2009: 421).

[37] For a modification, introducing the condition that the means contributes to the end, Clérico (2001: 35).

[38] This shows that the 'logic of promotion' must be non-monotonic. On non-monotonic reasoning, see Prakken (1997); Nute (1997); Hage (1997); Wang (2003), although not with regard to the problem discussed here.

### 2.4.2 Inference Rules for Normative Judgements and Statements

The logic of normative judgements and statements is concerned with the inference rules with respect to the results of balancing. The special feature of normative judgements is that the definitively valid norms that are established as the result of a balancing are supported by normative arguments. Accordingly, inferences valid within a logic of normative judgements must preserve this support. Moreover, the definitive character of norms must also be preserved.

These requirements restrict the range of logical inferences. For as soon as a new normatively relevant property is introduced, logical inferences are no longer possible, and one must perform a procedure of balancing again. Since one cannot exclude in advance the possibility that a new property may be normatively relevant, one always has to determine whether it constitutes, or is relevant to, a normative argument. Hence, instead of using logical inferences, normative argument will proceed primarily by means of a sequence of balancing procedures in order to integrate new information.[39]

In addition, a further restriction stems from the incapacity of autonomous agents to determine by their individual judgements alone which norms are definitively valid and therefore count as binding norms on other agents. This precludes transforming, without further qualification, a normative judgement into a statement of definitive validity in the sense of a binding norm. On the other hand, it is true that a normative judgement implies the attribution of some type of validity to a norm. Which type of validity, however, needs to be specified.[40]

Nevertheless, there are some logical relations. The various types of normative expression that present the result of a balancing are logically related, though not logically equivalent. Such relations hold between, first, priority statements and normative judgements and, secondly, between normative judgements and normative statements. The symbol '|' will be used to indicate that a sentence is being used to make a judgement or statement.[41]

The respective rules of argument are:

(IA4) A statement of the priority of one argument over another with respect to a particular norm implies a normative judgement to the effect that this norm is definitively valid.

$$|\,\mathrm{PRIOR}(\mathrm{ARG}_{\mathrm{Ni}}/\mathrm{ARG}_{\mathrm{y}}, \mathrm{N}_{\mathrm{i}}) \text{ -> } |\,\mathrm{O}\ \mathrm{VAL}_{\mathrm{DEF}}\mathrm{N}_{\mathrm{i}}$$

[39] Prakken (1997: 59) offers a similar characterisation of non-monotonic reasoning, as requiring to consider the entire amount of available information for every step in a derivation. The difference to the balancing suggested here is that one must not only consider the entire amount of available information but that the available information excludes inferring a result on the basis of the available arguments. The issue is not between local and global proof methods but that there is no proof method.

[40] See 4.3.2.3.

[41] See above 2.2.4, on Frege's judgement-stroke.

The reverse does not hold, for the same normative judgement may be justified by various sets of arguments and respective statements of priority.

(IA5) Within an ideal procedure of normative argument, a normative judgement of the definitive validity of a particular norm implies a normative statement of its definitive validity.

$$|\text{O VAL}_{\text{DEF}}\text{N}_{\text{i}} \text{ -> } |\text{VAL}_{\text{DEF}}\text{N}_{\text{i}}$$

This is the case for the reason that perfectly reasonable agents will accept exactly those norms that they ought to accept according to their normative judgements. This presupposes, however, that no competing normative views are present, for a conflict between normative views of autonomous agents would require a second-order balancing.

If one defines the validity of a norm as its acceptance in an ideal discourse, that is, an argumentative procedure in which all requirements of rational argumentation are fulfilled, the following rule holds:

(IA6) A statement of a definitive requirement of the definitive validity of a norm implies a statement that this norm is definitively valid.

$$|\text{VAL}_{\text{DEF}}\text{ O VAL}_{\text{DEF}}\text{N}_{\text{i}} \text{ -> } |\text{VAL}_{\text{DEF}}\text{N}_{\text{i}}$$

The reverse also holds in a perfectly justified normative system, for in such a system each definitively valid norm will be backed by a requirement for validity:

(IA7) A statement that a norm is definitively valid implies a statement of a definitive requirement of the definitive validity of a norm.

$$|\text{VAL}_{\text{DEF}}\text{ N}_{\text{i}} \text{ -> } |\text{VAL}_{\text{DEF}}\text{ O VAL}_{\text{DEF}}\text{ N}_{\text{i}}$$

Thus, a reasonable agent cannot accept the one without the other. Accordingly, in a perfect normative system a pragmatic equivalence holds between the requirements of validity of the first order and of higher order.

Finally, if a relative normative statement $|\text{VAL}_{\text{DEF-PROC}}\text{N}_{\text{i}}$ is made by someone who accepts the result of a particular justificatory procedure PROC, this relative normative statement implies a second-order normative judgement $|\text{OVAL}_{\text{DEF}}\text{N}_{\text{i}}$ as well as a first-order normative judgement $|\text{N}_{\text{i}}$.

(IA8) A relative normative statement $|\text{VAL}_{\text{DEF-PROC}}\text{N}_{\text{i}}$, stating and accepting the result of a particular justificatory procedure PROC, implies normative judgements $|\text{OVAL}_{\text{DEF}}\text{N}_{\text{i}}$ and $|\text{N}_{\text{i}}$

$$|\text{VAL}_{\text{DEF,PROC}}\text{N}_{\text{i}} \text{ -> } |\text{OVAL}_{\text{DEF}}\text{N}_{\text{i}}$$

$$|\text{VAL}_{\text{DEF,PROC}}\text{N}_{\text{i}} \text{ -> } |\text{N}_{\text{i}}$$

This is due to the fact that someone accepting the result of a particular procedure makes a wholehearted normative judgement, which is absolute in the sense that it is not merely a description of the content of a particular system of norms. The reference to the context of the balancing procedure hence can be eliminated from the internal point of view, that is, from the perspective of a participant.[42]

## 2.5 CONCLUSION

Central elements of the conception of normative language suggested here are the semantic conception of norms, which distinguishes norms as the meaning of norm-sentences from the ascription of validity to norms, the distinction between normative arguments, judgements and statements and, in the class of normative statements, direct normative statements, which are also called 'normative judgements', and statements of validity. Statements of validity can ascribe different types of validity, such as definitive validity, or validity as a normative argument. The normative character of arguments, judgements and statements is displayed by the implication of a requirement to apply and follow the norm to which they refer. Autonomous judgements can, however, only carry a claim of validity as an all-things-considered individual judgement, and, as an objective claim, validity as a normative argument, which is to be balanced against competing normative claims.

A crucial claim regarding normative arguments is that they do not have the structure of normative propositions, by contrast with normative judgements and normative statements. The 'non-propositionality thesis' implies that a new foundation for a logic of normative argumentation is needed, one that is not based on propositional logic. An analysis of which inferences are admissible with regard to normative arguments as well as to normative judgements or statements shows, however, that hardly any logical inferences are possible. Rather autonomous reasoning proceeds by way of sequences of procedures of balancing in order to integrate new information, not by way of logical inferences. Normative arguments, judgements and statements have, however, certain pragmatic implications, which obligate a rational agent who uses such expressions to accept certain consequences.

[42] On the notions of internal point of view and perspective of a participant, see Alexy (2002b: 25); Sieckmann (1990: 118 ff, 187 f).

# 3

# *The Concept of Normative Arguments*

NORMATIVE ARGUMENTS ARE the basic elements of autonomous reasoning. They include requirements as to which norm is to be accepted as definitively valid, in short, requirements for validity.[1] Normative argumentation in its most elementary form is, accordingly, a procedure whereby individuals make normative claims requiring that a particular norm be understood as definitively valid and, hence, that it be applied and followed.

> For example, in the case of offensive speech, the principle of free speech demands that the speech in question be permitted, and the principle of the protection of personal honour demands that insults be forbidden. Both include requirements respecting the validity of a particular norm, which are, respectively, the prohibition and the permission of the speech in question. The normative arguments claim that these norms be accepted as definitively valid.

Thus, normative arguments are claims to recognise certain norms as valid, not statements to the effect that certain norms exist or are definitively valid. Statements of the definitive validity of a particular norm exclude the definitive validity of incompatible norms. If, for example, offensive speech is definitively forbidden, it cannot at the same time be definitively permitted. Accordingly, normative statements must be consistent. One cannot rationally state, at the same time, the definitive validity of incompatible norms. Since normative arguments are used in just these conflict situations, they cannot have the structure of statements of the definitive validity of the norm on whose behalf the argument is made.[2]

## 3.1 STRUCTURE OF NORMATIVE ARGUMENTS

The negative characterisation of normative arguments, contrasting them with normative statements, calls for a positive characterisation of the structure and type of validity of normative arguments. Since they can neither be statements nor

[1] Accordingly, 'requirement for validity' should in general, if not indicated otherwise, be read as 'requirement for definitive validity'.

[2] See 2.3, as to the non-propositionality thesis. Although one finds attempts to analyse normative conflicts by means of normative statements or propositions, for example, by means of optimising requirements, prima facie or pro tanto norms, or defeasible norms, these conceptions weaken the content or the character of the validity of the respective norms in a way that makes them incapable of figuring as arguments in the situation of conflict. See Sieckmann (2011).

mere norms in a semantic sense without any attribution of validity, the only plausible alternative is that their claim to validity rests on higher order requirements for validity. With regard to each requirement for the validity of a certain order, there must be a requirement of a higher order that demands its definitive validity. Thus, an infinite set of requirements for validity will be necessary to constitute a valid normative argument.

For example, in the case of offensive speech, the principle of free speech demands that the speech in question be permitted. A normative claim of this sort must have some form of validity, but this cannot be the form of definitive validity. Its character of validity is that the normative claim included in it must again be supported by a requirement for validity of a higher order, indicating that one ought to accept the respective normative claim as valid, and so on. The result, by repeating this structure, is an infinite chain of reiterated requirements for validity, where each of them is supported by a requirement for validity of a higher order.

Accordingly, the central norm-theoretic thesis is that normative arguments have the structure of reiterated requirements for validity. A normative argument consists of a set of norms including:

(1) a norm N that is argued for;
(2) a second-order norm requiring the definitive validity of the norm N as the result of the balancing;
(3) a third-order norm requiring the definitive validity of the second-order norm;
(4) a fourth-order norm requiring the definitive validity of the third-order norm, and so on.

The possibility of saturating this structure is the specific criterion for the validity of normative arguments.

This conception of normative arguments is distinct from that of arguments as a set of premises from which a conclusion logically follows. The connection between normative arguments and the result of argumentation is not a logical conclusion but rather a procedural act of accepting what ought to be accepted. The procedural character of normative justification is an essential feature of autonomous reasoning, for autonomous individuals must be in a position to form their own normative judgements, and the validity of a norm must therefore depend, in some way, on the judgements of autonomous individuals. Thus, rational discourse or other forms of participatory procedures are not merely instruments for arriving at a correct or, at least, a better result. Rather, they are constitutive elements of normative justification. Since logical inferences do not reflect the structure of such procedures, the relation between argument and result must be defined in a different way. What is required is a procedural inference, which consists of accepting what one ought to accept.

The basic structure of normative arguments as requirements for validity of a particular norm can be represented as:

(1) $O\ VAL_{DEF}\ N$

'N' represents a norm individual, '$VAL_{DEF}$' predicates the definitive validity of a norm, and 'O' is the deontic operator for 'ought'. Hence, normative arguments contain a requirement that a norm N ought to be definitively valid.

This reconstruction leaves open the question of whether a norm of the structure (1) is used as a normative statement or a normative argument. If it were used to make a statement, it could not figure as an argument in a process of balancing. It would decide the question at stake and would then not be open to competing arguments. Consequently, one must interpret it a normative argument. Then, however, it is not clear what character of validity it has. If it were no more than a norm in a purely semantic sense, without any claim of validity, this would not suffice to introduce an argument into a balancing. Accordingly, normative arguments can neither be normative statements of definitively valid norms nor mere norms in a purely semantic sense.

The solution to this dilemma is to reiterate requirements for validity. A normative argument for N not only includes a second-order claim that N be understood as definitively valid, but also a third-order claim to the effect that the mentioned second-order claim be definitively valid, and so on. Thus we get structures of arguments such as:

(2) $OVAL_{DEF}$ OVAL N

(3) $OVAL_{DEF}$ $OVAL_{DEF}$ $OVAL_{DEF}$ N

and so on. That is, the structure of a normative argument contains an unlimited reiteration of requirements for validity. This can be represented as:

(4) . . . $OVAL_{DEF}$ N

A normative argument for N then presupposes that the validity of N be required at first, second, and any higher level. The argument contains the claim that N can be supported by an unlimited reiteration of requirements for validity.

For example, an argument for permission to utter a certain speech-act might be formulated as 'It ought to be permitted to say . . ., for everyone ought to have the right of free speech'. This argument consists of:

(a) a first-order requirement for validity:

It ought to be valid that (under circumstances C) one has the right to free speech,

(b) a second-order requirement for validity:

It ought to be valid that it ought to be valid that (under circumstances C) one has the right to free speech,

(c) a third-order requirement for validity:

It ought to be valid that it ought to be valid that it ought to be valid that under circumstances C one has the right to free speech,

and so on.

Hence, a normative argument refers to an infinite set of sentences that contain requirements for validity of ever higher orders with respect to the norm or normative state in question. Using i (being a number 0, 1, . . .) in order to indicate the level of N in a set of requirements for validity of ever higher orders, one can define normative arguments accordingly as follows:

> $DF_{NA}$: A normative argument for the definitive validity of a norm $N_i$ consists of a requirement for validity O VAL $N_i$, backed by an infinite set of requirements for validity of higher orders referring ultimately to the norm $N_i$.

A normative argument claims that it is possible to support the norm in question and each requirement for validity by means of a requirement for validity of a higher order. However, this claim is not part of the formulation of a normative argument. It is not possible to formulate an infinite structure completely. The claim of a normative argument belongs to the pragmatic level of argumentation. The claim on this level can be made explicit by formulating requirements for validity of higher orders. One might also consider the possibility of an unlimited reiteration of requirements for validity as an ontology to which normative arguments refer. However, this is not necessary for the use of normative arguments. The crucial point is that the possibility of reiterating requirements for validity of the respective norm determines the validity of normative arguments.

In sum, the claim of a normative argument and, hence, the criterion for its validity is that a particular claim can be supported by requirements for validity of ever higher orders. This is expressed by the structure:

$$\ldots \text{O VAL}_{DEF} \text{ O VAL}_{DEF} \text{ N}$$

The possibility of saturating this reiterated structure is the specific form of validity of normative arguments. That is, a normative argument is valid if an unlimited chain of requirements for validity of higher orders can support it.

## 3.2 ARGUMENT FOR THE REITERATION OF REQUIREMENTS FOR VALIDITY

Why should one accept this account of the structure of a normative argument, as distinct from that of normative statements? What sense does it make to reiterate requirements for validity? How normative arguments figure in balancing might become clearer by considering an example.

> A declaration that politician A is corrupt interferes with A's claim that his personal honour be respected. On the other hand, such a declaration is an instance of speech, and hence the speaker might well claim that this speech be permitted. The question is whether, given the circumstances of the case at hand, the speech in question is to be regarded as permitted or forbidden. Let us assume that we do not have a pre-established legal rule that covers this case. Accordingly, such a rule must be established by balancing the competing arguments. The arguments are, on the one hand, the right to free speech, requiring that the speech in question be permitted, and on the other hand, the

right to the protection of personal honour, requiring that the speech in question be forbidden.

Several aspects of this elementary case of balancing facilitate an understanding of the notion of normative arguments. A first point is that the formulation of the arguments in the above example shows that both arguments contain a reiteration of normative modalities. One argument suggests that a permission ought to be accepted as the result of the balancing, hence, as a definitively valid norm, and the other argument suggests that a prohibition ought to be the result. Accordingly, the arguments to be balanced have the structure of requirements for validity, that is, they include a normative requirement regarding a particular norm.

In addition, several arguments support this view. A first argument here is that normative arguments conceived as reiterated requirements for validity have the features necessary to figure as reasons in procedures of balancing. Secondly, the structure of normativity includes a reiteration of normative requirements. Thirdly, interest-based arguments have indeed such a structure, by contrast with authority-based arguments. Moreover, the reiteration of requirements for validity serves to make intelligible the logical structure of moral autonomy and makes it possible to develop a complete model of normative justification.

### 3.2.1 Structure of Balancing

A crucial problem of practical reasoning is how to understand balancing as a method of rational decision-making in its own right, not reducible to other forms of reasoning, such as the method of subsumption and deduction, the calculation of costs and benefits or any other type of inferential justification, which derives the result from given premises or criteria.[3] If balancing is to be regarded as a method in its own right, it must present a form of rational argumentation the result of which is not determined by presupposed and already established criteria, but which nevertheless makes it possible to claim the correctness of its result. Thus, it must be open in its result but nevertheless count as a justification of it. The latter requires that the balancing is based on arguments that make it possible for one to sustain a claim to the correctness of the resulting judgement. That is, there must be arguments for choosing a certain result, arguments that hold precisely in these conflict situations with other arguments and, moreover, imply that this choice is correct.

Accordingly, if balancing is to be a method of rational argumentation distinct from inferential modes of reasoning, it must have the following features:

(1) openness of the result, that is, there are no criteria sufficient to determine the result of the balancing;

[3] As to the thesis of the dichotomy of subsumption and balancing Alexy (2003: 433–49); Stück (1998: 405–19); Sieckmann (1990: 18 f).

(2) pro tanto conclusiveness of the normative arguments to be balanced, that is, a normative argument determines the result if there is no counter-argument;
(3) validity of the competing normative arguments in conflict situations, that is, the conflicting arguments are valid at the same time and remain arguments demanding a particular result in the case of conflict; and
(4) foundation of a claim of correctness as to the result of the balancing.

An initial point of importance is that the balancing of normative arguments is concerned with the decision as to which norm *ought to be accepted* as the result of the argumentation and, hence, ought to be accepted as definitively valid. This reflects the condition of the openness of balancing. The result is not derived from premises stating a criterion for the priority of one or another of the arguments in dispute.

By contrast, one might formulate arguments that directly state the existence of a permission or prohibition. That is, one might claim that in the case in question A *has* the right that the declaration that he is corrupt not be made and, accordingly, that it *is* forbidden. Or that the speaker *has* the right to speak thus and so and therefore his speech *is* permitted. This would assume that the argument is one of existing rights, permissions or prohibitions. Although we might talk in this way, and this may indeed be adequate if we discuss rights, permissions or prohibitions according to established rules, it misconceives the character of balancing to assume that this kind of argumentation is about existing rights. Genuine problems of balancing do not presuppose established rules respecting the question at hand but, to the contrary, presuppose that such rules do not exist or at the very least do not decide the normative issue in question.

> Accordingly, in the case of offensive speech the question is whether one ought to accept as valid the permission or the prohibition of the speech in question, given the facts of the case. A normative argument that a norm be accepted as valid, or put shortly,[4] be valid presents a requirement for the validity of the norm in question.

Secondly, the arguments to be balanced must respond to the issue, namely, that of which norm ought to be accepted as definitively valid. Thus, they comply with the second condition, that they are, taken on their own, pro tanto, conclusive, determining a result where no competing argument is applicable.

The crucial point, however, is the third condition, that normative arguments remain valid in the situation of conflict. In order to understand this, the reiteration of requirements for validity is required. The decisive argument for the construction of reiterated requirements for validity is that this structure makes it possible for one to explain how normative arguments retain their normative force in cases of conflict with other arguments. By contrast with normative statements, requirements do not presuppose that there be only one premise or consistent set

[4] This simplification rests on the assumption that the validity of a norm depends on its acceptance by autonomous agents. It applies only to norms within an autonomous morality. With respect to the justification of norms, however, one may well doubt that there is an alternative to the conception of individual autonomy.

of premises relevant to the judgement or decision to be taken. They do not claim to exclude the validity of other requirements. In addition, their normative force is not affected where competing requirement come into play. First, normative arguments do not lose their force because another argument receives priority over them. Normative requirements are not affected in their validity by the mere fact that they are not complied with. Secondly, also the fact that they encounter a contrary requirement does not affect their validity. In this respect, the feature of infinite reiteration is decisive. In a conflict of requirements with finite structure one might indeed conclude that a conflict of requirements of the same level cancels the conflicting requirements, so that a fresh decision is to be made. By contrast, this does not hold with respect to infinite structures of reiterated requirements of validity. Here, there is always another requirement that demands acceptance of the norm in question. Therefore, reiterated requirements of validity of this structure keep their normative force in the situation of conflict with other requirements.

In order to understand the force of normative arguments in the situation of conflict, one needs to explain what force normative arguments have when balanced with competing arguments. They include a norm but, in order to be used as an argument, this norm must be more than a norm in a purely semantic sense, that is, a norm expressed by a simple norm-formulation without any claim to validity. It must have some kind of validity. On the other hand, it cannot have definitive validity, for this would exclude a balancing of this norm. The third possibility is validity as a normative argument: $VAL_{ARG}N$. The validity of a norm as an argument is not actual, definitive validity but required validity, that is, validity that ought to be recognised. It includes the structure of a requirement for validity: $O\ VAL_{DEF}N$. In order to sustain this requirement as valid, although not as definitively valid, the requirement for validity must, however, be reiterated. One can call this type of validity an ideal 'ought', as opposed to a real or actual 'ought'.[5]

The fourth condition, the claim to correctness respecting the result of balancing, follows from the structure of requirements for validity. If an agent recognises a norm as definitively valid, as required by the prevailing argument, that is, the argument he regards as prevailing, then he must claim that this is the choice we ought to make, which is, in this sense, the correct choice. The claim to correctness respecting the results of the balancing is, therefore, a normative claim, consisting of the idea that the definitive validity of the resulting norm follows from what the agent recognising it ought to do.

Summing up, normative arguments with the structure of reiterated requirements for validity have the logical properties that are necessary for them to figure as reasons in the balancing of arguments.

[5] As to the notion of 'ideal ought', see Sieckmann (1990; 2011). See also Alexy (1979; 2009).

### 3.2.2 Structure of Normativity

The reiterative structure of requirements for validity conforms to the structure of normativity. Normativity is understood here as the normative validity of something,[6] for example, a norm, a system of norms or a speech act aimed at establishing a norm. One might even regard normativity as nothing other than the validity of a norm, and validity as the fact that a norm actually ought to be applied and followed according to its content. However, the term 'validity' is used in various ways, and not always in a normative sense.[7] Therefore, it seems to be necessary to speak of 'normative validity', in order to define normativity.

Normative validity has at least two implications. Claiming that a norm is valid in a normative sense must say, first, that this norm actually ought to be applied and followed and, secondly, that other agents ought to accept this norm as valid.

> For example, a legislator must claim that the issued norm ought to be applied and followed, and that the norm ought to be accepted as valid by other agents. If one of these claims is missing, one cannot understand an act as legislative, that is, as an act intending to give rise to a norm that commands normative validity.

If someone states that a norm is valid but adds that one may or may not care to follow this norm, as one wishes, this statement cannot be understood as attributing normative validity. A norm that is normatively valid cannot leave the question of what the norm addressee is to do open.

Similarly, if someone claims that a norm is to be followed but grants that there is no reason to accept this normative claim, one cannot understand this statement as one of normative validity. Normative validity presupposes that there is a reason to accept the norm in question as valid, and this reason must, moreover, be a strong reason, *requiring* the acceptance of the norm in question as valid, and not only justifying it as normatively possible or permitted.[8]

Accordingly, normativity has two conditions:

(i) The validity of a normatively valid norm must imply that this norm actually ought to be applied and followed.
(ii) Normative validity presupposes that other agents ought to accept the validity of the respective norm.

[6] Normativity may be understood in a wider sense, referring to everything that has to do with normative language, like statements or expressions of what one ought to do. See, eg, Wedgwood (2007); Thomson (2008); Stemmer (2008); Parfit (2006); for more comprehensive analyses of normativity, see Bertea (2009) on the normativity of law. However, for the following argument the aspect of validity is crucial.

[7] For example, if validity is defined as membership in a system of norms, it does not have any normative implications. Membership might be defined by formal or empirical criteria, such as, for example, being enacted by some legislative institution. Such criteria leave open the issue of whether one actually ought to follow the norms identified by these criteria. Accordingly, they do not confer validity in a normative sense.

[8] If one could offer only a weak reason, which allows for other positions as well, one cannot claim the respective norm to be normatively valid. A statement that leaves open other options to the addressees does not claim the stated norm to be binding on them.

Anyone making a claim of normative validity must be implying that these conditions are met.

Since these claims are normative claims about norms, they include a reiteration of deontic modalities. And since these normative claims again include claims to normative validity, the conditions stated above apply to them as well. Accordingly, normativity is characterised by a reiterative structure of normative claims. Any attribution of validity to a norm must be embedded in claims of the following structures:

(1) The validity of a norm N implies the validity of a requirement to apply this norm.

$$\mathrm{VAL}(N) \rightarrow \mathrm{VAL}\ O\ \mathrm{APPL}\ (N)$$

In this relation, the kind of validity is not specified. If its object is a definitively valid norm, the implication is the definitive validity of a requirement to apply this norm.[9] If it is valid as a normative argument, the implication is that there is a valid argument that one ought to apply this norm.

(2) If a norm N is valid, then there is also a valid requirement that the validity of this norm be accepted.

$$\mathrm{VAL}(N) \rightarrow \mathrm{VAL}\ O\ \mathrm{ACC}\ \mathrm{VAL}\ (N).$$

Since in autonomous reasoning acceptance of a norm means that it is regarded as valid, one may as well state this implication referring to a requirement of validity.

(2') If a norm N is valid, then there is also a valid requirement for the validity of this norm.

$$\mathrm{VAL}(N) \rightarrow \mathrm{VAL}\ O\ \mathrm{VAL}\ (N).$$

Again, this relation holds for definitive validity and validity as a normative argument, respectively. And since the requirement for validity is a norm, a higher order requirement for validity regarding its validity follows according to condition (2) or (2').

Whilst the first relation explicates the concept of normative validity, the second is a meta-theoretic statement on the structure of normative systems. No norm can be claimed to be valid without claiming the validity of a higher order requirement that this norm be valid. This holds both for definitive norms and for normative arguments. Since it applies to definitive norms as well, its demonstration of reiterative structure applies not only to normative arguments. Still, the reiteration of definitively valid norms is of little practical interest, for definitive validity demands action, not argument. By contrast, the reiterated structure of normative arguments makes it

[9] One must, moreover, distinguish between substantive definitive validity and procedural definitive validity. See 4.3.2.3.

possible for one to explain how they function in normative argumentation. Thus, the analysis of the structure of normativity supports the claim that normative arguments consist of sets of reiterated requirements for validity.

### 3.2.3 Structure of Interest-based Arguments

Another point in support of the construction of normative arguments as reiterated requirements for validity is that normative arguments based on interests do indeed have this structure. If one accepts the idea that interests imply a demand that they ought to be respected, then one will also have to assume that there is an interest in the validity of the norm that demands respect for those interests, and an interest in the validity of the higher order norm, and so on. The possibility of reiterating interest-based demands stems from two premises:

(1) An interest of an autonomous agent serves to justify a demand that this interest be realised and, consequently, justifies a corresponding normative argument on behalf of the definitive validity of the respective norm.
(2) Together with a first-order interest, there is an interest of a higher order in the definitive validity of the above-mentioned requirement for the validity of a norm protecting the first-order interest.

The first premise, stating that interests put forward by autonomous agents ought to be realised, can be justified by means of the conception of autonomous reasoning. Since the validity of a norm depends on the consent of autonomous agents, and since these agents, if reasonable, will not consent to an argument that treats their interests as irrelevant, the validity of a norm can only be established if it is recognised that the interests put forward by autonomous agents ought to be realised.

The second premise, which connects a first-order interest with a higher order interest in the validity of a norm protecting the first-order interest, follows as a requirement of rationality. The norm protecting the first-order interest serves to promote the realisation of this interest. This holds in the case of a conflict of interests where the normative protection serves to promote the realisation of the respective interest. This positive effect is demonstrated by the fact that arguments about norms actually take place. If norms were irrelevant to the realisation of interests, such disputes would not make sense. Therefore, at least in general, the second premise holds.

Based on these premises, one can develop the reiterative structure of normative arguments. In order to do this, some determinations are in order:

INT(Z): There is an interest of an autonomous agent in a state of affairs Z.

$VAL_{ARG}OZ$: The requirement of Z is valid as a normative argument.

INT($VAL_{ARG}OZ$): There is an interest in the definitive validity of the requirement of Z.

The reiteration of requirements for validity then results as follows:

| | |
|---|---|
| (1) $INT(Z)$ | |
| (2) $INT(Z) \rightarrow VAL_{ARG}OZ$ | |
| (3) $INT(Z) \rightarrow INT(VAL_{DEF}OZ)$ | |
| (4) $VAL_{ARG}OZ$ | Inference from (1), (2) |
| (5) $INT(VAL_{DEF}OZ)$ | Inference from (1), (3) |
| (6) $INT(VAL_{DEF}OZ) \rightarrow VAL_{ARG}OVAL_{DEF}OZ$ | Inference from (2), $Z = VAL_{DEF}OZ$ |
| (7) $VAL_{ARG}OVAL_{DEF}OZ$ | Inference from (5), (6), etc. |

In general, a requirement for validity of level i+1 can be generated by inserting for Z, that is, as the object of the interest in question, the definitive validity of a norm requiring the realisation of Z as defined at level i.

This structure holds for teleological arguments in general. If the validity of a norm serves to guide action, and if the fulfilment of the required action serves a particular goal, then the validity of the norm is demanded as a means of fulfilling this goal. Interests, however, are special, for in an autonomy-based theory they must necessarily be accepted as a basis of valid arguments. Interests are whatever autonomous agents demand to be realised and respected in procedures of normative justification. One must acknowledge these claims, at least in principle, if there should be any chance to find a result that must be accepted by the autonomous agents involved. On the other hand, goals not based on interests of autonomous individuals require an independent justification, and it is not clear whether such a justification is available.[10]

### 3.2.4 Structure of Autonomy

The paradox of autonomy results because autonomous decisions must be self-determined and therefore cannot be derived from already existing norms, but nevertheless must be bound by norms in order to constitute some form of self-legislation. The second requirement implies that the validity of norms is independent of its acceptance by the norm addressees, the first makes validity depend on individual acceptance.

The conception of normative arguments purports to resolve this problem. The structure of balancing normative arguments can explain both aspects of

[10] Autonomous interests are the primary and, presumably, the only source of normative arguments. By contrast, arguments directly referring to religious or traditional authority, which are not supported by autonomous interests, do not have the structure of reiterated requirements for validity. Such arguments refer to an authoritative act that claims to be a final justification and are not meant to contribute to an argumentation. Thus, an interesting result of the conception of normative arguments as reiterated requirements for validity is that exactly those claims are disqualified as normative arguments that have been the main target of the reason-based tradition of enlightenment.

autonomous morality. The idea is that autonomous judgement consists in establishing a priority relation among conflicting normative arguments.[11]

> If, for example, one must decide whether an insulting speech is permitted or forbidden, the principles of the right to free speech and of the protection of personal honour collide. One might decide that if the speech in question is primarily meant to harm another person, the principle of the protection of personal honour deserves priority and, consequently, the insulting speech is forbidden. Thus, one establishes a conditional priority of the principle of personal honour over that of free speech, given the general circumstances or context of the case.

This priority relation cannot be deduced from objective criteria. Rather it requires a normative judgement. The judgement is bound by normative arguments requiring a particular result of the balancing. Thus, autonomous judgement is normatively bound, at least from the internal perspective of the agent conducting the balancing. Whatever the judgement will be, it is required by the normative argument that prevails, given the facts of the case. Consequently, when making a judgement based on the balancing of normative arguments, one must claim that this judgement is correct in the sense that it is required by the prevailing normative argument. If one decides that insulting speech is permitted, this is owing to the principle of free speech and not to the wish of the party taking the decision.

> For example, if the definitive validity of a norm fulfils what is required by a normative argument, then the argument counts in favour of this norm. The unrestricted permission of free speech fulfils the principle of free speech, and therefore this principle constitutes a normative argument in favour of this permission. If a permission of free speech is recognised only under certain conditions, that is, in a subclass of the set of cases to which the principle of free speech applies, this conditional permission is again required by the principle of free speech. It is true that this principle requires more than a conditional permission, but permitting free speech in some cases is better than a complete prohibition, and each case in which a permission of free speech is indeed recognised improves the normative situation from the perspective of the principle of free speech.

From the perspective of the competing principle, the reverse situation is at hand. But the agent believes, in the case at hand, that the principle of free speech weighs more heavily than the competing principle. Accordingly, this principle determines the agent's normative view. The competing principle only affects the relative strength of the normative position held by the agent favouring the principle of free speech. Thus, the agent must present his normative position as required by the principle of free speech and must claim that he is recognising as valid what the weightier argument requires.

It is at the same time true that in a case of genuine balancing, there are no criteria of priority that determine that the agent give priority to the principle of free speech. In this respect, the agent must represent his decision as free. He could

[11] See 2.2.4.

have decided otherwise. No predetermined norm compelled him to give priority to the principle of free speech. If he had arrived at the opposite position, he would claim the competing principle of personal honour to be weightier in the case in question, and his decision would be bound and required by this principle. But as things stand, he believes the principle of free speech to be weightier, and he must draw the corresponding conclusion from this view.

The structure of normatively bound decision-making is exactly what characterises the structure of autonomous morality. The conceptual requirement that a moral choice be both free and at the same time bound by moral standards is fulfilled by the structure of balancing normative arguments.

### 3.2.5 Trilemma of Normative Justification

Another reason to interpret normative arguments as reiterated requirements for validity is that this structure provides a basis for meeting the sceptical strategy that would have one attacking every argument by asking why one ought to accept it. If someone suggests that one has, given condition C, the right to free speech, the sceptic will ask why. If the proponent answers with an argument, the sceptic will once again respond with a 'why'-question, and so on. This leads to the well-known 'Münchhausen'-trilemma to the effect that every argument ends in a circle, an infinite regress, or the breaking off of all argument.[12] The account of normative arguments in terms of reiterated requirements for validity may serve as a defence against the sceptic's strategy of asking 'why'-questions, for this account is based on the possibility of adducing an unlimited number of arguments.[13] Hence, one can answer any 'why'-question with a new argument. The proponent is, then, never forced to concede that he can give no further argument.

One might object that the reiteration of requirements for validity only leads to an infinite regress, which is one horn of the 'Münchhausen'-trilemma. This might indeed be correct. But who is faced with the problem of this regress? The role of normative arguments in a justificatory procedure is distinct from that of normative statements. The aim of adducing a normative argument is not that of ending argument but that of commencing or continuing with it. For this purpose it is necessary to show that the argument in question must be considered and cannot be rejected at the outset by questioning its validity. The necessity of taking an argument into account is established if the argument can be supported by arguments of ever higher order, that is, if one is able to reiterate the requirement for validity $OVAL_{DEF}N$ at any higher level of argument. If this is possible, then any

[12] See Albert (1980: 13).

[13] There are various means of coping with this problem. See, eg, Buchwald (1990: 232 ff). The question, however, as to whether the trilemma of justification can be resolved within the framework of deductive reasoning is beyond the scope of the present analysis. The point here is that autonomous reasoning presents a complete model of normative justification, a model in which the trilemma of justification does not arise.

question as to why one should consider the argument in question can be answered, and as soon as this becomes clear, the sceptic's strategy of asking 'why'-questions loses its sense. Accordingly, the only way to counter an argument of this reiterated structure is to present counter-arguments, and hence to enter into argument.

By contrast, normative statements claim to state what is definitively valid. They claim to state the result of an argumentation and, thus, to complete it, and not to commence or to continue it. This difference is important, for the sceptic's strategy of 'why'-questions has effects for normative statements that are different from those for normative arguments. If someone makes a normative statement, thus claiming to bringing an argumentation to an end, he must be able to support this claim in a finite number of steps. Otherwise, he loses the argument. If, by contrast, someone commences an argumentation with a normative argument, the sceptic's strategy will never lead to the difficulty of the need to adduce a new argument. A first-order requirement for the validity of N is different from a second-order requirement, and so on. Each of them is supported by the possibility of reiteration. Hence, the proponent can always present a new argument. This might not make good sense. But this is not the proponent's problem. It is the sceptic who blocks further argumentation by provoking a reiteration that seems to make little sense and serves only for meeting the sceptic's strategy of repeating 'why'-questions. This blockade, however, is irrational. Therefore, one cannot rationally ask 'why'-questions that demand further arguments where the proponent is able to present a normative argument supported by reiterated requirements for validity.

Consequently, the reiteration of requirements for validity leads to an infinite structure, where each requirement for validity is backed by another one of higher order. This does not undermine the position of the proponent, however, but that of the sceptic. Thus, the structure of normative arguments as reiterated requirements for validity provides the key to a complete model of the justification of norms, beginning with interest-based normative arguments and leading to statements of definitively valid norms.

## 3.3 OBJECTIONS AND PROBLEMS

Various objections have been raised to the characterisation of normative arguments as reiterated requirements for validity.

Robert Alexy claims that reiteration does not explain the argumentative force of principles or normative arguments (2000: 294 ff). He describes the relation between normative sentences expressing norms in a purely semantic sense Op, and normative statements VAL Op as an oscillation between two inadequate alternatives: as a pure norm in a semantic sense, Op says too little to be an argument, but as a normative statement VAL Op, it says too much, for it excludes weighing and balancing. Reiteration, Alexy concludes, does not constitute an argument. The reconstruction of the reiteration as an oscillation between norms in a semantic sense and normative statements misses, however, the point of reiteration as an infinite structure.[14] Alexy replaces an *infinite* logical structure by an oscillation between two finite structures. Since a finite structure need not have all the properties of an infinite structure, his argument is inconclusive.[15]

Thomas Zoglauer argues that the reiteration of modalities does not serve to resolve a normative conflict (1998: 146 ff). This, however, is to fail to understand the point of the reiteration. It is not meant to resolve normative conflicts but to constitute normative arguments. He also objects that the collision of normative arguments does not amount to a contradiction (1998: 148). This, again, fails to understand the point of the notion of normative arguments, which is to construct a collision of norms that is not a normative contradiction, such that colliding arguments can be valid at the same time.

Peng-Hsiang Wang, by contrast, has doubts that there is a difference between conflicts between normative statements and those between normative arguments (2010: 29 ff), disregarding, however, the distinction between definitive validity and validity as an argument. Respecting the content of the norms, it is true that there is no difference between conflicts of normative statements (or definitive norms) and conflicts between normative arguments (or norms valid as an argument). In both cases, a conflict between norms exists if their requirements cannot be completely fulfilled at the same time. The crucial difference stems, however, from the distinct claims to validity connected with normative statements and with normative arguments. The incompatibility of norm contents has different consequences in the two cases, namely, where the norms in question are claimed to be definitively valid, and where the norms are merely valid as an argument.

Wang also suggests that the reiteration of deontic modalities is superfluous within a formal system of deontic logic.[16] In his argument he begins, however, by ignoring the difference between definitively valid norms and norms valid as an argument. The logical system that he proposes includes only a single type of norm, in particular, definitive norms expressed by normative propositions. It should not come as a surprise that on this basis the argumentative function of the reiteration of requirements of validity cannot be understood.

Nils Jansen suggests that the conception of reiterated requirements for validity OOp contains an equivocation where the sense of 'ought' is concerned, for the first-level operator O expresses a legal or moral ought and the second-level operator a

[14] It is important to distinguish the formulation of a normative argument, which must be finite, and the infinite structure to which the normative argument refers. One might interpret this reference by means of the idea that normative arguments refer to a normative world that is structured by reiterated requirements for validity, thereby presupposing a specific normative ontology. Or, from a procedural point of view, one might say that normative arguments demarcate a point at which it does not make sense to ask for further reasons; here, the only way to proceed in the argumentation would be either to accept the argument or to present counter-arguments.

[15] It is interesting to note that Alexy, in his own analysis of an ideal 'ought', arrives at premises that provide for the creation of a reiteration of deontic modalities. See Alexy (2009: 25), premise (7): O OPT Op $\leftrightarrow$ $O_i$p, and (2009: 30), premise (16): O OPT p $\rightarrow$ $O_i$p. On this point, see Sieckmann (2011: n 65).

[16] Wang (2010: 29 ff). This shows, on the other hand, that the reiteration of deontic modalities as such is not a real problem, by contrast with, for example, the view of Weinberger (1996: 162 n 14).

normative argument (1998a: 98 n. 92). The equivocation is avoided, however, by making explicit the character of validity by means of the predicates $VAL_{DEF}$ and $VAL_{ARG}$.[17]

Jansen also claims that an argumentation addresses not the question of which norm one should accept but the question of, for example, which rights one has (1998: 97). Although it might be true that normative argumentation is often understood as being about the existence of norms, rights or normative positions, it would, however, be wrong to think of this as the only form of normative argumentation. The balancing of normative arguments cannot be interpreted in this way; rather, it is aimed at establishing which norm ought to be recognised as valid. Accordingly, the model of normative arguments understands balancing as a constructive enterprise that does not presuppose the existence of substantive definitive norms.

## 3.4 CONCLUSION

The construction of normative arguments as sets of reiterated requirements for validity appears to be adequate to explain the special type of validity of normative arguments, as arguments capable of being balanced against each other and at the same time figuring as arguments for a certain result of the procedure of balancing. Accordingly, normative arguments are reasons that demand a particular result but can collide with other arguments and, where they do, must then be balanced against competing normative arguments. By contrast, normative statements express that a certain norm is definitively valid (or that a norm is valid in some other sense).

Normative arguments are distinguished from normative statements, first of all, at a pragmatic level. Using a normative sentence as a normative argument is different from using it in making a normative statement. The use of a norm-sentence as a normative argument is indicated by the symbol '. . .', expressing the claim that one is able to adduce further requirements for validity of ever higher order. The formulation of the normative argument itself is a finite linguistic expression. The normative argument consists not only of one such expression but of an infinite set of requirements for validity of ever higher order. Consequently, the structure of a normative argument can be represented as:

$$. . . O\ VAL_{DEF}\ N$$

The content of a normative argument is defined and, thus, distinguished from other normative arguments by a norm-formulation N. The logical structure of a normative argument is that of a requirement for validity O VAL $N_i$ (i being a number 0, 1, . . . which indicates the level of N in a set of requirements for validity

[17] See already Sieckmann (1997b: 352 ff; 1994: 239 f).

of ever higher order), backed by an infinite set of requirements for validity of a higher order referring to the same norm. At a pragmatic level, a normative argument is defined as the use of a normative sentence with the claim that it can be supported by requirements for validity of ever higher order. Accordingly, a complete normative argument would consist of this set of requirements for validity of a particular norm $N_0$, its elements being the norms $N_1$: O VAL $N_0$, $N_2$: O VAL $N_1$, . . ., $N_j$: O VAL $N_i$.

This analysis is concerned with normative arguments as used in argumentation. Using a normative argument is different from making a statement that something is valid as a normative argument. Such a statement respecting the validity of a normative argument must be distinguished from a statement that a norm is definitively valid, as the result of a procedure of balancing. In order to draw this distinction, a predicate '$VAL_{ARG}$' for the validity as a normative argument has been introduced.

# 4

# *The Justification of Norms*

A FUNDAMENTAL PRINCIPLE of practical reason is that no norm can be regarded as valid without justification. The demand for justification provides the foundation of critical moral and legal thinking. Its content remains ambiguous, however. The aim of justification might be to show that a certain normative view is defensible, that a normative claim can legitimately be made against other agents, or that a norm is actually binding and definitively ought to be applied and followed by its addressees. In which sense the requirement for justification is to be understood and to what extent it can be complied with are themselves issues in the analysis of autonomous reasoning.

The conception of autonomous reasoning understands the balancing of competing normative claims as lying at the core of the justification of norms. Such claims constitute normative arguments. The result of the balancing is bound by these arguments although it is not completely determined by criteria applicable by means of logical inferences. Therefore, balancing includes an autonomous decision or judgement. The resulting structure of the justification of norms, normative decisions or judgements reveals the structure of autonomous reasoning, that is, the justification of normative judgements by means of the balancing of normative arguments. These judgements are at the same time free but also required by normative arguments and are, in this sense, autonomous. Thus, the balancing of normative arguments is the core of autonomous reasoning and also–since it is the only way of justifying norms–normative justification.

Three issues of the justification of norms must be distinguished: first, how to establish normative arguments by means of claims put forward by autonomous agents; secondly, how to get from normative arguments to autonomous judgements; thirdly, how to get from autonomous judgements to normative statements about objectively valid and binding norms. Autonomous justification by individual agents provides only the starting point for the construction of the objective validity of norms. Autonomy implies that autonomous agents may make their own judgements of what they think is correct. The agents may, however, hold incompatible normative views as to which norm ought to be accepted as valid, and their autonomous judgements may diverge. The problem of objective validity is how to overcome a divergence between competing individual judgements with an eye to establishing a commonly binding norm that everyone must reasonably accept.

Subsequently, the structure of normative justification will be outlined. In the following chapters, the problem of the structure of balancing and that of the claims to correctness and objective validity will be discussed in greater detail.

## 4.1 STRUCTURE OF NORMATIVE JUSTIFICATION

An example will help to illustrate the structure of normative justification. A typical normative problem is whether smoking should be permitted in public places. The problem may be resolved in different ways. One possible solution is the norm:

N1: Smoking is permitted in public places.

Different arguments may be advanced in favour of this norm, in particular, the interests of smokers in enjoying this aspect of their lives, or interests in raising the capacity to work by smoking. The contrary norm is:

N2: Smoking is forbidden in public places.

This norm can be supported by other arguments, for example, the interests of non-smokers in clean air, in avoiding health risks, and in a safe environment. The corresponding normative arguments can be presented as the principles of individual liberty, efficiency, wellbeing, health care, and the protection of the environment. Thus, a balancing of interests and of the corresponding normative arguments is required. Some people may believe that N1 should be valid, others that N2 should be chosen, some may favour a compromise, for example, that smoking ought to be forbidden in closed public rooms but permitted in the open air. The decision will depend on what is achieved respecting the fulfilment of the competing arguments, and what relative weight is to be assigned to these arguments respecting the degree of their fulfilment or non-fulfilment in the case at hand.

The relative weight of competing normative arguments in a concrete case is defined by the extent to which the fulfilment of one of them is necessary to justify a certain loss of fulfilment of the conflicting argument. The greater the relative weight, the more that will be required for the fulfilment of the competing claim. The problem is how to determine the relative weight of normative arguments. There are no fixed criteria for the attribution of relative weight to conflicting arguments. If there were, one could apply these criteria directly instead of engaging in a balancing of conflicting arguments, and the process of balancing would then be redundant and without justificatory force. If there is a case of genuine or autonomous balancing, the relative weight of the arguments depends on a judgement of the person doing the balancing. Hence, the balancing of normative arguments essentially requires a personal judgement. It is an expression of autonomy.

The determination of which norm is definitively valid will also have to take into account the normative views of other people.

> For example, if many people, including smokers, think that one should not smoke in public, this will itself constitute a reason to think that the prohibition of smoking (N2) is the correct solution.

Thus, the balancing will depend on the normative views of the agents involved. Accordingly, balancing normative arguments is a reflective process in which individuals take into account their normative conceptions. On the basis of this normative material, consisting of conflicting arguments and individual normative conceptions of the agents involved, a solution must be found as to which norm ought to be definitively valid. It is important to distinguish this mutually reflective process from the simple process of balancing arguments. Whereas the simple balancing of arguments can be analysed in terms of an optimisation model, the mutually reflective balancing of individual normative conceptions is more complex.

Summing up, balancing decisions resolve a conflict between normative arguments by establishing a priority among these arguments and a corresponding norm as the result of the procedure of balancing. There are no positive criteria from which the correct result might be inferred. Instead, the result of a balancing is established by the judgement of an autonomous agent. Since there are no criteria that can adjudicate between diverging judgements, a solution can only be found in a rational argumentation among agents with different normative views. This argumentation may lead to a reasonable agreement as to which norm ought to be accepted as valid. Whatever arguments are used, however, there is no guarantee that reasonable people will reach such an agreement.

This openness of the balancing of normative arguments raises doubts about the claims to correctness and bindingness that can be made regarding a norm recognised as valid. If one must acknowledge at least the possibility of reasonable disagreement, how can one hold any position to be the correct one? And how can one regard a commonly accepted solution as binding on its addressees? These questions require a multilevelled conception of normative justification.

The central elements of normative justification by means of autonomous reasoning concern the justification of normative arguments, judgements and statements. A complete theory of normative justification must, however, include several issues that go beyond the basic elements found in the balancing of arguments. It must address at least the following issues:

(1) the status of the justification: is it necessary to ask for justification, to accept the idea of autonomy, and to give arguments?
(2) the rules of argumentation: the model of justification requires rules of argumentation on how a correct argumentation is to proceed which, again, need justification;
(3) autonomy rights: a right of autonomous agents to put forward normative arguments must be acknowledged, thus creating an obligation on the part of other autonomous agents to take these arguments into account in their reasoning;

(4) the introduction of arguments: normative arguments must be put forward claiming that the definitive validity of a particular norm ought to be accepted as the result of a procedure of balancing;
(5) normative judgements resulting from the balancing of normative arguments: in cases of conflict, normative arguments must be balanced against competing arguments and an autonomous normative judgement is required on the question of which norm ought to be recognised as definitively valid;
(6) the solution of conflicts among normative conceptions of individual autonomous agents: normative judgements of autonomous agents may conflict, and if a common norm is needed, one must decide which of the norms ought to be held as collectively binding. This requires intersubjective reflection that integrates competing individual normative judgements;
(7) the issue of the objectivity and bindingness of norms: since the views stemming from intersubjective reflection are still found at the level of individual normative judgements, criteria of objectivity are required in order to decide whether there is a norm that must be accepted by all reasonable agents as definitively valid and hence binding;
(8) the legitimacy of subjective normative statements about binding norms: the necessity of having a binding norm might justify a normative statement even if the criteria of objective validity do not suffice to justify the definitive validity of the norm in substance;
(9) the availability of authoritative justification: the definitive validity of norms might be established by authoritative decision if the authority itself is objectively justified. This step transforms the question of justification of a substantive norm into a question of the justification of a legislative or judicial authority.

These issues do not form a sequence that must be followed in a justificatory procedure. For example, authoritative justification is not the completion of normative justification. One may once again encounter conflicting normative arguments, one may have to depend on normative judgements, may require intersubjective reflection, and may face the problem of objective validity.

In order to treat these issues systematically, they can be classified according to their procedural or substantive character. Procedural issues pose the question of whether it is necessary to enter into a normative discourse, the rules of such a discourse, and the right of autonomous individuals to introduce their claims and normative views into such a discourse. Substantive issues[1] are the interest-based normative arguments, the individual normative judgements on the correct solution to the normative problem, and normative statements about collectively binding norms. Issues of the objectivity, legitimacy and authority in making normative statements may well be relevant with regard to each of these issues.[2]

[1] Substantive issues concern the possible result of an argumentation, as distinct from procedural rules guiding the argumentation. One should note, however, that procedural rules themselves can be made the object of argumentation, and accordingly can figure as a substantive issue.

[2] For a more detailed treatment of issues of the objective validity of norms, the legitimacy of normative statements, and the justification of authoritative decision, see 4.3.3, 6.4.

## 4.2 PROCEDURAL ELEMENTS OF NORMATIVE JUSTIFICATION

### 4.2.1 Necessity of Argumentation

The result of autonomous reasoning depends on which norm autonomous agents accept as valid. Thus, the consent or dissent of these agents is crucial for establishing valid norms. This is to say that a rational discourse is a necessary condition of the justification of statements of the definitive validity of norms.[3] One can support this conclusion by various additional arguments. First, the process of intersubjective reflection requires a discursive justification not only in the sense that people must communicate in order to convey their interests and views to others but also as an element of the justification of norms. It requires not only knowledge about other people but also about the mutual exchange of normative views referring to each other, which will be possible only by means of discourse. Secondly, a pragmatic or instrumental reason in favour of discourse is that the search for consent or acceptance will be promoted by discourse. At the very least, without a discourse between agents of differing views, it will be unlikely that a commonly accepted solution can be found. Thirdly, there is a moral reason for the necessity of discourse. Individual autonomy is respected only if the autonomous agents are allowed to arrive at their own decisions and, where a collective decision is required, to take part in a discursive procedure together with other agents involved.[4] However, the main argument for the necessity of rational discourse is that the justification of statements of definitive validity must refer to the consent of autonomous agents. Thus, this justification will not be possible without discourse.

This form of necessity is, however, relative to the project of normative justification. A different issue is whether it is necessary to engage in this project. The most fundamental challenge to normative justification is the question of why one ought to be moral[5] or, more generally, why one ought to accept any norm at all as valid, in the sense that it ought to be applied and followed.[6]

Some authors suggest that people must inevitably engage in a normative discourse, and thus recognise autonomy rights of other people.[7] There are various accounts that attempt to establish that one must necessarily accept at least some norms. Most prominent among these accounts are transcendental-pragmatic arguments suggesting that we are necessarily involved in communicative practices, that these practices necessarily presuppose certain norms, such as the right

[3] On discourse as an instrument of rational justification, see Alexy (1989a); Bäcker (2008).

[4] See also Habermas (1996, orig. 1994: 118 ff, 134).

[5] The question of why one ought to be moral is ambiguous. It might refer, as in this context, to the issue of whether to engage in normative reasoning. One must distinguish, from this, the issue of whether one ought to follow norms established as valid by normative reasoning. The second issue is that of the bindingness of norms.

[6] This question can be asked for epistemic or for anarchical reasons. A sceptic might hold that no norms exist. An anarchist might claim a fundamental liberty that must not be restricted by any norm.

[7] See Apel (1973); Habermas (1991); Alexy (1995).

to take part in a discourse, or liberty and equality within discourse. A problem that arises with this account is that of showing that participation in communicative practices including such rights truly is inevitable.

In order to show that any reasonable agent must accept the necessity of a rational discourse on normative issues one might argue that if a discursive justification is based on balancing, which is open as to its results so that one cannot count on objective criteria but must rely on the rational acceptance of autonomous beings, taking part in a discourse does not sacrifice interests[8] but rather opens up the possibility of legitimating one's claims by means of a discursive justification. Consequently, there is an advantage in taking part in a rational discourse – and an objective interest, which any reasonable agent making normative claims must have. This suffices to establish that everyone must accept rational discourse as a method of justification. Claims or action that cannot be justified this way cannot claim to be legitimate; their enforcement would amount to brute force. Whether one prefers to take resort to brute force instead of rational justification is, however, an empirical decision, which is not determined solely by arguments. Still, one has to insist that it cannot be justified without arguments.

Normative justification does not depend, however, on the argument for its necessity. Still, to engage in normative argumentation is the only possible way to answer normative questions, for no one can claim to have direct access to moral truth, and those who do not take part in a normative discourse have no voice on normative issues.

### 4.2.2 Rules of Argumentation

The structure of normative argumentation is determined not only by substantive rules of argumentation but also by rules of procedure. Procedural rules of argumentation have been elaborated in the theory of ideal discourse.[9] Though the distinction between substantive and procedural rules is not altogether clear and some rules may be classified either way, at least some procedural rules do indeed structure rational argumentation. Their justification refers to the fact that they present necessary conditions of normative justification. However, where requirements of rational justification conflict, a balancing of such requirements may be necessary in order to determine the rules of argumentation.

First of all, one must assume that claims to normative validity require a justification by means of argument. Therefore, for those who make normative assertions or claims, a burden of argument must be accepted.

[8] See Sieckmann (1997a). This certainly holds if consent is the criterion of normative validity, such that any individual has a veto-position with respect to the definitive result of discourse. Later on, reasonable convergence will be suggested as the criterion of binding norms instead of consent. Still, participation in discourse offers the chance of vindicating one's normative claims, which anyone who relies on the justifiability of his claims will appreciate.

[9] Alexy (1989a: 297 ff).

(A1) Whoever makes a normative claim must be prepared to present a conclusive argument on the question of why making this claim is justified.

A conclusive argument is one that supports the claim in question and suffices definitively to justify it where there is no counter-argument. It need not preclude the possibility that there are reasons for alternative solutions, even prevailing ones. The legitimacy of making normative claims does not presuppose that these claims will inevitably prevail, thereby winning the argument. It requires, however, an argument that is sufficient to sustain the claim in itself.[10] The necessity of presenting arguments for normative claims precludes not only normative claims that do not have any justification but also references to an intuitive recognition of norms or to supposed moral evidence that cannot be based on reasons and, in general, any foundation that does not reflect the autonomy of individual agents.

A second rule of argumentation of utmost importance from the perspective of autonomous reasoning, is the rule of the exchange of arguments:

(A2) If an autonomous agent has offered a structurally valid normative argument, someone who wants to object to the argument must offer a structurally valid counter-argument.

'Structurally valid' means that what is offered as an argument has the formal features of a normative argument. Every argument with proper formal features offered by an autonomous agent is relevant to the argumentation. Its substantive validity is not at issue, for this is the object of subsequent argumentation. What is required is that the argument consists of a set of reiterated requirements for validity. On the other hand, the counter-arguments can but need not be normative arguments. They may attack the premises or presuppositions of a normative argument as being incorrect.

According to the stated rule, if a structurally valid normative argument has been presented, the proponent is not required to present further arguments in order to support the first argument, as long as no valid counter-argument is presented. This rule excludes the strategy of a sceptic who demands an ever greater number of new arguments by asking again and again why one ought to accept the argument proffered.[11]

The rule of the exchange of arguments might be buttressed with the requirement that everyone has to present all of his normative arguments completely. This would ensure that the argumentation immediately engages in a procedure of balancing. On the other hand, the possibility of splitting up the argument makes it possible to introduce a requirement of coherence. There are different ways to structure normative argumentation, namely, an overall balancing of all arguments presented, or a step-by-step procedure offering single arguments and counter-arguments, establishing prima facie priorities among them, introducing new arguments and counter-

[10] One can understand this as a requirement of coherence. The argument offered must match the alleged claim.

[11] The justification of this rule follows from the solution of the trilemma of justification. See 3.2.5.

arguments, which might modify the prima facie priorities, and so on. Normative justification should fulfil a requirement of coherence with respect to different structures of argumentation. The requirement of coherence is:

(A3) The result of the argumentation ought not to depend on the chosen procedure or presentation of arguments chosen.

Without this requirement, the result of a normative justification might well turn on arbitrary circumstances, which a rational justification must avoid. As long as such divergences exist, a problem remains to be resolved, and one cannot claim that one or another of the possible normative statements has been definitively justified. This leads to the stated requirement of coherence. As a consequence, different procedures ought to be used to counter-check the result of an argumentation. Moreover, theories not complying with this requirement are not sufficient to meet the demands of normative justification.

### 4.2.3 Autonomy Rights

Autonomous reasoning requires recognition of certain autonomy rights. Its structure requires the recognition of rights regarding the procedures of justifying norms:

(a) the right to form interest-based claims and normative arguments based on them;
(b) the right to form normative judgements based on the individual balancing of normative arguments by the agent himself;
(c) the right to form normative judgements based on intersubjective reflection of competing normative judgements, taking into account the normative judgements of other agents as well, in order thereby to determine which norm ought to be recognised as collectively binding.

Autonomy also demands that the right of autonomous agents not to be subject to a norm that he or she rejects as morally wrong be recognised. This right, however, may conflict with the need to have a collectively binding norm, and it might, accordingly, be subject to restrictions. Thus, one has to distinguish between autonomy rights that are strictly valid and those that are valid only in principle.

In addition to rights concerning the participation in autonomous reasoning as such, autonomy rights include the right to live in accordance with one's own interests, life plan or normative convictions. Again, such a right to personal autonomy may be subject to limitations and holds primarily as a right in principle. The extent to which it holds definitively must be determined by means of the balancing of conflicting rights, goods or principles.

In any case, the right to put forward normative arguments and judgements must be acknowledged by all agents. Without recognition of this right, normative justification would not be possible. Every normative conception and normative system must recognise this right. This follows, for the justification of norms must ultimately refer to the criterion of the consent of autonomous agents, and this consent will not be forthcoming if the arguments and judgements of autonomous agents are not considered as relevant. If the arguments of autonomous agents are disregarded, these agents, entirely reasonably, will reject the result of the argumentation, and acceptance of the proposed norm will not be achieved. Thus, if normative argumentation is to have a chance to succeed, individual autonomy must be recognised and autonomous agents must have a right to introduce normative arguments and judgements based on the balancing of such arguments. Thus, the following thesis holds:

> (A4) Individual autonomy implies that every agent has a right to introduce into the discourse normative arguments as well as those normative judgements that stem from the balancing of such arguments.

This right not only makes it possible for one to introduce arguments without having to prove their correctness, but it includes also a normative power[12] that enables autonomous agents to change the normative situation within the justificatory procedure. By putting forward a normative argument, they create an obligation on the part of other agents to take into account the proposed argument in their own reasoning.

## 4.3 SUBSTANTIVE ELEMENTS OF NORMATIVE JUSTIFICATION

With respect to the contents offered in autonomous reasoning, a normative justification includes normative arguments as well as various types of normative judgements and statements based on the balancing of these arguments. Thus, normative argumentation consists of attributing different types of validity to norm-sentences, attempting to establish, step by step, stronger forms of validity – initially, normative arguments, then, definitively valid norms as stated in the all-things-considered judgements of individual agents and, finally, collectively binding norms. Since normative argumentation aims at establishing the definitive validity and bindingness of norms, an analysis of necessary conditions of how statements of definitive validity and bindingness might be justified will manifest central features of normative justification and of the arguments, judgements and statements employed in it.

### 4.3.1 Normative Arguments and their Implications

Normative justification begins with normative arguments introduced by autonomous agents, demanding a particular solution to a conflict of interests.

[12] A normative power is the capability intentionally to determine the normative situation, analogous to a legal competence in the Hohfeldian sense. See Hohfeld (1923: 23 ff). On Hohfeld, see Alexy (2002a: 155).

For example, a smoker may appeal to the interest in liberty as a reason for permitting smoking, while an opponent appeals to the interest in the protection of health, insisting that smoking be prohibited. Such arguments may be defeated by counter-arguments, but they must lead to a certain normative decision where there are no counter-arguments.

One might say, ideally, that if there were no obstacles to realise legitimate normative claims, the suggested norm ought to be accepted as definitively valid. Whether this conclusion actually follows will depend, however, on the relevant arguments and the circumstances of the actual case.

#### *4.3.1.1 Foundation of Normative Arguments*

The foundation of the validity of normative arguments put forward by autonomous agents is their autonomy, in particular, the competence or normative power to introduce such arguments into discourse. This normative power provides a formal justification of the validity of normative arguments and avoids the necessity of resorting to a substantive justification independently of argumentation. It is legitimate for autonomous agents to put forward interest-based claims without any need to give a substantive justification. Hence, one must accept as a rule of argumentation:

(A5) If an autonomous agent claims that a particular norm be accepted as valid and this claim is not defective in formal respects, then other agents must take this claim into account in their reasoning and must treat it qua normative argument as valid.[13]

The formal justification of normative arguments circumvents the problem of showing how it is that individual interests have objective value. It suffices that an autonomous agent claim respect for his individual interest in order to adduce a valid argument, the only condition being that it is possible to transform this argument into a definitively valid norm that might be accepted as binding on all addressees. This condition requires that the arguments be consistent with the principles of their own justification. The justification of normative arguments is, in principle, the competence of autonomous agents to put forward such arguments. This gives rise to two requirements of universalisability: autonomous agents must accept the competence of other agents to put forward normative arguments, and the arguments they offer must, in theory, without regard to the specific interests of other agents, be acceptable to each autonomous agent.

Consequently, the competence to introduce normative arguments must be universally recognised. Accordingly, there is at least one class of normative argument that each reasonable agent must accept, that is, arguments based on individual interests of autonomous agents.[14] On the other hand, not everything can be

[13] This rule is similar to that of the exchange of arguments (A2), but it has a different foundation. It is based on autonomy, whereas the rule of exchange is founded on the need for a reasonable argumentative procedure.

[14] For a similar argument, see Tugendhat (1998: 49). One may doubt whether there are any values not based on the interests and needs of people. If there are, they can be defined as something that has a value and ought to be realised. The strength of this requirement is determined by that value.

accepted as a normative argument. Since normative arguments make claims about what other agents ought to accept as a valid norm, and since these agents also are autonomous, interest-based arguments must themselves comply with a requirement of universalisability. In particular, a valid normative argument cannot aim at the violation of the interests of other autonomous agents, for this would undermine the basis of its own validity.[15]

The conception of autonomy as a normative competence circumvents problems of substantive justification at the level of normative arguments, but nevertheless constitutes a framework for establishing valid arguments. Any of the alternative models of justification would require a substantive justification, which, however, they cannot provide, for there is no reason why autonomous beings should accept an alternative that does not respect their autonomy. Therefore, if one has an interest in the rational justification of norms, one must accept the competence of autonomous agents to put forward normative arguments.

#### *4.3.1.2 Pragmatic Implications of Normative Arguments*

According to the claim to validity of normative arguments, someone putting forward a normative argument must accept various implications. These implications are not logical in character, but pragmatic. That is, they are implied in what is claimed by someone making a normative argument. First, since normative argumentation aims at establishing the definitive validity of norms, one must accept as a basic requirement the specific relevance of the normative arguments to the issue in question:

> (A6) A normative argument for the definitive validity of a norm N must hold that if there should be no counter-argument one must accept that N is definitively valid.

If this condition is not met, what is offered as an argument is at best an incomplete or contributory argument.[16]

Normative arguments require that one accept and realise them to the extent possible with respect to competing arguments.[17] This is a consequence of the basic rule that a normative argument may only be set aside if a counter-argument prevails over it. If there is no such counter-argument and, hence, it is possible to follow the argument at hand, one has to do so. Thus, normative arguments have the normative force of optimisation requirements:

> (A7) A normative argument for the definitive validity of a norm N must be realised, with regard to competing arguments, to as great an extent as is possible.

[15] See 1.3.2. For example, sadistic interests purporting to do to people precisely that which they do not want, are precluded. Another example of an exclusion of interests is the preclusion of external, as against personal preferences, see Dworkin (1978: 277). However, this preclusion cannot be established by the basic principles alone.

[16] On the notion of contributory reasons, see Hage (1997).

[17] On the notion of 'optimisation requirements', see Alexy (2002a: 47).

Another implication of making normative arguments follows from the requirement of the universalisability of normative arguments:

(A8) A normative argument must claim that it is possible in theory, without regard to empirical aspects of the agents concerned, that each reasonable agent accept it as a valid argument.

Since normative arguments demand acceptance of a norm as definitively valid, this implies that the norm suggested by such an argument must be acceptable as a definitively valid norm. By the same token, it is not allowed that normative arguments suggest norms that could not be reasonably accepted as definitively valid. Thus, a requirement of universalisability holds in the sense that only those results are possible that might draw the consent of all autonomous agents involved.

Universalisability requires not only that arguments put forward be acceptable to others, but also that arguments based on the interests of other agents be accepted. This follows from the requirement of the internal consistency of interest-based normative arguments, for one cannot claim that his interests constitute a normative argument, while denying at the same time the relevance of individual interests for normative argumentation. Hence, a third implication of normative arguments is that of the consideration of individual interests:

(A9) An autonomous agent putting forward a normative argument based on an individual interest must acknowledge the normative relevance of individual interests to the argumentation in general.

This goes beyond the negative condition that a normative argument cannot have content that directly denies the relevance of individual interests to normative justification, requiring, then, respect for the interest-based claims of other agents.[18]

### *4.3.1.3 Interests, Conceptions of the Good Life and Normative Arguments*

Normative arguments are based on the interests of autonomous agents. This is understood here as an analytical relation. The interests of autonomous agents are exactly what these agents require to be respected by other agents, and the content of a normative argument put forward by an autonomous agent defines his or her interest. No assumptions are made as to which interests autonomous agents will put forward. However, such interests must be legitimate in the formal sense of universalisability explained above[19] and, in addition, they ought to form part of a coherent life plan or conception of the good life.

The transition from interests to normative arguments requires two steps: the transition from an anthropological concept to a normative one, and the integration

[18] This is important because one might hold that there is no obligation to comply with the wishes of other individuals. This needs clarification. Although individual wishes, interests or needs as such do not create a definitive obligation, they do constitute a relevant normative argument in general practical discourse, as far as they comply with the condition of universalisability. Such arguments are again arguments for the recognition of normative arguments as morally or legally valid.

[19] See 1.3.2., and below 4.3.1.1.

of volitional claims, which may be based, for example, on desires, into a coherent conception that a reasonable agent could hold and claim to be respected by others. Following the two steps from interests to normative arguments, the construction of a normative justification can proceed in either of two ways. One might base normative arguments directly on individual interests and integrate these arguments by means of balancing into a coherent normative conception; or one might integrate individual interests into a coherent conception of the good life and consequently base normative arguments on these conceptions, requiring that each of them be respected and realised in a procedure of balancing.

The constructions are not, however, equivalent. The second construction presents two problems of balancing, first, the balancing of the interests of one individual and, secondly, the balancing of diverse individuals' competing conceptions of the good life. This differentiation makes it possible to introduce a requirement of equal respect for the conceptions of good life of autonomous beings, which is not implied by the first construction. The first construction balances interests according to their weight or importance.[20] This favours agents who have many interests or assign great weight to their interests. Thus, it does not result in an equal treatment of autonomous agents, who, therefore, can legitimately object to this form of argument. Accordingly, a theory of normative justification must require that autonomous agents develop coherent profiles of their interests in the form of a life plan or a conception of the good life. Thus, a requirement of coherence applies:

(A10) Normative arguments of autonomous agents must be based on coherent conceptions of interests or life plans.

Furthermore, one can introduce as a requirement of morality that these individual conceptions of the good life must be given equal weight in forming autonomous normative judgements on the question of which norm is to be accepted as definitively valid. Equal weight, however, presupposes that the respective conceptions are coherent and fully elaborated. Where this is the case, one cannot deny that equal respect must be given to these conceptions.

Normative arguments do not themselves make it possible to state the definitive validity of a substantive norm.[21] An important restriction on individual autonomous judgements is that a statement of what people ought to do is justifiable only if all of the relevant arguments have been considered and integrated into a coherent normative conception, which includes judgements on what a person ought to do in cases in which his or her interests conflict with those of others. Before this is done, no statement of definitive validity would be correct, for a necessary element of its justification is still missing. Hence, stating the validity of a normative argument does not yet imply that its content ought actually to be realised, but only that it ought to be balanced against competing arguments.

[20] This would be the way utilitarian theories treat the problem. It is rightly criticised for not taking into account the separateness of persons. See Rawls (1971: 27, 29).

[21] Although their definitive normative content can be expressed in the form of an optimising requirement, see Sieckmann (1990: 75, 86; 1992: 151); see also Peczenik (1989: 94).

### 4.3.2 Autonomous Normative Judgements

The balancing of normative arguments results in autonomous judgements or, emphasising that individual agents make these judgements, individual normative judgements. They include a claim of an autonomous agent as to which norm ought to be accepted as definitively valid and, accordingly, as collectively binding in a society.[22] An autonomous judgement has the following features:

(1) It puts forward a norm, thereby attributing validity to it.
(2) It results from the balancing of normative arguments.
(3) It claims that everyone ought to accept this norm as valid.

Autonomous judgements form part of an individual normative conception that integrates competing interests, conceptions of the good life, and related normative arguments. In addition, the structure of normative arguments implies a claim that the norm required by the argument be recognised as valid. In the case in which an autonomous judgement in fact recognises this norm to be definitively valid, this judgement is required by the normative argument supporting it.

#### *4.3.2.1 Basic Justificatory Relation*

As a consequence, normative judgements include two claims, first, that the validity of a norm stems from the result of a certain procedure of balancing and, secondly, it should be recognised as valid, for it is required by the stronger argument. The elements are interrelated, for the claim that one argument is stronger than competing arguments can only be established as the result of a balancing. It depends on the weighting of the competing claims.

> If someone holds, for example, the view that the prohibition of smoking is supported by the stronger argument, than this judgement expresses the relative weights of the principle of the protection of health and of that of individual liberty in the particular case. These weights, however, are attributed by the one making the judgement. Hence, the judgement makes explicit the result of the balancing. On the other hand, someone giving priority to the protection of health must claim, owing to the logical structure of normative arguments as requirements for validity, that this result is required by the stronger argument. From an external point of view, one might say that the agent claims the result to be required by what *he believes* to be the stronger argument. From the point of view of the agent himself, however, what he believes to be the stronger argument *is* the stronger argument.

[22] Only judgements based on balancing are understood here as individual normative judgements. In a wider sense, normative arguments that a certain norm be valid can also be regarded as including a normative judgement as to the validity of this argument. Judgements based on the balancing of arguments, however, have a status in a justificatory procedure different from normative arguments, for they contain a claim as to which substantive norms ought to be applied and followed as definitively valid. Therefore, they should be clearly separated from the simple introduction of normative arguments into discourse.

Therefore, although no fixed criteria are available in order to determine priority among the competing arguments, whatever one establishes as the result of the balancing of normative arguments must be claimed to be required by the stronger argument and it must be claimed, too, that this is the result that everyone ought to accept.

This type of justification is to be distinguished from justification by logical inferences and from the justification of actions as being permitted. A special feature of this reasoning is that the inferred result is based not on a logical inference but on a normative relation. That is, the inference that a particular norm is valid follows from complying with the requirement that one ought to accept this norm as valid. It is a procedural act of accepting what one ought to accept. This may be characterised as a procedural inference.

Logical inferences also occur within autonomous reasoning, but they are not specific to it. For example, one can formulate as a basic premise of the justification of normative judgements:[23]

> (BJ) If a norm N represents a valid normative argument for a concrete normative consequence R in a particular case C and there is no conflicting norm $N_i$ applicable to this case or, alternatively, all conflicting norms have been excluded or overridden in this case, then the norm N', with C as condition and R as normative consequence, is in this case definitively valid.

The conclusion that a norm is definitively valid depends on the condition that there is no conflict between this norm and other norms. One can distinguish three situations in which no conflict exists. First, there may be no actual normative conflict in the first place. In this instance, no conflict arises simply because there is no conflicting argument. It can be stated, then, descriptively, that there is no conflict of norms. The second and third situations can be set out as an alternation. There may be a conflict of norms that is removed normatively, either by excluding the applicability of one of the conflicting norms or by giving priority to one of the applicable norms over the others. According to these three cases marking freedom from conflict, the inference from the validity of a norm N as a normative argument for a particular conclusion N' to the definitive validity of the concrete norm N' is possible in three ways.

> (BJ.1) If a norm N is valid as an argument for a particular norm N', and if there is no norm that is incompatible with it, then N' is definitively valid.

> (BJ.2) If a norm N is valid as an argument for a particular norm N', and if all the norms $N_i$ that are incompatible with N' are excluded, then N' is definitively valid.

> (BJ.3) If a norm N is valid as an argument for a particular norm N', and if N receives priority in case of N' over each norm $N_i$ that is incompatible with N in the case of N', then N' is definitively valid.

The most interesting case is that of (BJ.3), for it refers to a priority relation and therefore presupposes a balancing of competing arguments. The case in which

[23] This corresponds to the rule of argumentation (A6).

there is no incompatible norm applicable does not create a problem, and the case that incompatible norms are excluded is not elementary but presupposes that norms have already been established regarding the exclusion of certain norms.

The rule (BJ.3) makes clear why logical inferences are of little interest in a conception of normative justification. It shows that one of the conditions of the antecedent, the priority between N and $N_i$ regarding N', requires a balancing that establishes the definitive validity of the norm in question in the particular case. Although one can distinguish between predicates of priority and of definitive validity, in fact both refer to the same balancing. The presentation of normative argumentation in the form of premises and logical inferences is possible but may be misleading, for it conceals the real character of the justification.

Rule (BJ.3) presupposes that if incompatible normative arguments occur and none of them is excluded, a priority relation must be determined. If a norm N receives priority, then N is definitively valid. If there is a norm that collides with N and if N does not receive priority, then N is not definitively valid. If, in addition, one cannot conclusively state that another norm has priority over N, this is a case in which one is unable to determine whether N is definitively valid. Moreover, if, in addition, no priority of a competing norm can be established, then the normative situation is indeterminate. In this case, it does not follow that a permission to apply any of these norms is definitively valid. This is owing to a second characteristic of the conception of normative justification.

Normative justification requires more than that it is simply permitted to hold a norm to be valid or to make a particular decision. Whilst one might well justify a simple action by showing that it is permitted, a normative justification must include a claim to the effect that one *ought* to accept a particular norm or decision on the basis of reasons.

> For example, a smoker when reproached may defend her smoking with the claim that it is not forbidden to smoke. Contrariwise, a law or judicial decision that forbids smoking cannot be justified on the ground that there is no norm prohibiting this normative act. The justification of a normative decision requires positive reasons that show why this decision ought to be accepted as correct.[24]

The correctness of a normative decision does not imply that this is the only correct solution. An alternative might be justifiable as well. All that is required for a decision to be deemed correct is that every reasonable person must accept the correctness of this decision in the weak sense that there are valid reasons in favour of it and that there would be no mistake in taking the decision. However, every individual agent who holds a particular view must claim that his or her view is

[24] One should note that a stronger conception of justification also applies when the question arises as to why one is smoking. This cannot be justified by a pure permission but only by giving positive reasons in answering the question. Hence, the structure of justification does not differ between decisions and simple actions. Still, the concept of justification is ambiguous. It may be understood merely as conformity with the relevant norms or, in a stronger sense, as an argument for doing something. Whilst a weak justification may be used with respect to acts and simple decisions, a norm restricting liberty requires a strong justification.

correct in the strong sense and ought to be followed by all reasonable agents. Since, however, all autonomous agents make such normative claims, and since no one can claim one's own position to be superior to the other positions,[25] all that can actually be required is that each of these autonomous views be understood as correct in the sense of being justified and not affected by mistakes.

> For example, a legal regulation might forbid smoking in public places for reasons of public health. At the same time it might be possible to defend as reasonable as well the decision not to enact such a prohibition. But someone who decides to issue this prohibition must claim that it is required by the stronger reasons and, hence, ought to be accepted by any reasonable agent.

Thus, the justification of a normative judgement as correct does not preclude the possibility that alternative decisions may also be seen as justified on the basis of reasons. In order to exclude normative alternatives, a justification of the objective validity of a particular norm or decision is required, by contrast to a merely subjective justification that an individual agent can offer.

#### *4.3.2.2 Autonomous Judgements and Definitive Validity*

As a consequence of the non-exclusionary character of normative judgements, the claim to validity of autonomous judgements is subject to two limitations. First, such judgements cannot purport to state existing norms. Since there are no criteria that completely determine the result of a balancing decision, the decision requires an autonomous choice in fixing the relative weights of the competing arguments and in establishing a priority among them. Secondly, since the autonomy of other agents precludes the possibility that someone else determine the definitively valid norms for them, individual autonomous judgements cannot settle the question as to which norm is definitively valid and hence binding. Accordingly, an individual agent cannot state the definitive validity of a norm in the sense of a direct action-guiding statement.

This, however, seems to contradict the structure of balancing, which says that the result of balancing will be a determination of which norm is definitively valid.[26] In addition, it seems also to contradict the idea of autonomy. Since autonomy includes the right to make normative judgements independently of what other people may think, it must be legitimate for autonomous agents to form normative judgements based on the balancing of interest-based arguments, disregarding the normative views of others. Such a judgement is stronger than a mere normative argument, for it claims to state a valid norm as the result of a balancing.

One might interpret such a judgement as a statement of the definitive validity of a norm according to an individual's normative view. This would not be correct, however, for a reasonable agent knows that on the basis of a balancing of individual interests alone, and without consideration of the normative judgements of

[25] That is to say, as long as he cannot demonstrate the other position to be mistaken.

[26] See 1.3.3, 2.2.4.

other agents involved, one cannot assume the definitive validity of the norm that one is proposing.

What then becomes of the right of autonomous agents to take judgements by and for themselves on the validity of norms, without regard to the normative views of other agents? It seems that autonomous agents can make statements of definitive validity only in the sense that a certain norm is the result of autonomous balancing, although not binding on other agents. This requires distinguishing between definitive validity and the bindingness of a norm. This distinction can be made in terms of procedural and substantive definitive validity.[27]

### *4.3.2.3 Procedural and Substantive Definitive Validity*

Definitive validity presupposes, on the one hand, that a norm is the result of a complete justificatory procedure, and it implies, on the other hand, an obligation actually to apply and to follow this norm. In this sense, statements of definitive validity imply directly action-guiding statements. One can, however, distinguish a procedural from a substantive notion of definitive validity. Procedural definitive validity only requires that a norm be the result of a complete justificatory procedure, with no arguments remaining to be considered. A norm is definitively valid in a procedural sense if it results from a complete balancing including all relevant arguments, that is, an all-things-considered judgement of a particular agent. One can represent this as:

$$\mathrm{VAL}_{\text{DEF-PROC}}\mathrm{N}$$

By contrast, substantive definitive validity implies that a norm ought to be applied and followed actually and without further argument. It may be represented as:

$$\mathrm{VAL}_{\text{DEF-SUBS}}\mathrm{N}$$

The important point is that substantive definitive validity implies a direct action-guiding statement. An individual normative judgement does not suffice. An objectively valid statement is required, one that is valid for all norm-addressees.[28] By contrast, procedural definitive validity does not have this implication. This allows autonomous agents to state their normative views as definitively valid, this being the result of their individual reasoning all-things-considered, claiming that other agents ought to follow this judgement, but without interfering with the autonomy of other agents. Thus, normative judgements include or imply three elements:

[27] See 1.3., 2.2.2.

[28] A stronger form would be validity for all autonomous agents. This, however, does not seem to be required for an immediate action-guiding statement.

(1) An individual normative judgement, proposing a norm N, represented as:

$$\vdash N$$

(2) A normative statement of procedural definitive validity of N, that is, the validity of N as the result of a specified procedure, in particular, a balancing by agent A, represented as:

$$\vdash VAL_{DEF\text{-}PROC(A)}N$$

(3) A normative claim against other agents to the effect that they ought to accept N as definitively valid, constituting a normative argument, which may be stated in the following form:

$$\vdash VAL_{ARG}\ O\ VAL_{DEF\text{-}SUBS}N$$

Since in this interpretation normative judgements and their implications do not conflict with the autonomy of other agents, the following rule holds:

> (A11) Autonomous agents may form normative judgements based on their individual balancing of the relevant arguments and then claim that other agents ought to accept this judgement.

Owing to their autonomy, other autonomous agents need not accept the normative position put forward with such a judgement. Nevertheless, the agent who holds this position must regard its rejection as wrong, normatively speaking, and according to his own view.

> With respect to the example of the prohibition of smoking, the smoker and her opponent both have the right to make normative judgements on the result of the balancing of the relevant arguments, and both must accept each other's statements as legitimate though wrong, and each will claim of her judgement that other agents ought to accept it.

In addition, where it is a matter of determining collectively binding norms, autonomous agents must consider the normative judgements of other agents as valid normative arguments within their reasoning. Thus, the following relation holds:

> (A12) Normative judgements of autonomous agents constitute normative arguments in the course of reasoning of other agents on the bindingness of norms.

On the other hand, normative judgements do not imply statements of substantive definitive validity.[29] A correct normative judgement from an individual's point of view has to make explicit, first, the agent (A) who forms the judgement

[29] See 2.2.2.

and, secondly, the interests and judgements that have been considered in this judgement. At an initial stage, this comprises individual interests (I) but not the normative judgements of others. That is, it will be a judgement stating that according to the normative conception of agent A, which is based on the relevant individual interests I, the norm N is definitively valid. Such a judgement can be represented as:

$$VAL_{DEF\text{-}PROC(I,A)}N$$

The agent will regard this judgement as correct and therefore claim that other agents accept it as well. This claim encounters, however, the right of other autonomous agents to judge freely on their own. In addition, since at this stage only interests of other agents have been taken into account, but not their normative views, it is not yet justified to claim that other agents ought to apply and follow the proposed norm.

In addition, a statement of definitive validity requires, as a necessary condition of its legitimacy, that the normative judgements J of the other autonomous agents have been taken into account. Since autonomous reasoning presupposes that the validity of norms depends on recognition of their validity by autonomous agents, the normative views of these agents are relevant arguments in determining which norm is valid. A judgement that reflects the views of other agents will include the point that according to the normative conception of agent A, based on the relevant individual interests I and normative judgements J of the agents involved, N is definitively valid. An intersubjectively reflected judgement can be represented as:

$$VAL_{DEF\text{-}PROC(I,J,A)}N$$

At this stage, an agent may claim that other agents ought to apply and follow the proposed norm. Since all arguments and views have been taken into account, so that nothing remains to do for an autonomous agent in order to form a normative judgement, one must recognise at this stage his or her right to judge which norm ought to be regarded as definitively valid and, therefore, ought to be applied and followed.

> (A13) Intersubjectively reflected normative judgements based on individual balancing of the relevant arguments, including those following from the normative judgements of autonomous agents, justify claims as to which norm ought to be accepted as definitively valid and hence be applied and followed.

However, this is still no more than an individual normative judgement. Since other agents may also make similar judgements and may arrive at incompatible results, even taking into account the judgements of other agents does not allow one to state the substantive definitive validity of a norm with the implication that this norm is binding on other agents.

### 4.3.3 Statements of Binding Norms

Autonomous judgements and the corresponding statements of procedural definitive validity must be distinguished from statements of substantive definitive validity, which imply not only that a norm is the result of a successfully completed argument, but also that this norm ought actually to be applied and followed and, hence, is binding on its addressees. The justification of such statements must ensure that this claim to bindingness is justified. It must show that each reasonable agent must accept the claim to bindingness that is at issue as legitimate, although he might not accept the proposed norm in substance.

From this, certain necessary conditions for justifying statements of substantive definitive validity of a norm follow:

(1) An autonomous judgement stating the norm in question is required.
(2) The judgement must stem from correct individual reasoning.

That is, the justification of the judgement offered by the agent in question must comply with the requirements both of correct balancing and of the reflection of the diverse normative conceptions of all autonomous agents concerned. These requirements apply already to statements of definitive validity in the procedural sense.

In addition, the justification for the bindingness of a particular norm has two further conditions:

(3) In a procedural respect, a discursive justification is required, including not only individual reflection but also a mutual, intersubjective reflection on the part of the autonomous agents involved on their respective normative judgements. Thus, the agents must ask which norm ought to be accepted as binding with regard to the situation of diverging normative views.
(4) In a substantive respect, the norm in question must be supported by a reasonable convergence of autonomous agents in their judgements coupled with their need to have a commonly binding norm.

The need for a discursive justification follows, for no one can individually determine which norm is binding on other autonomous agents. In order to achieve this, a compromise between diverging normative positions in one's own individual normative conception will not suffice. No other agent must accept norms as binding that are only the product of another individual's judgement. Of course people might agree by chance on what ought to be recognised as definitively valid and, hence, as a binding norm. If, however, there is no agreement, then the judgement of one individual, even if made after consideration of all the relevant arguments, cannot be binding on other agents. This follows from the principle of autonomy, which requires that autonomous agents shall not be subject to the judgement of other agents. Thus, there emerges an important constraint on autonomous reasoning:

> (A14) An autonomous agent cannot determine by his individual normative judgement alone which norms are collectively binding.

As a consequence, and in addition to a complete individual balancing of arguments, a discursive justification is required in order correctly to make statements of definitive validity and bindingness. Norms cannot be established as binding by monological reasoning alone. Rather, all autonomous agents involved must be included in the procedure of argumentation, mutually taking into consideration the individual normative judgements of all participants. This is necessary not only in order to acquire information about the interests and normative views of the agents involved, but also because a claim to the bindingness of the norm cannot be justified without reflexive reference to the normative conceptions of all autonomous agents concerned.

For example, the smoker and her opponent have to take into account the normative judgements of each other, and they have to form a normative conception on the question of which norm ought to be definitively valid regarding this situation of dispute.

Moreover, these conceptions must be judged according to their rational acceptability and to the weight that should be given to them.

For example, one might question whether the judgement of a smoker is affected by an addiction to smoking that stands in the way of rational judgement. On the other hand, this addiction might establish a special urgency of the smoker's interest that must be taken into account also at this second-order level of balancing.

In summary, among the individual normative judgements one must distinguish intersubjectively reflected conceptions from individual normative conceptions that are not based on intersubjective reflection. Intersubjectively reflected conceptions may be called normative conceptions in a strict sense – or moral conceptions, as distinct from personal ethics.

The intersubjectively reflected normative judgement is a judgment of a higher order. Still, it is an individual judgement, for everyone will hold his own view, which can diverge from that of other agents. The definitive normative claim of such judgements is still restricted to the requirement that other agents ought to recognise the respective norm as definitively valid or, at a higher level, that such a claim be recognised as definitively valid. It may have some independence and stability where changes in individual normative judgements are concerned, for a change in the normative judgement of one individual may, even in his view, not affect the normative judgement based on intersubjective reflection. But intersubjective reflection does not yet support a normative statement of substantive definitive validity of the form $VAL_{DEF\text{-}SUBS}N$.

Substantive definitive validity, or bindingness, of a norm can be established if the proposed norm is supported by the criterion of reasonable convergence, presupposing, in addition, that the need for a commonly binding norm can be justified. Reasonable convergence means that, based on rational argument, the definitive validity of a particular norm is accepted by an increasing majority of the agents.[30] That is, rational discourse leads to a tendency to accept this norm as

[30] In more detail, see 6.4.2–6.4.4.

definitively valid. A reasonable convergence precludes the claim that an incompatible norm could be binding as well. If, in addition, a commonly binding norm is needed, reasonable agents must accept that this norm is stated to be binding on all its addressees, including those who reject this norm in substance. Thus, it justifies a claim to bindingness.

> (A15) A norm may be claimed to be binding if it is supported by reasonable convergence of autonomous agents and, in addition, a commonly binding norm is needed.

One should note, however, that this justification only *permits* proponents of a norm to claim this norm to be binding on all its addressees. It does not exclude that opponents claim this norm to be wrong. Thus, what can be stated as definitively valid is the permission to claim a norm to be binding, in the case that the conditions for claims of bindingness are met.

## 4.4 CONCLUSION

Summing up, what is necessary in order to establish binding norms is that autonomous agents develop both individual normative conceptions by means of the balancing of interest-based normative arguments, and intersubjectively reflected conceptions as to which norms are binding.

Intersubjective reflection requires taking into account the conceptions of all other autonomous agents involved which, again, requires intersubjective reflection. This, in turn, requires a discursive justification. Statements of definitive validity in the sense of bindingness are justified if a reasonable convergence among autonomous agents results from rational argument as to which norm ought to be seen as definitively valid and hence binding and, in addition, a collectively binding norm is needed.

All this displays the structure of autonomous reasoning as a procedure of argumentation in which different types of validity are attributed to norm-sentences, on the one hand, by individual normative judgements, on the other hand, by normative statements aiming at establishing a definitively valid and binding norm by means of argumentation. In both cases, the necessary steps in argumentation must be taken in order to establish a definitively valid and binding norm. Thus, normative argumentation is a process of transforming claims to validity of a certain type into stronger claims to validity, which again may be confronted with competing claims, in particular, normative arguments and individual normative judgements. It is an oscillating process, which might be successful in establishing a norm as definitively valid and binding, although this is by no means necessary. And even where such a result is achieved, this might at any time be called into question again.[31]

[31] Accordingly, one might qualify the results of autonomous reasoning as defeasible. However, this must not be understood in the sense that a non-monotonic logic applies. Autonomous reasoning includes non-inferential elements of judgement or decision-making, establishing a result with a type of validity that is different from that of the arguments. See Sieckmann (2003b).

# 5

# *Autonomous Balancing*

THE BALANCING OF conflicting normative arguments forms the core of autonomous reasoning. Since it is free but at the same time bound by normative reasons, it represents the structure of autonomy. Hence, the analysis of the structure of balancing is important not only in itself but also in order to understand autonomy. In addition, the relation between autonomy and rationality requires clarification. If autonomous decisions were completely arbitrary, the idea of autonomy could hardly form the basis of law and morality. Thus, a central issue arises, namely, the respects in which autonomous judgement is constrained by standards of rationality and the extent to which a rational justification of norms or normative judgements is possible. Accordingly, an analysis of this structure and of the criteria that apply to balancing is required.

## 5.1 CONCEPTIONS OF BALANCING

To avoid misunderstandings, various conceptions of balancing must be distinguished. In particular, the conception of autonomous balancing presented here contrasts with balancing as calculation and balancing as interpretation.

### 5.1.1 Balancing as Calculation

The conception of balancing as calculation describes balancing as the application of criteria that determine a preference relation among conflicting goods.[1] This might even take the form of a mathematical calculation.

> For example, one might ask what number of policemen is optimal in order to protect public places from vandalism. If the number is too great, the costs will be greater than the damage they will prevent. If it is too small, the damage will be more costly than the policemen. The optimal number of policemen will lie somewhere in the middle, and, given the relevant empirical data, this can be calculated.

A form of calculation is suggested by utilitarian or consequentialist theories, which refer to criteria such as happiness, utilities or individual preferences in order to determine the correct rules or decisions.[2] However, the data that we find

[1] See, eg, Hurley (1989); Broome (1991).
[2] See Sen and Williams (1973: 1 ff); Parfit (1984: 24 ff).

in moral or legal problems will not ordinarily lend themselves to mathematical calculations.[3] In another form of calculation that one finds in the theory of rational decision-making, the concern is with the aggregation of individual preferences according to predetermined criteria that result in a collective preference.[4] This approach, however, is not viable under certain plausible conditions, as demonstrated by Arrow's paradox.[5]

Still another approach to balancing as calculation is presented by Robert Alexy's 'weight formula'. This formula for the balancing of principles includes variables for the abstract weights of principles, the respective intensities of infringement of these principles, and the reliability of empirical premises, and makes it possible for one to infer the priority among conflicting principles in a particular case.[6] It requires that the values of the abstract weights, degrees of fulfilment and reliability of premises be determined. Where this is the case, a calculation becomes possible. The problem, however, remains how to determine these factors. This problem arises, in particular, with respect to the abstract weights of principles.

In general, formal or axiomatic theories of rational decision-making can be interpreted as an analysis of balancing as calculation. The correct result of balancing, if there be one, follows from given axioms, premises and rules of calculation. This approach encounters problems, however, when applied to moral or legal cases. It is therefore important to note that the conception of autonomous balancing suggested here differs from that of balancing as calculation.

### 5.1.2 Balancing as Interpretation

Balancing and subsumption are regarded as distinct forms of legal interpretation and application.[7] If interpretation is understood in a wide sense, balancing may be regarded simply as one mode of interpretation among others. One can, however, juxtapose balancing and interpretation if one regards interpretation as a deductive or inferential form of reasoning, and balancing as reasoning with conflicting arguments, which, accordingly, cannot be either deductive or inferential in some other form.[8] Since balancing cannot adequately be represented as a form of logical inference, treating it in this way is to forgo the essence of balancing.

[3] There are, however, suggestions in this direction. See, eg, Hofmann (2007) and Trapp (1988), who argues that a requirement of rational balancing is that it can be represented within a mathematical model (1988: 396).

[4] See Hurley (1989: 55 ff); Kern and Nida-Rümelin (1994).

[5] See, eg, Hurley (1989: 227 ff); Kern and Nida-Rümelin (1994: 27 ff).

[6] On the 'weight formula', see Alexy (2002a: 408 ff). An even more detailed elaboration one finds in Bernal Pulido (2004; 2006a; 2006b). For a critical discussion, see Brożek (2007a: 107 ff; 2007b); Atienza (2006: 172 ff); Riehm (2006: 66 ff); Sieckmann (2010b).

[7] On the relation between balancing and interpretation, see also Stück (1998); Alexy (2003).

[8] Logical inferences need not be deductive. However, I will disregard the dispute about deductive and non-monotonic reasoning. Both are types of inferential reasoning, which is opposed to autonomous balancing.

By contrast, balancing as interpretation suggests that balancing takes place in the course of applying abstract criteria that frame the decision. For example, one might use such premises as these: the solution must be optimal, or reasonable, or the principle with the greater objective weight or importance in the circumstances of the particular case determines the result. Balancing then consists of determining what is optimal or reasonable, or what counts as the objective weight of the conflicting principles in the particular case. The problem with this approach is that it will work only if criteria are available that determine which solutions are optimal or reasonable, or that answer the question of the weight of a principle in a particular case. If, however, one faces a genuine problem of balancing – requiring autonomous balancing – there are no predetermined criteria for determining the objective weight of the colliding arguments; these are only established by the balancing itself. Accordingly, conceptions of balancing as interpretation have to assume that the solution to the balancing problem has already been predetermined by certain criteria of priority among the competing arguments. If this should be true, then autonomous balancing will not apply. The burden of argument lies with those conceptions that treat balancing as some sort of interpretation. If they do not succeed in this respect, then to conceive of balancing as a kind of interpretation is to conceal the real structure of the problem without having contributed to its solution.

It should be noted, however, that the conception of balancing as interpretation is not without interest for a theory of normative argumentation. For example, legal argumentation will to a great extent consist of arguments based on previously established rules of priority. A purely autonomous judgement will take place only in borderline cases of legal reasoning, where, for example, a new problem must be resolved, or where former solutions are questioned, or where the validity of positive law is cast into doubt. From a practical point of view, interpretive balancing may be of greater importance in legal reasoning than autonomous balancing. Interpretive balancing, however, presupposes that some rules of priority have been established as definitively valid. Thus, autonomous balancing is the primary case of normative argumentation.

### 5.1.3 Autonomous Balancing

The conception of autonomous balancing does not presuppose premises that substantively determine the balancing of normative arguments. Rather, in its core it consists in establishing a priority relation among the conflicting arguments. According to this conception, the structure of balancing includes three elements; first, the arguments to be balanced against each other, secondly, the procedure of balancing aimed at establishing a priority among the conflicting arguments and, thirdly, the definitive norm that stems from the balancing decision.

For example, a legal system might include a norm sanctioning insults, to the effect that, if someone says of another person that he is a liar, this will in general count as an insult and hence be legally forbidden. However, one might argue about the issue. On the one hand, there is the right to personal honour, which demands protection against insults. On the other hand, there is the right to free speech, which requires that everyone be allowed to say what he thinks. These rights cannot both exist without qualification. Hence, we have a conflict of rights. Both rights apply to the case but they cannot both dictate the outcome. They can hold only in principle, requiring a certain solution, but to be weighed and balanced against other arguments. In order to determine a definitive solution, a priority must be established between the competing arguments.

The priority will depend on the facts of the case and on the relative weight of the competing arguments. Thus, the balancing requires not only the conflicting arguments but also supplementary arguments concerning the relative weight and the degree of fulfilment or non-fulfilment of the requirements included in the conflicting arguments.

For example, one might assume that if the offensive assertion was false, the right to personal honour deserves priority. Even if the assertion was sincere but nevertheless wrong, and there are no special circumstances that legitimate the offensive speech, the right to personal honour will be given priority over that of free speech. Another priority rule might be that, if the offensive speech, forming part of an electoral campaign, is to be understood as a drastic way of criticising the political opponent, the right to free speech deserves priority over that of personal honour.

The determination of the priority is, of course, a matter of evaluation. What is of interest here is only the structure of this type of argumentation.

Autonomous balancing includes at least two competing normative arguments. At least in the legal context,[9] they usually are called 'principles' in the sense that they express norms that are valid only in principle. In the example above, these are:

$P_1$: Everyone has the right to free speech.

$P_2$: Everyone has the right to personal honour.

The principle $P_1$ implies a requirement of a particular normative consequence, namely, that the speech be permitted (R). The principle $P_2$ implies a requirement of the opposed consequence ($\neg$R). The normative situation comprises of a number of facts of the case $F_1, \ldots, F_n$. A subset of these facts forms the condition (C) according to which one principle receives priority over the other with respect to the normative issue of whether certain speech be permitted or forbidden.

The priority relation can be defined in various ways, as a priority among principles or between possible results. One may state a priority among the conflicting

[9] By contrast, in moral discourse the term 'principle' is often used to refer to norms of strict validity. One can explain the difference by noting the fact that principles are often seen as important norms of general character, and that in law, in order to count as legally valid, a normative argument must be sufficiently strong to establish an obligation of law-applying organs to take into account this argument in their legal reasoning. Important arguments usually have a wide range of application, so that they may well be called 'principles'. By contrast, in moral reasoning any interest-based claim of an autonomous agent might count, but not all such claims will qualify as principles. See Sieckmann (2010a).

principles with regard to a certain result, that is, a certain legal consequence, and certain conditions. This can be represented as (see also Alexy 2002a, 53):

$$\mathrm{PRIOR}(P_1/P_2)C,R$$

In the example: the principle of free speech receives priority over the principle of personal honour, on the condition that the speech is not false, where permitting the speech in question is at issue.

One may also state a priority with regard to the legal consequences, that is, the possible solutions of the balancing. Such a priority depends on certain conditions C and on the conflicting principles or normative arguments. Thus, the notation will be:

$$\mathrm{PRIOR}(R/\neg R)C,P_1,P_2$$

In the example: on the balancing of the principles of free speech and personal honour in the case of speech that is not false, the permission of speech receives priority over its prohibition.

The second notation makes clear that the conflicting principles figure as reasons for a particular result of the balancing, whereas the first notation represents principles as the objects of the balancing. Both notations are possible. However, the second notation conforms better to the idea of normative arguments as reasons for particular results of a balancing.

The priority among the competing arguments determines which rule commands the case in question. This rule supports the consequence R under a certain condition C:

$$R/C$$

or it may support the opposite consequence non-R under some condition C:

$$\neg R/C$$

The important point is that this rule is established only as the result of the procedure of balancing, and is not derived from predetermined criteria. Since it is based on the reasoning of an autonomous individual (A), the type of validity of the result where, for example, R is chosen, is the following:

$$\mathrm{VAL}_{\mathrm{DEF},A}(R/C).$$

Thus, the result is an individual normative judgement or statement. In spite of this subjective character, there are nevertheless formal criteria of correct balancing that judgements based on balancing must comply with.

## 5.2 THE MODEL OF OPTIMISATION

The central problem of balancing is how to justify a priority among normative arguments in conflict, that is, to justify the result that the balancing ought to have. This depends on the criteria of correct balancing. These criteria can be made explicit by means of a model of optimisation.[10] According to this model, the determination of the priority among normative arguments must render an optimal solution. Again, optimality is defined by a criterion of equilibrium. A solution is optimal if it results in a state of affairs where the conflicting arguments are considered to be of equal weight, that is, where one is indifferent as to the respective gains and losses in the fulfilment of the conflicting requirements.

Figure 5.1 illustrates the structure of a balancing problem.[11]

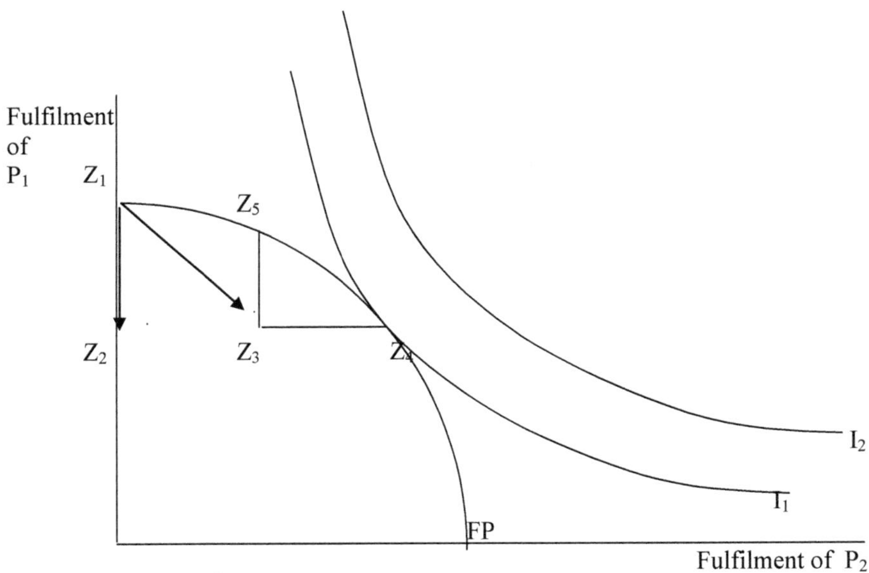


**Figure 5.1: Optimality**

When a conflict between two principles $P_1$ and $P_2$ occurs, the greater the possible degree of fulfilment of the one principle, the lesser the possible degree of fulfilment of the other principle. This is displayed in Figure 5.1 by the curve FP connecting the factually possible solutions. It displays the 'Pareto-Optimality Frontier', that is, the solutions that comport with the criterion of Pareto-optimality. Respecting these solutions, it is not possible to improve on the fulfilment of one of the conflicting principles without diminishing the fulfilment of the other.

[10] The idea of optimisation is ambiguous and contested. For a critique, see, eg, Slote (1989); Wimsatt (2006). It seems, nevertheless, at least possible to integrate critiques, such as the suggestion that one should choose a second-best solution, into a more complex model of optimisation. Also it is not clear whether the critiques against optimisation apply to the model of autonomous balancing proposed here.

[11] See also Hurley (1989: 70); Steiner (1994: 164); Jansen (1997: 29ff).

For example, the greater the extent to which speech is permitted, the lesser the extent to which personal honour is protected. The factually possible, feasible solutions can be represented by a curve that connects the points combining a certain degree of the fulfilment of $P_1$ with the highest possible degree of the fulfilment of $P_2$ that is compatible with the former.

In addition, combinations of a certain degree of fulfilment of $P_1$ and of $P_2$ must be evaluated. Obviously, a complete fulfilment of $P_1$ and $P_2$ would be best, and the complete non-fulfilment of both would be worst. Combinations between these extremes can be ordered in classes of combinations to which someone is indifferent, that is, which one evaluates as equally good. This evaluation results from weighing up a certain loss in the fulfilment of $P_1$ with a certain gain in the fulfilment of $P_2$, for example, a certain loss of protection of personal honour and a certain gain in free speech. The points representing combinations evaluated as equally good can be connected by indifference curves. The higher an indifference curve is placed in this bundle, the better the combinations represented by this curve.

There will be a bundle of indifference curves that do not touch or intersect but that lie on top of each other. Some of these indifference curves will at some point or set of points intersect with or touch the curve of factually possible combinations. The indifference curve that does not intersect but only touches the curve of possible combinations is the best available indifference curve. The points situated on both curves are the optimal solutions of the balancing problem.[12]

The elements of this model of optimisation are an adaptation of the criterion of Pareto-optimality, the idea of indifference curves, and the definition of optimality based on both of the former elements.

### 5.2.1 Criterion of Pareto-Optimality

The criterion of Pareto-optimality defines as optimal those states of affairs that cannot be changed without worsening the position of at least one of the persons involved. In order to apply this criterion to normative arguments, instead of considering the positions of persons, one has to consider the degree of fulfilment of the claims or principles included in normative arguments.[13] Accordingly, solutions are Pareto-optimal if and only if they cannot be changed without diminishing the degree of fulfilment of at least one of the principles involved. Any gain on part of one principle that is involved must result in a loss in the fulfilment of a conflicting principle.

[12] As to this model, see Hurley (1989: 70); Barry (1990: xxxviii, 7); Steiner (1994: 164); Sieckmann (1995: 49 n 19; 2004); Jansen (1997: 29 ff); (1998a: 112 f); Rivers (2007).

[13] This goes beyond the original meaning of the Pareto-criterion and also beyond its use in economics and practical philosophy. However, the criterion explicates a central feature of rational decision-making when choices between incompatible options must be made. There is no need to restrict it to the positions, utilities or preferences of individuals.

In Figure 5.1, Pareto-optimal solutions are represented by the concave curve, bending to the right. The drawing of this curve is arbitrary. It may be drawn as a straight line as well. Also, Pareto-optimal solutions need not form a continuous line. It may be the case that in fact only some discrete solutions can be realised. If, in an extreme case, only those solutions lying on the axes are possible, the balancing would then amount to an all-or-nothing decision. Still, it would be a balancing of normative arguments.[14]

### 5.2.2 Indifference Curves

The points representing solutions evaluated as equally good can be connected by an 'indifference curve'. These solutions are hypothetical, not actual combinations of degrees of fulfilment of the conflicting principles. The indifference curves will run from northwest to southeast, that is, each indifference curve will be falling. Since the agent doing the evaluation will not prefer any one of these points to another point of this curve, he will be indifferent to each of the solutions represented by one curve. He would prefer, however, solutions above this curve to those on the curve.

In Figure 5.1, the indifference curves are represented by convex lines, bending to the left, away from the origin of the scheme. Like that of the Pareto-optimality curve, the drawing is arbitrary.

### 5.2.3 Optimality

The ensuing definition of an optimal solution to a conflict of arguments results as follows. Optimal solutions represent those points situated on the Pareto-optimality frontier as well as on the highest accessible indifference curve, where the indifference curve abuts with the Pareto-optimality curve but does not intersect with it. The points situated on both of these curves are the optimal solutions of the balancing problem. Indifference curves intersecting with the Pareto-optimality curve cannot be optimal, for there is a superior indifference curve that does not intersect but abuts with the curve of possible combinations. The points on the abutting indifference curve are evaluated as better than those on a lower indifference curve. In addition, the points that are situated also on the Pareto-optimality curve represent solutions that are in fact possible. On the other hand, points on indifference curves above the Pareto-optimality curve are in fact not accessible. They cannot be solutions to the balancing problem. Thus, the optimal solutions must be those situated on both curves, that is, the Pareto-optimality frontier and the highest accessible indifference curve.

[14] Therefore one should not restrict the concept of principles to norms that can be fulfilled in degrees, as suggested by Alexy (2002a: 47 f).

## 5.3 CRITERIA OF BALANCING

The basic requirement of balancing is that of choosing an optimal solution. The problem with this requirement is that the criterion of optimality is not applicable independently of the balancing. The choice between possible solutions of a balancing or, as one might also say, between the conflicting arguments in the respective case, is determined by the optimal solutions. These depend on the relative weight attributed to the principles in conflict as well as on the extent of their realisation or non-realisation by means of the alternative solutions. The weighting of the conflicting principles is to be determined, however, by the balancing itself and cannot provide a criterion for this decision.

Nevertheless, there are criteria of correct balancing. The balancing of normative arguments must follow criteria of rationality, if this balancing is to count as a rational justification of a normative judgement. There are some general requirements of rationality, such as those of consistency and coherence, of correctness of the empirical premises, and of supervenience in the sense that the reasoning should be related to conceivable, empirically verifiable data. Moreover, the optimisation model includes specific requirements of correct balancing.

### 5.3.1 Requirements of Correct Balancing

The optimisation model offers two negative criteria, negative in the sense that they do not determine a correct solution but merely point out possible mistakes. The first of these follows the criterion of Pareto-optimality:

> (B1) Solutions that restrict a principle unnecessarily, without any gain for a conflicting principle, are inadmissible.

In such a case it would be possible to find a better solution respecting the latter principle without loss to the former principle. An optimal solution must be situated on the curve indicating the Pareto-possibility frontier. In Figure 5.1, $Z_2$ and $Z_3$ are not Pareto-optimal. $Z_2$ is the result of a restriction of $P_1$ with no gain regarding $P_2$. $Z_3$ receives some degree of the fulfilment of $P_2$, but $Z_4$ and $Z_5$ (as well as the solutions on the Pareto-optimal frontier) between them are clearly better (Pareto-superior) to $Z_3$.

> (B2) The indifference curves must be negatively sloped, that is falling, running from northwest to southeast. They must not be either horizontal or vertical.

This follows, for the fulfilment of a valid requirement must be evaluated positively. Hence, a solution that does not gain anything for the one principle but is worse with respect to a conflicting principle cannot be evaluated as equally good. The second criterion is similar to that of Pareto-optimality; it is applied, however, not to factual possibilities but to the evaluation of hypothetical solutions.

Decisions that violate these conditions are mistaken. This, however, does not answer the question of how a correct, optimal solution is determined. In order to do this, one must try to formulate preference rules. One then confronts the problem, however, that it is not clear how to determine the relative weight and the degrees of fulfilment of the competing arguments. Still, one can analyse the factors entering into the balancing in order to establish certain constraints on autonomous balancing and develop arguments for this balancing.

### 5.3.2 Factors of Balancing

In order to find a rational basis of balancing, one can develop preference rules and preference orderings case by case, making clear which criteria are applied in balancing decisions, and then try to provide a rational justification for the application of these criteria, which refers to standards that are independent of the balancing problem to be decided. In this approach, certain requirements of coherence are applied, which are specific to the balancing of normative arguments. In the last instance, balancing relies on general criteria of practical rationality as developed in theories of practical argumentation.[15]

The first step, however, is to formulate the factors in balancing. Two types of factors can be identified. These are the degrees of fulfilment of the competing claims and the relative weights assigned to these claims, both directed to the concrete case to be decided. They form the basis of the criteria of correct balancing according to the model of optimisation.

#### *5.3.2.1 Degree of Fulfilment*

In Figure 5.1, the degrees of fulfilment of the conflicting principles are represented along the axes. The closer a point representing a solution is to the origin, the less the respective principle is fulfilled. Degrees of fulfilment may be interpreted in different ways. One can refer to the degrees of fulfilment of the respective principles achieved or lost by a certain balancing result, compared with what would result from the contrary decision. Or one might refer to the overall fulfilment of the conflicting principle. The second option encounters the problem, however, that one must refer to the level of complete fulfilment of a principle, which may be difficult to determine and might even not exist in the case of a normative ideal that does not have a maximum of fulfilment. The first option is more elementary and, moreover, is all that is required in order to determine the degrees of fulfilment of the conflicting principles. It determines the degree of fulfilment (or non-fulfilment) of a principle by establishing what is gained or lost by a balancing result with respect to the level of fulfilment of the respective principles that is given.

[15] See Alexy (1989a); Buchwald (1990); Bäcker (2008).

For example, the prohibition of insulting speech draws out a certain degree of the fulfilment of the principle of free speech, and adds a certain degree of fulfilment to the principle of the protection of personal honour.

These factors may be represented as:

$$\Delta FM(P_1,N) \text{ and } \Delta FM(P_2,N)$$

#### 5.3.2.2 *Relative Weight of Principles*

The relative weight of the conflicting principles determines what normative importance is attributed to the degree of fulfilment of conflicting requirements. It is determined only in relation to a conflicting requirement,[16] and can be represented as:

$WR(P_1,P_2)$: the relative weight of $P_1$ against $P_2$, and

$WR(P_2,P_1)$: the relative weight of $P_2$ against $P_1$

Since the relative weight of a principle may depend on the degree to which a principle is fulfilled or not fulfilled,[17] it should be stated in relation to the given level of fulfilment which, again, may be represented by the balancing results in question, that is, the norm N. However, reference to N may not suffice, for the balancing may depend on factors of the case at hand that are not represented by the conditions of application and the normative consequence of N. Therefore, it seems advisable to refer to all the circumstances that enter into the case to be decided, which are presented by C. The relative weight of conflicting principles can then be represented as:

$$WR(P_1,P_2,C,N) \text{ and } WR(P_2, P_1,C,N)$$

The relative weights of the principles are correlated in reverse order. If one represents them with numbers x and y, the following equation will hold:

$$x = 1/y$$ [18]

[16] See Barry (1990: 7 n 2).

[17] Some authors suggest that the relative weight of a principle increases with the diminishing degree of fulfilment. See Alexy (2002a: 195); Jansen (1997). Although this may indeed be plausible in many cases, it is not clear that it constitutes a conceptual feature of balancing. Against this position, see Sieckmann (2009b: 64 f).

[18] Mathematical functions may be of help in monitoring the coherence of the balancing. As long as their use is confined to this purpose, and they are not used as a method of calculating the correct result of the balancing, there are no fundamental objections to their use in presenting arguments of balancing. See Sieckmann (2010b: 114 ff)

An important point is that the relative weight of a principle is not an intrinsic property but depends on the other principle involved in a conflict.

> For example, the relative weight of the principle of liberty depends on whether it collides with the principle of the protection of health or with economic arguments, such as, for example, that smoking in a tenant's flat may mean that the flat must be repainted more often. In the first case, the relative weight of the principle of liberty will be rather low, in the second case much higher.

The relative weight of a principle also depends on the circumstances of the case, for example, the strength of interests involved, and on the importance that certain principles are deemed to have in a society.

### 5.3.3 Relative Weight in a Particular Case

By means of the concept of the relative weight, a third criterion for correct balancing can be formulated. It refers to the concept of the relative weight (or relative importance) of a principle in a particular case, that is, with regard to all relevant circumstances of the case that one has to decide.[19] The relative weight of a principle in a particular case is a function of its relative weight and of its degree of fulfilment or non-fulfilment in a particular case. The degree of fulfilment of the respective principles depends on the solution chosen, that is, a particular norm N or its opposite, ¬N. Thus, the balancing result depends on four factors, which means that the priority of principles is determined by a function *f* of these factors.

> For example, in a conflict between free speech and the protection of personal honour, the chosen norm may be N: permission of the speech in question, or ¬N: prohibition of this speech. This alternation may be represented as N/¬N. Since norm N, however, already determines this alternation, it suffices to mention N. The priority relation among the principles $P_1$ and $P_2$ regarding circumstances C depends, then, on the degrees of fulfilment and the relative weight of the principles involved.

Accordingly, the following rule of balancing holds:

> (B3) The priority among conflicting principles $P_1$, $P_2$ regarding a possible result N in circumstances C is a function of the difference of fulfilment (ΔFM) that the choice of N or ¬N makes to the fulfilment of $P_1$ and $P_2$, respectively, and the relative weight (WR) of $P_1$ against $P_2$ in circumstances C regarding N.

The relative weight of a principle in a particular case will be greater, the greater the relative weight of this principle, and the greater the degree of fulfilment or non-fulfilment of the principles brought about by the balancing decision. A balancing decision will determine a particular solution and, thus, the degree of fulfil-

[19] In this context, 'particular case' does not mean an individual case. Since the circumstances of the case are certain features described by means of predicates, the object of the decision will usually be a case in a generic sense, comprising a set of individual cases, and its result will accordingly be a general rule with a more or less extensive scope of application.

ment or non-fulfilment of a principle. Alternative decisions will lead to alternative degrees of fulfilment or non-fulfilment. The greater the degree of non-fulfilment brought about by the decision is, the more difficult it is to justify this decision. This is reflected by the relative weight of a principle in the particular case. Accordingly, the following requirement of coherence holds for the balancing of principles:

> (B4) The greater the degree of non-fulfilment of a principle to be justified, the greater the relative weight of a conflicting principle in the particular case must be in order to justify the degree of non-fulfilment of the first principle.[20]

From this, more specific rules follow. Since the relative weight of a principle in a particular case is proportional to the relative weight of the principle and to the degree of fulfilment or non-fulfilment to be decided upon, the justification of an increase in the non-fulfilment of one of the principles requires an increase in one of the other factors.

### 5.3.4 Abstract Weight of Principles

The weakness of the criterion of the relative weight of principles is that, according to the analysis above, relative weight is determined only by means of the balancing itself. It only explicates the priority that is established among the conflicting principles; it cannot, however, itself serve as a criterion to determine such a decision. A stronger conception of balancing attributes weight to principles independently of actual balancing. The difference of such an abstract relative weight of a principle is that it has to be established independently of the balancing decision to be made, so that it does not merely explicate which relative weight has been attributed in a balancing. This abstraction allows one to use the relative weight as (part of) a criterion for balancing judgements.

Another step in order to strengthen the force of balancing as a method of rational justification is to define the weight of principles not with regard to a pair of principles standing in conflict, that is, as a relational weight, but as the weight assigned to each principle separately. The difference is that the relational weight of a principle must always be correlated with that of the conflicting principle. If it is high, the relative weight of the conflicting principles must be low. If it is medium, the relative weight of the conflicting principles must also be medium. By contrast, one might attribute weight to principles independently of a particular conflict with a competing principle. It seems plausible that a principle that always or in many cases receives, for example, a high relative weight is seen as having a high abstract weight in a non-relational sense.

[20] Alexy (2002a: 102) has called a similar relation the 'law of balancing' (*Abwägungsgesetz*), although it is not clear whether this is meant in the same sense as is being used here. Alexy seems to understand this relation as expressing also the increase of the relative weight with a diminishing degree of fulfilment of a principle.

If, for example, the principle of free speech is almost always given high relative weight compared with competing principles, one can also assign great weight to it without reference to competing principles.

Still the non-relational weight of a principle is a relative weight in the sense that it refers to the relative strength of the principle in conflict with other principles. Such an assignment of a non-relational abstract weight differs from, but is related to, the relational weight of the respective principles. A principle of high non-relational relative weight will have high relational relative weight in conflict with a principle of medium relative weight, but in the event of a conflict with a principle that has high abstract relative weight as well, the relational relative weight for both of them will only be medium.

The conception of an abstract weight of a principle fits intuitions regarding the balancing of normative arguments.

For example, the rights to life, physical integrity and health are of great weight regardless of the rights or principles they conflict with. However, if such a right collides with a right of the same type, both will have the same relational weight.

With the attribution of an abstract weight to principles independently of a concrete balancing decision, a different construction of balancing decisions becomes possible. One can now attach values to the gains and losses respecting the fulfilment of a principle, which will be called 'values of fulfilment' of the principles in question. A certain degree of fulfilment of a principle will correspond to a certain value of fulfilment VF of the respective norm N in case C with regard to one of the principles, $P_1$, involved in the balancing. This value will depend on the abstract weight WR of the respective principle $P_1$ against the competing principle $P_2$ and the degree of its fulfilment. The abstract weight may depend on external factors, for example, the extent to which a society deems as urgent attributes to the interest protected by the principle in question, and will not be the same in various contexts of decision. In any case, the following relation holds:

(B5) The value of fulfilment of a principle is positively correlated to the degree of its fulfilment and its relative weight.

The value of fulfilment of a principle regarding the facts of the case is its weight in the concrete case.

In addition, one can define an overall value of fulfilment of a certain solution, that is, of the resulting norm N, which depends on the values of fulfilment of the competing principles in conjunction.

(B6) The value of fulfilment of a particular balancing result N is positively correlated to the values of fulfilment of the respective principles in conflict.

A solution that achieves the highest value of fulfilment is optimal. Thus, one can define optimal solutions as those that achieve a maximum (MAX) in the overall value of fulfilment:

DFOPT: Optimal results of the balancing of principles are those with the greatest overall value of fulfilment with respect to the particular case.

Instead of the value of fulfilment, one can as well refer to the concrete weight or importance of the conflicting arguments respecting a particular result in a particular case. This is appropriate, in particular, in order to be able to state criteria of priority among conflicting principles.

The guiding criterion of the balancing is that of choosing an optimal result. Accordingly, the following rules of balancing hold:

(B7) The result of the balancing of principles must present an optimal solution to the particular case.

Or, equivalently:

(B7') One must choose, as result of the balancing of normative arguments, the solution with the highest value of fulfilment that can be achieved by the particular decision.

(B7") One must give, as result of the balancing of normative arguments, priority to that argument with greater weight (importance) in the concrete case.

Accordingly, the following rule of priority holds:

(B8) In a conflict of $P_1$ and $P_2$ concerning case C and consequence R, priority must be given to the principle the fulfilment of which achieves the higher value of fulfilment in the circumstances of case C.

The consequence R defines the norm N that may or may not be the result of the balancing. Instead of values of fulfilment, one can speak of the weight or importance of a principle $P_i$ in a particular case C regarding the consequence R, namely:

$$WR(P_i,N,C,R)$$

The representation of the balancing as a comparison of values of fulfilment, weight or importance in the particular case reflects common intuitions. What is more, it implies further, comparative rules of balancing. These apply *ceteris paribus* on the basis of a comparison of cases. Thus, the following relations hold:

(B9) If $P_1$ receives priority over $P_2$ in case $C_1$, and in case $C_2$ the value of fulfilment of $P_1$ is greater than in $C_1$, then, *ceteris paribus*, $P_1$ receives priority over $P_2$ in $C_2$.

Since the value of fulfilment of a principle depends on the degree of fulfilment and the abstract weight of the principle in question, rule (6) is the basis of more detailed rules:

(B10) If $P_1$ receives priority over $P_2$ in case $C_1$, and in case $C_2$ the degree of fulfilment of $P_2$ is smaller than in $C_1$, then, *ceteris paribus*, $P_1$ receives priority over $P_2$ in $C_2$.

(B11) If $P_1$ receives priority over $P_2$ in case $C_1$, and in case $C_2$ the abstract weight of $P_1$ is greater than in $C_1$, then, *ceteris paribus*, $P_1$ receives priority over $P_2$ in $C_2$.

(B12) If $P_1$ and $P_2$ are of equal relative weight in case $C_1$, and in case $C_2$ the abstract weight of $P_1$ is greater or the degree of fulfilment of $P_2$ is smaller than in $C_1$, then, *ceteris paribus*, $P_1$ receives priority over $P_2$ in $C_2$.

Such coherence rules are not applicable, however, if the *ceteris paribus* condition is not met. This will be the case if the degrees of fulfilment and the abstract weights of $P_1$ and $P_2$ vary in different directions, that is, the change of one factor favours $P_1$, the change of the other factor $P_2$.

### 5.3.5 Criteria of Abstract Weight

The evaluation by means of values of fulfilment or by appeal to the importance in the concrete case does not offer criteria that make it possible for one to determine abstract weights of principles, values of fulfilment of single principles, and overall values of fulfilment of solutions that stem from balancing decisions. Rather, it presupposes that these factors are determined. The rules of balancing stated above present side-constraints of correct balancing, not directives that guide balancing. The determination of the factors of balancing forms part of the balancing itself, and statements of weights and values of fulfilment only explicate the assumptions underlying a balancing judgement. Although this contributes to the conception of balancing as a form of rational justification, balancing would offer a stronger form of rational justification if the factors involved in the balancing could be determined not only *ex post*, explicating a decision taken, but *ex ante*, figuring as criteria for the balancing decision. Hence, the question is whether there are criteria, or at least arguments,[21] to determine these factors of balancing.

With regard to the abstract weight of principles,[22] three criteria contribute to its determination: the strength of interests that back the principle in question, other principles that support a principle involved in a conflict, and prior decisions establishing preference relations among principles.

The interdependence of the abstract weight of principles and the strength of interests backing these principles stems from the fact that individual interests are the primary source of the validity of principles. Autonomous individuals demand that their interests be respected and thus require the acceptance of those corresponding principles that protect these interests. Since these interests can be more or less strong, the abstract weight of the corresponding principle will differ accordingly.

[21] One should not expect to find a consistent set of criteria of weights and degrees of fulfilment, but rather various arguments for a particular determination of these factors which, again, may conflict. Thus, problems of balancing may also occur with respect to the determination of the factors of balancing. This will not necessarily be the case, however, and in any event a more precise and elaborate determination of the factors of balancing contributes to the rationality of balancing.

[22] The following is limited to this aspect, because it seems the most problematic. By contrast, it seems clear that at least in some cases one is able to determine degrees of fulfilment or non-fulfilment in an objective manner.

Thus, the weight of normative arguments can be judged according to the importance of reflected interests. The importance of an interest is in first place determined by the needs of the person having that interest. These needs can be more or less strong or urgent. One can take the strength or urgency of an interest as a criterion of the prima facie importance of the interest. This evaluation may need revision, however, with respect to the interests of a person over the long run or with respect to her conception of the good life. The importance of an interest that is assigned to it after a process of reflection can be called the value of that interest.

The evaluation of interests can be carried out by the party whose interest is at stake, but also by other agents. Furthermore, criteria for the rational evaluation of interests may be introduced. Hence, one can distinguish subjective evaluations and different kinds of 'objective' evaluations of interests. At the level of autonomous normative judgements, only subjective evaluations are necessary. The preference relations reflect the relative strength or weight of the conflicting arguments, or the value of what it is that, according to these arguments, is to be realised. The balancing forms a part of the development of a conception of the good life. Someone developing such a conception employs his own judgements on the value of things and the relative weight of arguments. These judgements can reflect the evaluations of other agents as well, for example, the weight they attach to their interests. But they need not. Someone may think that his own evaluations are best, and that, for example, the interest in smoking counts for very little, no matter how smokers themselves evaluate their interest in smoking. However, any reasonable agent must consider the empirical strength of needs and preferences.

Hence, the problem of aggregating preferences or interests is not as great a problem as one might think. The problem of intersubjective comparisons of utilities can be resolved where only one agent is judging. He can always make judgements about preference aggregations, provided that he has all the relevant information, or at any rate thinks he does. Since the balancing of normative arguments leads to norms that state what one ought to do (according to the agent judging), an autonomous agent can make normative statements about what one ought to do, and how conflicts of interests ought to be resolved.

One might refer to the strength of interests, not only as a subjective evaluation, but also as an objective argument. First, as a critical argument, the strength of interests might be used to show that the weight a proponent attributes to an argument does not correspond to the strength of the interests on which it relies. This would only be an internal critique questioning the validity of an argument. Since in this context the strength of an interest is regarded as an empirical factor, such an argument does not suffice to establish a normative solution but can only point out mistakes in proposed solutions.

Taken as a positive argument, the strength of an interest may be introduced as an objective evaluation. This is possible on the basis of the criterion of the strength of reasonable convergence.[23] If someone places certain weight on an argument

[23] See 6.4.2.

owing to the corresponding strength of a supporting interest, this is a claim as to which evaluation one ought to accept as commonly binding. As such, it can be judged according to the degree to which it fulfils criteria of rational justification and according to the strength with which the agents involved hold this conviction. If such judgements lead to a reasonable convergence of autonomous agents as to the evaluation of the respective argument, the argument can claim a certain form of objective validity. Hence, an objective evaluation is possible – though not in all cases, but in some, where reasonable convergence results.

Backing by other principles gives a principle additional weight, although this must not be understood as an addition in a mathematical sense. For example, since the principle of free speech is fundamental with respect to the functioning of democracy, it is supported by the principle of democracy. Accordingly, it receives in general a greater weight than conflicting principles, and claims to free speech get prima facie priority against other claims.

> This is exemplified by the *Lüth* case and decisions following it,[24] in which the German Constitutional Court held that, owing to its relation to democracy, freedom of speech deserves greater relative weight by comparison with competing rights, and also by the *Lebach* case where the Court held that in general the broadcasting of a documentary film about a crime must be permitted, even though this may affect an undisturbed personal development of the delinquents.[25] It is only owing to the special circumstances of the case that this prima facie priority of free speech was reversed and the broadcasting prohibited.

A third criterion for the abstract weight of a principle is the reference to preference relations established in other cases that display the abstract weight assigned to the principles in question. If, for example, a principle was accorded priority in many other cases of conflict with various principles and these conflicting principles are of some weight, one can then assume that the prevailing principle has a great abstract weight. This of course presupposes that the abstract weight of the other principles is already known. Hence, the reference to other cases is an argument of coherence, not an ultimate criterion for the abstract weight of principles.

## 5.4 THE INDETERMINACY OF BALANCING

The criteria of balancing do not positively determine a certain solution, although they preclude some solutions. This indeterminacy of balancing stems first of all from the evaluative character of the weighting of principles that is represented by the indifference curves. One can, however, also find indeterminacy in other respects of the balancing.

A first type of indeterminacy may be called structural indeterminacy.[26] Even if someone has completed a balancing with all necessary information, this need not

[24] BVerfGE 7, 198 – Lüth; 61, 1 – NPD Europas.
[25] BVerfGE 35, 202 – Lebach.
[26] See also Alexy (2002a: 310) on 'structural discretion'.

lead to a single solution. The criterion of optimality may be indeterminate, owing to the fact that several solutions are optimal at the same time.

> For example, with respect to the protection of free speech, various regulations for the protection of personal honour might be possible, and one might well judge these regulations to be equally good, for the loss in free speech is compensated by an increase in the protection of personal honour, and vice versa.

A second type of indeterminacy stems from epistemic reasons.[27] One might not be able to determine a single solution owing to the fact that one does not have sufficient knowledge for a completely determined judgement that is based on balancing. The necessary empirical knowledge for determining the degrees of fulfilment of principles might not be available, or such degrees might not have been defined with sufficient precision. This will yield an epistemic indeterminacy of the balancing decision.[28] Several solutions will be regarded as equally good; one does not have information that would justify a finer discrimination.

> For example, the risks to public health stemming from a certain disease might not be well understood; following the relevant probabilistic assumptions, different solutions may appear to be correct.

A third kind of indeterminacy arises when the normative judgements of reasonable agents differ. Their judgements may differ in evaluative respects as well as in their empirical assumptions. Here the reason is not the structural or epistemic indeterminacy of individual judgements based on balancing; rather, it is the impossibility of making objectively valid judgements in these respects. The possibility of differing judgements of different agents may be called discursive indeterminacy, by contrast with the structural or epistemic indeterminacy of monological reasoning. Discursive indeterminacy implies that not only one but, indeed, several judgements based on balancing may reasonably be held. It is not a first-order indeterminacy within the structure or criteria of the balancing itself, but a second-order indeterminacy with respect to the procedure of rational argumentation, and of the available criteria of objectivity.

A fourth kind of indeterminacy arises in legal or other institutionalised systems where competences of decision-making are distributed and, therefore, competences to make authoritative judgements exist. In such a system a judge might deem himself able to justify a certain judgement based on balancing but nevertheless see himself obligated to respect the normative views of other organs in the legal system, for example, the legislature or administrative organs. Thus, he might be hindered from deciding as he deems correct at a substantive level, bound, as he

[27] See Alexy (2002a: 310).

[28] Alexy (2002a: 420) also regards the indeterminacy of the relative weight of conflicting principles as a case of epistemic indeterminacy. This does not, however, seem to be correct, for establishing the relative weight of a principle is not a cognitive act but an autonomous determination. Autonomous agents may make such determinations without an epistemic foundation. By contrast, it would be incorrect to make a statement, for example, that some event is highly probable, if one does not have sufficient information to justify the statement.

is, to respect the competences of organs that have made different decisions on the same matter, or he might at least be permitted to defer to the alien judgement. In such cases, the role of judicial review[29] needs to be defined.

The case of indeterminacy owing to competing competences of other decision-makers is different from that of discursive indeterminacy. The respect for competences of other organs serves as a reason to forbear from deciding according to one's own substantive normative views. Within a free discourse, without competence on the part of particular agents to make certain authoritative decisions, discursive indeterminacy means that all agents will remain committed to their own judgements, and the discourse will not lead to a unique solution. By contrast, competence respective to forming authoritative judgements may require that agents who are subject to these competences forbear from applying their own judgement even though this judgement may well be justified as correct. The indeterminacy owing to the competence to hand down authoritative judgements is the result, for the normative situation becomes dependent on the judgements of other agents. Again, it is not a first-order indeterminacy but a second-order indeterminacy, stemming from features of authoritative systems with different organs and competences that make necessary a second-order balancing on the question of who ought to have the competence to make a binding decision.

Authoritative competence may apply with various degrees of strictness with respect to the bindingness of the norms issued by the authority. These norms may be strictly binding or merely binding in principle. Furthermore, an authoritative competence may apply in two cases: first, with respect to judgements that are justifiable in a rational discourse and, secondly, with respect to incorrect judgements, those that cannot rationally be justified. Since authority is defined as the power to make decisions that are binding apart from their substantive correctness, the second case cannot be excluded as a merely theoretical possibility. Whether a legal system makes use of it, and what degree of strictness is claimed, is an issue of positive law.

The authority to make judgements that are in principle binding on other organs may be represented by formal principles.[30] These principles require that one is to follow the decision of another organ. For example, one might propose the requirement that courts are to respect the balancing of constitutional principles by the democratically elected parliament, for, so the proposal goes, this balancing is political in character, and parliament has greater legitimation where deciding the issue is concerned. In this case, we encounter the need to balance between competing conceptions of constitutional interpretation, that favouring the parliament and that favouring the court. Although the court may believe that the substantive reasons in favour of one solution are stronger, the principle of democracy requires that the decision of the parliament be respected. This requirement is not absolute, however, for the court might understand the argument on behalf of its normative

[29] See Rivers (2006), (2007); Sieckmann (1990: 152 ff; 1998: 60 ff).

[30] On the notion of formal principles see Alexy (2002a); Sieckmann (1990;, 2009a), (2009b). See 9.3.1.

view as sufficiently strong to outweigh the requirement that the interpretation of the parliament be respected.

## 5.5 CONCLUSION

The analysis of balancing as a problem of optimisation provides for a fairly precise account of the formal structure of the balancing of principles and, more generally, normative arguments, as well as of the criteria and factors bearing on it. It also makes clear, however, that the criteria of correct balancing will often not suffice to determine the result of such a balancing. They will exclude certain results as mistaken, and this might in turn even require the recognition of certain norms as definitively valid, or the balancing might lead to clear results in some cases, given the circumstances of the case. In other cases, however, there will be no clear result. Therefore, the indeterminacy of balancing remains an essential feature of this type of reasoning. This should neither surprise us nor be seen as a defect. It simply reflects the element of choice that is essential to autonomous reasoning, and it therefore supports the thesis that the balancing of normative arguments is the characteristic feature of autonomous reasoning.

# 6

# *Claims to Correctness, Validity and Objectivity*

THE STRUCTURE OF the balancing of normative arguments can be regarded as 'the logic of autonomy'[1] owing to the fact that judgements based on balancing are free but at the same time also bound by normative arguments. This may be called the 'autonomy thesis'. Individual autonomy, however, implies that normative judgements are subjective, personal and agent-relative, and cannot as such claim to be objectively valid such that they bind others. Hence, the problem remains, namely, how claims to objective validity can be justified by means of autonomous reasoning. Objective validity, by contrast with subjective validity, must in some way be independent of individual normative judgement. It is not clear, however, how this, in keeping with a conception of autonomous reasoning that makes any normative justification depend on individual judgements, is possible.

The problem breaks down into two issues: first, the conception of objective validity requires clarification; secondly, the capacity of autonomous reasoning to establish objectively valid results must be analysed. The issues are interrelated. It makes no sense to use a conception of objective validity that is not appropriate for normative argumentation. In this respect, objectivity as truth or as correspondence with reality seems to be inappropriate for autonomous reasoning, for the balancing of normative arguments is not about discovering a normative reality. Rather, it is about constructing it. Therefore, one must ask, first of all, which claims are included in normative argumentation, what is required to justify these claims, and which norms, according to the claims involved in normative argumentation, must be accepted or cannot be accepted.[2] Accordingly, the claims implied in autonomous judgements and the possibility of justifying these claims require closer analysis.

[1] This should not be confused with the positivist's thesis of the autonomy of law. On this thesis, see Postema (1996).

[2] This is a strategy also used by transcendental-pragmatic arguments, which claim to explicate the presuppositions that anybody who seriously participates in argumentation must accept along with their implications. However, the analysis of presuppositions of normative argumentation suggested here is not concerned with the question of whether particiption in normative argumentation is necessary.

## 6.1 CLAIMS TO CORRECTNESS

A most fundamental and abstract claim implied in normative judgements is that of the correctness of the judgement. Beginning with the question of what counts as correct, more specific claims can be identified. In particular, one can ask what is required to justify a normative judgement or statement and then conclude that someone making such a judgement or uttering such a statement claims that the conditions necessary to justify it have been met.

However, the concept of a claim to correctness is ambiguous. It might be understood as a claim to truth or to something similar to truth, and it would then be seen as an epistemic claim.[3] By contrast, in a normative sense one might understand a claim to correctness as the claim to do what is right or required.

### 6.1.1 Epistemic Correctness

Epistemic correctness may be understood in various ways. A strong version interprets it as ontological correctness, that is, a sentence is true if it corresponds with reality. This may be called a strong correspondence theory of truth. Its criterion of truth is the recognition of facts. Applied to normative justification, this would imply that it is possible to know which norms exist. A weaker correspondence theory submits that if one accepts a normative statement as true, one is thereby assuming that there is a corresponding normative fact. According to this view, facts are merely stipulations by means of which we interpret statements.[4] The claim of truth in this weak, merely semantic sense, means no more than that the assertion of p implies the assertion that p is true. This semantic thesis can be combined with an epistemological thesis to the effect that the truth of a sentence can be judged without reference to corresponding facts, for example, by means of a rational discourse.

According to these distinctions, claims to truth can take different forms:

(1) Truth as a semantic claim: making a statement implies a claim that this statement is true.
(2) Truth as a purely ontological claim: making a statement implies that there is a fact that makes this statement true, whether or not one is able to verify this fact.
(3) Truth as a weak epistemic claim: making a statement implies that one can justify the statement on cognitive grounds, which need not refer to corresponding facts.
(4) Truth as a strong epistemic claim: making a statement implies that one can justify the statement by reference to some corresponding fact.

[3] A claim to correctness in an epistemic sense is referred to in Alexy's thesis that people necessarily make claims to correctness in their arguments or statements. This thesis of a necessary claim to correctness is used in order to justify moral norms or discursive rights. See Alexy (1995: 132 ff); also Habermas (1998, orig. 1996: 62 f). The claim to truth is also the focus of Dworkin (2006: 2 ff); Pavlakos (2007); Somek (2006).

[4] One might even use the concept of truth without referring to facts. See Patterson (1996).

The strong epistemic claim appears to be too strong, at least with respect to normative argumentation. Normative statements cannot be justified by referring to a corresponding normative fact. Consequently, the ontological claim seems to be without any relevance to normative reasoning. The assumption of normative facts that correspond to normative statements, though it may be harmless, cannot be used to justify the statement in question. Accordingly, it seems reasonable to understand the claim to truth of normative statements as a semantic and weak epistemic claim.

Whatever version of a claim to truth one adopts, the content and claims connected with normative statements require that they be used in a way that is compatible with the assertion of their truth. One might call this requirement a claim to logical truth-likeness. If, for example, one makes a statement that one ought not to kill, one cannot at the same time reject a statement that it is true that one ought not to kill. It includes also a claim to the logical consistency of the normative statements that an agent makes or accepts. Normative statements must, moreover, be compatible with the purely ontological claim that a corresponding fact exists. If one makes a statement, for example, that smoking is forbidden, it must be possible to assume that in fact it is forbidden to smoke. This implication is weak but nevertheless not without interest. It requires that in order to be able to make correct normative statements one must remove normative conflicts and must try to construe a 'normative world' with logical properties comparable to those in the world of empirical facts. This requires, moreover, a certain stability of normative judgements in the sense that they cannot depend solely on evaluations but must have empirical backing, for mere evaluations might change at any moment.

However, epistemic correctness is not an adequate interpretation of the claim to correctness of normative judgements based on the balancing of normative arguments. Since this balancing is not determined in its result by pre-established criteria and hence autonomous agents may come to different results, these judgements do not display the necessary features of truth. In particular, one cannot preclude the possibility that incompatible normative judgements are equally justified. Consequently, individual normative judgements cannot be regarded as statements of normative facts, and hence cannot be claimed to be true.[5]

### 6.1.2 Normative Correctness

Normative judgements based on the balancing of normative arguments are connected with a claim to normative correctness. One can speak of normative

[5] Alexy (2007b: 333 ff) argues that the claim to truth still serves as a regulative idea, providing orientation to the argumentation. Truth as a regulative idea of discourse does not, however, suffice to justify a claim to the truth of particular statements. By the same token, a wanderer needs an orientation but cannot claim, with his first steps, that he has already arrived at his destination.

correctness in the sense that an action corresponds to a requirement and is therefore correct.[6]

> For example, speech-acts may be said to be correct if they conform to communicative conventions. The acceptance of an argument, too, may be said to be correct if it should be accepted as a good argument. The acceptance of a norm as valid can be said to be correct if it ought to be accepted as valid.

This claim to normative correctness may hold in a stronger or a weaker sense. The weaker form consists in the compatibility of an act with the applicable norms. In this sense, an act can be correct if it is compatible with the relevant norms, notwithstanding the fact that one might have acted otherwise. Similarly, normative judgements can be said to be correct if they are compatible with the relevant norms. A stronger form is that of normative necessity, that is, an act is correct because it is normatively required. A normative judgement is correct if it is required by the relevant norms. Whilst the weaker version of normative correctness allows for different solutions, the stronger version points to a required solution. This requirement may hold definitively or only in principle. The strong claim to correctness of a definitive requirement is similar to the claim to epistemic correctness, for it precludes competing solutions. Even this stronger claim does not, however, imply that from the perspective of someone making a normative judgement, there cannot be reasonable disagreement about the correct solution. By contrast, stating the truth of a proposition precludes, according to the content of this statement, the possibility that incompatible propositions may correctly be held to be true.[7]

Normative justification requires a weak claim to correctness with respect to the requirements of formal rationality, combined with a strong claim to normative correctness where the proposed norm is concerned, which includes the requirement of the validity of this norm. Such requirements for validity offer a justification of norms that is different from a justification of them by means of logical inference. The normative justification is not based on a logical inference stemming from a set of premises and concluding with a normative statement. Rather, its point is a justification of a norm on the ground that its validity (and its acceptance by a reasonable agent) is required by the prevailing normative arguments.

## 6.2 CLAIM TO CORRECTNESS OF AUTONOMOUS JUDGEMENTS

The claim to correctness of an autonomous judgement includes the point that this judgement, although free and not predetermined by established norms, is required by the stronger of the competing normative arguments and, hence, ought to be accepted. This claim includes, in accordance with the requirements of normative

[6] See Tugendhat (1993: 19 n 3).

[7] It is important to note that this reflects the claim included in the statement itself. From the perspective of an observer, reasonable disagreement will be possible if there are no objective criteria to validate one of the respective statements and disqualify all the others.

justification, formal and normative elements. An agent making a normative judgement must, first, claim that the judgement complies with the formal requirements of a correct balancing and, secondly, that it is required by the stronger of the competing normative arguments and is therefore the judgement that one ought to make or accept.

These formal and normative claims to correctness are distinct from a third claim to correctness, a claim to correctness in a substantive respect, that is, that the judgement is true or correct in a sense that is similar to being true. As pointed out above, correctness in this third sense cannot be claimed for individual normative judgements, for an autonomous agent must be aware that other agents may legitimately propose different judgements. Hence, only the formal and the normative claim to correctness are appropriate for individual normative judgements.

With respect to the normative claim of autonomous judgements, one can distinguish three claims:

(1) the claim to correctness included in individual normative judgements;
(2) the claim of the validity of norms based on the intersubjective reflection of individual agents, which is procedural definitive validity; and
(3) the claim to substantive definitive validity (bindingness or objective validity) of the norm in a sense that goes beyond individual normative judgements.

The specific content of the claims to correctness, validity and objectivity will depend on what is necessary in order to comply with these claims. Addressing this issue requires an analysis of the basic structures and necessary contents of such claims, and the rational constraints they must comply with.

### 6.2.1 Normative Judgements as the Result of Balancing

Normative judgements include a claim that the result of the balancing be accepted as definitively valid. A first problem is the relation of this claim to that included in a normative statement.

For example, the result of a balancing might be expressed as:

(1) In situation C, the principle of liberty deserves priority with respect to the question of whether smoking ought to be permitted.

This can be expressed in the form of a normative requirement:

(1') In situation C, smoking ought to be permitted.

On the other hand, one might make a normative statement:

(2) In situation C, smoking is permitted.

Within the structure of balancing normative arguments, the normative statement, that is, (2), of what is actually permitted, prohibited or required is not included in the normative judgement, namely, (1) or (1'), but complies with the normative requirement expressed by that judgement. The step from the normative judgement to a normative statement requires a procedural act of determining which of the norms is definitively valid.

The content of such a normative statement needs clarification, however. The problem is this. According to the definition of normative validity, a statement of the validity of a norm implies that it ought to be applied and followed by the norm-addressees. Hence, it claims to be binding on the norm-addressees. However, the result of balancing normative arguments, even if based on intersubjective reflection, will be an *individual* normative judgement. Consequently, different agents may hold different normative views. In so far as this is a matter of autonomy and does not violate formal requirements of rational balancing, all these views must be accepted as possible and legitimate. Consequently, one cannot make a normative statement of an intersubjectively binding norm in an individual normative judgement.[8]

On the other hand, autonomous agents may form normative judgements based on the balancing of all relevant arguments, including the consideration of the normative views of other agents. The result claims definitive validity in the sense that it is supported by a complete procedure of justification, that is, definitive validity in a procedural sense.[9] If all substantive arguments *and* all competing views of other agents have been taken into account, there is nothing left which could cast in doubt the agent's view. One cannot deny the right of autonomous agents to claim definitive validity for such a normative judgement. What has to be denied, however, is the binding character of this judgement for other agents. Because of their right to autonomous judgement, they cannot be subject to the judgements of other agents. The normative situation is then the following:

(1) Autonomous agents can make normative judgements and corresponding statements of definitive validity.
(2) These statements imply claims to the effect that other agents ought to follow their normative judgements.
(3) These claims confront other agents' rights to autonomous judgement.
(4) No competing claim is superior to the others.
(5) Consequently, all judgements claim definitive validity, but no judgement can claim to be binding for other agents.

What remains is the claim that the definitively valid norm be applied and followed in the case of the agent himself. Nevertheless, the agent might argue that it makes no sense to follow a norm that is in general not followed. This, however, is a different issue.[10]

[8] See 4.3.3. Such a statement might be interpreted as an elliptical form of a personal view, to be presented as, for example, 'I think that N is valid'. If, however, non-relativised validity cannot be established by an individual normative judgement, it is not justified to make a normative statement to this effect. Therefore, a rational agent cannot make it.

[9] See 4.3.2.3.

[10] A moral person will probably remain true to his or her own normative view. Nevertheless, even if someone considers a norm to be morally right, there may be legitimate practical arguments for not following the norm if practically no one else is doing so.

Accordingly, individual normative judgements can state the definitive validity of norms in the procedural sense if they are based on balancing and the intersubjective reflection of all relevant arguments and normative views. They cannot, however, claim to state definitively valid norms in the substantive sense, that is, intersubjectively binding norms. Validity according to an individual normative judgement means that a norm is valid in the sense that it is the result of a correct balancing. This implies that someone who took a balancing decision claims, first, the formal correctness of this decision and, secondly, that the respective norm ought to be accepted as valid. A normative judgement stating the result of a balancing can only be understood in this weak sense, not in the strong sense of a statement of an intersubjectively binding norm.

### 6.2.2 Claim to Normative Correctness

The claim to the correctness of normative judgements can therefore be stated as follows:

> (C1) One who makes a normative judgement based on the balancing of normative arguments must claim the formal correctness of his judgement in accordance with the requirements of rationality and its normative correctness in the sense that the stated norm ought to be accepted as definitively valid.

Of crucial importance for the conception of autonomous reasoning is the claim to the normative correctness of normative judgements, which is a subjective, not intersubjectively binding claim to normative correctness. The necessity of such a claim is also supported by the structure of normative arguments as reiterated requirements for validity. If one normative argument is preferred to another that conflicts with the first argument, this is owing to its greater relative weight in a given situation C. Thus, the resulting priority relation and the corresponding norm R/C are required by the prevailing argument. This argument demands that the stated norm be understood as valid. Thus, a normative judgement includes a requirement that the priority of one argument over another ought to be accepted. Since this is the implication of the prevailing normative argument, it has the status of a normative argument. Its structure is:

$$\ldots \text{O VAL(R/C)P1,P2}$$

At any rate, the prevailing argument requires an even wider-ranging norm, one that reaches to the complete norm-content of the normative argument, that is, . . . O VAL(R). The norm established by the balancing decision is, however, limited to the range of application in which the argument receives priority, as represented by condition C.

> For example, the principle that health risks ought to be avoided requires that smoking in general be forbidden, and this includes a demand that it be forbidden in public

> spaces. As far as this principle is recognised as prior, the norm it requires is recognised as valid. Hence, although recognition of the norm is the result of an autonomous judgement (only partly determined by requirements of rationality), someone who claims a normative argument's priority over a conflicting argument must claim that the resulting norm is normatively required and ought to be valid, and that this is required by the normative argument that enjoys priority.

A problem might arise where someone is not able to decide between conflicting arguments in a given situation. He might regard both as being of equal relative weight in the case in question, so that different solutions appear to be equally good. If it should be necessary to take a decision on pragmatic grounds, this decision will not be based on a preference between the conflicting arguments, but rather on a formal preference, established on the ground that it is necessary to take a decision. A normative judgement based on this formal preference does not carry a claim to the normative correctness of its content. Accordingly, two kinds of preferences must be distinguished: a formal preference without substantive justification, and a substantive preference based on the relative weight of arguments in a given situation.

Nevertheless, the possibility of tie cases being decided by a formal preference does not exclude claims to the normative correctness of judgements based on balancing. A reasonable agent must have at least some substantive preferences. She cannot be indifferent to all cases of conflict. Some solutions are clearly better than others, for example, where it is the case that one principle can be fulfilled to a much higher degree than a conflicting principle of approximately equal relative weight. In some instances one principle will clearly have priority, in others the conflicting principle, and a third class of cases will render a decision difficult. But a line has to be drawn somewhere. Therefore, reasonable agents will make at least some normative judgements with claims to normative correctness.

In summary, a normative judgement based on the balancing of normative arguments carries a claim not only to formal correctness in the sense of compliance with the standards of rational decision-making, but also a claim to normative correctness in the sense that it is required by the prevailing normative arguments. Autonomous agents cannot avoid making such claims in their normative judgements.

## 6.3 CLAIMS TO DEFINITIVE VALIDITY

The claim to the normative correctness of autonomous judgements has further implications. As pointed out above, normative argumentation must aim at establishing definitively valid and hence binding norms. Intersubjectively reflected normative judgements may claim to state definitively valid norms, implying that every autonomous agent ought to recognise the definitive validity of a proposed norm and ought to apply and follow it. Although this claim is curtailed by the competing and equally valid claims of other agents, it makes applicable certain requirements that must be met if a definitively valid and hence binding norm is to result. The analysis of what the necessary conditions for a successful argumentation are reveals the claims that are implied in normative judgements about definitively valid norms.

### 6.3.1 Correctness of the Balancing

Anyone who claims the validity of a norm as the result of a balancing of normative arguments must claim the formal correctness of his autonomous decision according to standards of rational balancing. The claim to formal correctness includes, more specifically, the claim to correct balancing:

(C2) Normative judgements must claim to be based on a correct balancing.

This presupposes that the balancing is based on valid normative arguments, that all relevant arguments have been taken into account, and that the decision is based on a correct procedure of balancing.[11]

Moreover, requirements of coherence apply to normative judgements. First of all, an interest-based normative argument is valid only if individual interests are put forward not in isolation but as part of a coherent individual conception of the good life. Otherwise it would be possible for an agent to attribute the utmost importance to each of his interests, and this would make it impossible to find an acceptable solution. In addition, the requirement of intersubjective reflection demands that a coherent account of the competing normative views of individual agents be developed.[12] Finally, the normative judgement itself must be presented as a coherent solution of the balancing. Thus, a requirement holds:

(C3) The balancing must claim to present a coherent solution to the conflict of normative arguments that it encounters.

Thus, the balancing must comply with the general requirement that coherent preferences be formed. This includes two more specific requirements, which in law are usually recognised as requirements of equal treatment:

(C4) Normative judgements must be guided by the same arguments, that is, one must apply a normative argument to all cases to which it is applicable.

(C5) A normative judgement must follow a normative argument as long as there is no sufficient reason for a contrary judgement.

### 6.3.2 Mutual Respect for Autonomy

In addition, one cannot claim autonomy for oneself, whilst denying the autonomy of other agents who are capable of autonomous judgement. The claim that every

[11] As to the requirements of correct balancing, see 5.3.

[12] See 4.3.1.3.

autonomous agent ought to recognise a particular norm as valid can be sustained only if it stems from an argumentation that respects the autonomy of all agents involved. Thus, the following requirement holds:

(C6) One who makes an autonomous judgement must recognise the equal right of other autonomous agents to make such judgements.

The justification of the requirement that individual autonomy be respected begins with the assumption that the result of the balancing is not derived from other norms or criteria and also that it does not express a normative truth that everyone must accept whatever his or her interests and normative views might be. On the contrary, it is the result of an autonomous decision on the part of the one who is conducting the balancing. From his or her perspective, the decision is required by the prevailing argument. But this prevalence is established by an autonomous judgement and can claim validity against others only as such, not owing to the fact that the argument really is of greater weight than the competing arguments. Since autonomy is presupposed in making an autonomous judgement, it must be recognised by anyone making such a judgement. One who reflects on his normative judgements will therefore acknowledge the autonomy of other agents as well.

The recognition of autonomy means that every autonomous agent has the competence to balance normative arguments and to make normative judgements based on this balancing. Furthermore, it cannot be ruled out from the very beginning that different autonomous agents reach different results. Should such a divergence among autonomous judgements arise, no one can claim the superiority of his or her own judgement as against that of other autonomous agents. Thus, normative judgements can command validity only as individual judgements, which leaves open the possibility that other agents may well hold different views according to their right to autonomy.

### 6.3.3 Universalisability and the Criterion of Consensus

Where the criteria of validity are concerned, autonomous reasoning underlies two requirements for the justification of intersubjectively binding norms.

(C7) Autonomous judgements must reflect the consent[13] of autonomous agents as the aim of discourse.

One cannot regard the interests and normative views of this or that autonomous agent as irrelevant to the argument. Accordingly, a norm can only be justified as

[13] Consent in this sense is rational consent, that is, consent based on rational argumentation. Since factual consent or dissent may be unreasonable, it has no bearing on the issue of the validity of norms. On the other hand, rational consent is not merely ideal consent. What is required is that autonomous agents actually accept the validity of a norm and that this acceptance be based on rational argumentation.

definitively valid if it is at least theoretically possible for any reasonable agent to accept this norm as definitively valid. If someone proposes a norm that is not in this sense universalisable, he cannot claim that other agents ought to accept it. Hence, the judgement must fulfil a requirement of universalisability in the weak sense that it not be precluded, for reasons theoretical in nature, that the suggested norm find the general consent of reasonable agents.

> (C8) Autonomous judgements can only propose those norms as definitively valid that might find the consent of other autonomous agents.

The claim to find the consent of autonomous agents is a necessary condition of a legitimate claim of the intersubjective validity of norms and for the bindingness of norms. One who claims that a norm is in substance objectively valid and hence intersubjectively binding must assume that this norm will find the consent of every autonomous agent whose judgement is not objectively mistaken. In this sense, norms must be claimed to be universally valid if they are to be regarded as binding. For lack of epistemic criteria of moral truth, there is no other way to resolve the conflict between, on the one hand, the claim of an agent that other agents ought to accept the norm proposed by him and, on the other hand, the requirement that the autonomy of other agents be respected.

Thus, normative validity in this sense cannot be established apart from the normative views of the norm-addressees. Dependence on consent does not, however, imply that consent must figure directly as the criterion of the validity of norms, and it does not imply that complete consent is required either. Rather, it means that autonomous reasoning on the validity of norms must strive for the consent of autonomous agents. In particular, one can state the following conditions of the validity of norms:

(i) Normative arguments or judgements must refer to norms that every autonomous agent might possibly accept as valid. A norm that cannot find the consent of all autonomous agents under any circumstances cannot be the object of a valid normative argument or judgement.
(ii) The binding character of a norm requires a justification addressed to the autonomy of autonomous agents, for it restricts their autonomy. The justification can only come from rational acceptance by autonomous agents.

It is important to note that autonomous judgements must necessarily claim to be capable of finding the rational consent of all autonomous agents, although individual agents cannot claim substantive definitive validity for their normative judgements and, moreover, it may well be true that no norm can actually be established as binding.[14] Nevertheless, normative argumentation finally aims at establishing binding norms and therefore must aim at consensus of autonomous

[14] One should also note that norms might be established as binding, not because they are correct in substance but because a commonly binding norm is needed and there is no rational alternative to it. In this case, a complete consensus is not necessary, but the criterion of reasonable convergence may be adopted. See below 6.4.2. This does not, however, guarantee that a binding norm can be established.

agents. This holds also for normative judgements of individual agents, for they claim recognition from anyone else.

### 6.3.4 Intersubjective Reflection

Besides the coherence of one's own normative conception, anyone who claims a norm to be intersubjectively binding has to take into account the normative conceptions of other agents as well. Thus, an important requirement on judgements that purport to state which norms ought to be accepted as collectively binding is that of intersubjective reflection.

> (C9) Normative judgements as to definitively valid norms can only be established on the basis of intersubjective reflection, considering also the normative views of other autonomous agents in order to determine which norm ought to be accepted as collectively binding.

First of all, every agent must develop a conception of what norms she thinks best. Since, however, autonomous agents may come to diverging judgements, everyone must also take into account the fact of reasonable disagreement. Therefore, in order to state what norm ought to be valid in a society, it does not suffice to make up one's own mind about the best solution at a first level; one must also consider which norm is best in a situation in which different people hold different views about the norms that ought to be valid and, hence, binding for all.

> For example, with respect to the issue of whether one ought to acknowledge the right to smoke in public places, one must judge not only whether one would oneself accept such a right, considering all relevant interests and normative views. In addition, one must form a second-order judgement about what ought to be accepted as binding in a situation of diverging views on the question of whether smoking ought to be prohibited.

Hence, one must consider the views of other autonomous agents and ask what would be an acceptable rule for all in a situation of reasonable divergence. Accordingly, intersubjective reflection in individual normative judgements is required, everyone taking into account the judgements of everyone else.

An intersubjectively reflected conception provides an answer to the question of which norms are universally or collectively binding. It is a moral conception in a strict sense, by contrast with the moral aspects contained in individual normative conceptions.[15] By taking into account each other's normative conception, agents will develop such moral conceptions. Accordingly, the mutual respect for one another's moral conception is required in order to justify statements of definitive validity or bindingness. This also follows from the demand to treat all agents as autonomous persons.

[15] See 4.3.3. Similar distinctions can be found in various forms, however, offering quite different approaches. See the distinction between private and collective decision-making in Habermas (1991: 116), and also the idea of a political conception of justice, in opposition to that of a comprehensive religious, political or moral doctrine, in Rawls (1988: 252 f; 1985: 224 ff).

A moral conception is necessary if one wishes to provide a conclusive statement on the question of which norms are definitively valid and binding. Consequently, normative judgements must strive for compliance with the above-mentioned demands, that is, the correctness of balancing, mutual respect, universalisability and intersubjective reflection, and, moreover, a normative statement that proposes a substantive definitive validity of a norm must claim that these requirements are actually fulfilled.

## 6.4 CLAIMS TO OBJECTIVE VALIDITY

The claims to the correctness of balancing, mutual respect, universalisability and intersubjective reflection are necessary requirements for the justification of normative statements of binding norms. Compliance with them is not, however, sufficient to justify such statements. The justification of statements of the bindingness or objective validity of a norm requires a different basis from that of the claims of individual normative judgements and their implications. It cannot proceed by explicating the requirements that individual normative claims must fulfil, for definitive validity is something that cannot be claimed on the basis of individual judgements alone; it requires an independent foundation. First of all, the conception of objective validity must be clarified.

### 6.4.1 Notion of Objective Validity

Objective validity may be defined in two dimensions, that of rational justification and that of bindingness, or substantive definitive validity. A norm may be called objectively valid because it is rationally justified in substance,[16] or because it is binding on its addressees. On the one hand, these are interrelated. If a norm is not rationally justified, its addressees might reject it, consequently, one cannot regard it as binding. What is more, there is no alternative to demonstrating the objective validity of a norm by means of a rational justification. On the other hand, these aspects are not identical. It seems possible, depending on the notions of objective validity and rational justification, that a norm can be rationally justified in its substance without being binding.

The notion of rational justification is linked to that of correctness. The justification of a norm shows that it is correct. In accordance with the weak and strong interpretation of normative correctness,[17] there are various conceptions of rational justification. The justification of objective validity requires a strong inter-

[16] Substantive rational justification must be distinguished from a merely formal justification, drawing on the necessity of having any norm whatsoever (for example, traffic rules determining on which side of the street one has to drive). A formal justification may be objectively valid, but this does not affect the objective validity of the norm in substance.

[17] See above 6.1.2.

pretation, showing that some norm or normative judgement is required by the prevailing arguments. The strong version of justification allows, however, for diverse interpretations. A perfect rational justification presupposes that all requirements of rationality be met. If the justification of a norm meets this criterion, the norm is without any doubt objectively valid. However, rational justification need not be perfect. An approximative conception of rational justification demands that an argument meets standards of rationality to as high a degree as possible. The more an argument complies with this demand, the greater its degree of rationality. Approximative rationality does not, however, guarantee objective validity in the strong sense that everyone must accept the result of the argument. Hence, one might ask what the relation between rational justification and objective validity is and, in particular, what is meant by 'objective validity'.

Conceptions of objectivity differ as to their epistemological demands and ontological commitments.[18] A conception with strong ontological commitment defines objectivity as correspondence to normative facts.[19] If one prefers to avoid an ontological commitment to the existence of normative facts, one can at least identify certain conditions of objective validity that assimilate the definitive validity of a norm to a normative fact.[20] These are:

(1) a requirement of consistency, that is, if a norm N is definitively valid, its negation ¬N is not definitively valid;
(2) the exclusion of the objective validity of contrary norms, that is, the criteria of objective validity cannot be fulfilled by norms Op and O¬p at the same time;
(3) the requirement of stability, that is, one must expect that the definitive validity of a norm will not be lost solely owing to a change of attitudes and apart from relevant change of circumstances.

These conditions assure that normative statements can be used like statements of facts,[21] which basically follow the same logical rules as descriptive statements.

A strong epistemological conception defines the objective validity of a norm by means of its intersubjective validity, that is, in the sense that everybody must reasonably accept this norm as valid. Since this conception, like the ontological conception, must include the conditions of consistency, exclusivity and stability, one can regard these conditions as a common core of strong conceptions of objectivity. It is

[18] Various distinctions have been made. See, eg, Moore (2004); Marmor (2001); Bayon (1991).

[19] 'Fact' is used here as the meaning of a true statement, not necessarily restricted to the empirical world. See Sieckmann (1997a: 30). More precisely, the validity of a norm is stated as a fact by a true normative statement. For a defence of treating norms as facts, see Heidemann (1997).

[20] See above 6.1.1.

[21] According to the characterisation of objective validity of a norm as a normative fact, principles, being normative arguments to be balanced against conflicting arguments, can be objectively valid only with regard to the requirement that they be considered in procedures of balancing and be fulfilled as far as possible. It is only this normative content that can be stated as a normative fact if the respective principle is valid. In addition, principles used as normative arguments have a normative content that goes beyond that of normative statements. This normative claim cannot, however, be qualified directly as objectively valid.

also clear, however, that these conceptions of objectivity are incompatible with autonomy, for they leave no room for self-legislation.[22]

By contrast, a minimalist account of objective validity requires only that a statement of a norm be justified in a way that makes it more than a merely subjective opinion. Objective validity in a minimal sense means that the acceptance of a norm or a normative judgement is not merely a subjective matter; rather, its validity is in some way independent of individual acceptance. This independence may be reflected in a negative or in a positive sense. Negatively, a norm might not be valid despite being individually accepted as valid, as, for example, when an individual normative judgement is subject to rational critique and shown to be incorrect. Positively, a norm might be valid despite the fact that it is not being individually accepted as valid. Objectivity in this sense means that the norm in question is binding on its addressees.

Autonomous judgements meet certain minimal requirements for objective validity. They are objective in the negative sense that they are subject to rational critique according to the standards of correct balancing. Consequently, their correctness can be judged according to criteria that are independent of the individual judgement itself. In addition, autonomous judgements include a claim to normative necessity. This claim is a claim to objectivity in the positive sense of bindingness, but it is only a subjectively valid claim. Nevertheless, it renders applicable those requirements for the rational justification of norms that must be met if the claim to objective validity ought to be justified. Thus, the claim to normative necessity extends the possibility of rational critique.

An interesting question remains, however. Can autonomous reasoning establish norms that are objectively valid in the positive sense of being binding on their addressees? According to the analysis offered above, the bindingness of a norm is defined as follows:

> DFbind: A norm is binding on an individual norm-addressee if it is valid apart from the individual's acceptance of its validity.

A central characteristic of autonomous reasoning is that norms cannot be established as binding by individual reasoning.[23] Since autonomy includes the right to one's own normative judgement, no agent by his individual normative judgement alone can claim that a norm is binding on an agent who rejects the validity of this norm. If it is to be possible to establish binding norms, collective

[22] Moreover, even weaker criteria such as that of the strength of rational acceptance are not able to restrict autonomous choice. See Sieckmann (2003a).

[23] More precisely, two types of individual normative judgement must be distinguished, first-order judgements based on the balancing of interest-based claims and second-order judgements addressing the question of which norm is to be definitively valid with regard to the conflicting normative views of autonomous agents. One might call the first type an all-things-considered judgement and the second an all-perspectives-considered judgement. Since no one, on his own, can establish a norm valid for other autonomous agents, a judgement regarding which norm is definitively valid must take into account the normative views of other autonomous agents; it can therefore only be a second-order judgement. Nevertheless, it will still be an individual normative judgement about definitive validity, not a statement of a binding and therefore objectively valid norm.

autonomous reasoning and the collective acceptance of these norms by autonomous agents will be necessary. Two forms of acceptance have to be considered here, consensus and convergence.

### 6.4.2 Criteria of Objective Validity

One might well think that consensus is the relevant criterion for the objective validity or bindingness of norms on the ground that it represents not only the highest degree of acceptance of a norm but also the only way to avoid an agent's being subject to a norm against his will. Consensus, however, cannot establish a norm as binding for autonomous agents,[24] for any agent who consented to the norm might change his mind, rejecting its validity and thereby destroying the consensus.

An alternative to consensus is the criterion of reasonable convergence. The convergence of autonomous agents on the validity of a norm consists in a prevailing and increasing degree of acceptance of the norm by the autonomous agents.

> For example, in a conflict between free speech and the protection of religious freedom that arises because members of a religion see their religious feelings violated by certain publications, some agents might give unconditional priority to free speech, some unconditional priority to the protection of religious freedom, and most of them will give conditional priority to free speech if there are adequate grounds for the speech in question, but they will give conditional priority to the protection of religious freedom if the speech in question is simply meant to offend or ridicule. Given this distribution of opinions and in so far as a commonly binding norm seems to be necessary here, some agents may arrive at an intermediate solution as the norm that ought to be accorded definitive validity. If this occurs, support for the intermediate solution increases, possibly encouraging other agents to accept the solution.

Thus, rational argumentation may create a tendency toward increasing acceptance of a certain result, which may be reinforced by further argument. In order to establish a binding norm, such convergence must also be reasonable, that is, it must be the result of a process of intersubjective reflection that includes not only correct individual balancing but also the reciprocal consideration of the normative conceptions of other autonomous agents.[25] Accordingly, we can introduce the

[24] This also holds for modified criteria for consensus, such as the criterion that every reasonable agent might possibly consent to a norm or the criterion that every reasonable agent would consent to the norm. The first of these is too weak to establish a binding norm because incompatible norms might meet this criterion. The second one, if used as a criterion for normative validity and not as an empirical prediction, presupposes criteria that determine the result in a way that excludes autonomy as self-legislation.

[25] A similar idea is suggested by Rawls (1995: 141 n 16). The requirement of intersubjective reflection is crucial for this definition. Without such intersubjective reflection, the general acceptance of a norm does not provide a reason to follow the norm. If, by contrast, a norm is supported by reasonable convergence, there is at least a reason to regard it as binding. A tendency toward increasing support for a particular norm might be reversed by counter-arguments or by changes in circumstances relevant to the justification. If, however, there are no arguments that might reverse a stable tendency toward increasing acceptance, the norm is justified according to the criterion of reasonable convergence.

following definition of reasonable convergence:

> DF$_{RC}$: A norm is supported by reasonable convergence if an increasing majority of the agents concerned accepts the norm as valid on the basis of a process of intersubjective reflection.

In what sense and to what extent can reasonable convergence establish objectivity? While it constitutes some form of objective validity, the perspectives of supporters and opponents of a norm differ on this point.

Supporters of a norm backed by convergence will claim that this norm is binding on them. For, from their point of view, it is valid independently of the judgements of individual agents. Even if someone were to change his opinion, this would not affect the validity of a norm backed by convergence. Therefore, the following thesis connects a claim to bindingness with the criterion of convergence:

> (BC) Norm-addressees who support a norm backed by reasonable convergence will claim that this norm is binding on them.

Reasonable convergence is insufficient, however, to support the claim that a norm is binding on opponents, those who reject the validity of the norm. For example, a restriction of the freedom of speech in order to avoid offence to religious beliefs might be backed by reasonable convergence. Nevertheless, someone, after considering all the arguments and different normative views on the issue, might reasonably hold that the correct balance between free speech and the protection of religion ought to allow even such insults. For him, the fact of reasonable convergence is only one argument in his deliberations. If, against this argument, he reasonably denies the definitive validity of the norm, reasonable convergence cannot again serve as an argument that the norm he rejects is binding on him. Such a claim would fail to respect his autonomy.

The claim that a norm is binding even on its dissenters requires, then, an additional justification. One might show that agents must accept reasonable convergence as the ultimate criterion for validity and must therefore restrict their individual autonomy. Alternatively, one might suggest that dissenters, though rejecting the bindingness of a norm, must reasonably accept the correctness of the claim to bindingness made by supporters of this norm.

### 6.4.3 Objective Correctness of the Claim to Bindingness

The condition of reasonable convergence, while excluding the bindingness of competing norms, does not establish the bindingness of the supported norms, for it may be the case that none of the competing norms can be claimed to be binding. This possibility is excluded where a commonly binding norm is required:[26] in this case a norm must be established that is binding on all agents. Even dissenters

[26] This corresponds to the liberal claim that norms cannot be justified merely on the basis of conceptions of the good life but only if they are necessary to regulate conflicts between individuals.

will then have to recognise the correctness of a claim that a norm backed by reasonable convergence is binding. Thus, the following thesis arises:

(BN) A norm can be correctly claimed to be binding even on its dissenters if two conditions are satisfied:

(1) The norm is backed by reasonable convergence.
(2) It is necessary that there be a commonly binding norm.[27]

This claim to bindingness follows from correct reasoning, so it is objectively justified in a cognitive sense.[28] Everyone must recognise the correctness of the claim that the norm backed by reasonable convergence is binding where a common norm is required. One should note, however, that the correctness of the claim to bindingness does not amount to objectivity in the sense that every reasonable agent must accept the norm as binding. It simply means that the result was established in conformity with standards of rational justification, and therefore may correctly be held.[29] Opponents may still hold a contrary view and criticise the generally accepted judgement, claiming that a competing norm be recognised as valid.[30]

### 6.4.4 Restricting Individual Autonomy

The argument for restricting individual autonomy begins with the supposition that commonly binding norms must be established. This aim often will not be achieved if individual autonomy has priority over the demands of rationality. And autonomous agents may favour their substantive normative views against demands of rationality, upholding a normative view that is not supported by the best rational justification, at least as long as there is no perfect rational justification of the norm in question.

For example, let us assume that a prohibition to eat animals is not supported by the best rational justification, at least according to the view of many agents. Nevertheless, even acknowledging the deficit in respect of its rational justification, agents may hold such a prohibition to be normatively correct and may demand its implementation. Thus, they balance demands of morality against those of rationality.

In order to assure the possibility of establishing a commonly binding norm in morality or law, one must reject the claim that the norms of the respective system

[27] The necessity of having a commonly binding norm is a normative issue that may, like the validity of a norm, be disputed. One finds such disputes, for example, in the demarcation of public and private issues.

[28] The justifiability or correctness of a claim to bindingness means that all requirements of rational argumentation are met. It amounts to a claim of discursive possibility, see Alexy (1989a: 294; 1991: 413), or to the defensibility of the claim to objective validity, which, however, is not analogous to truth.

[29] This amounts to a weak normative correctness in the sense defined above 6.1.2.

[30] This conforms to the thesis that one cannot prove the validity of a penal law to one who has violated the criminal law motivated by moral conviction (*Überzeugungstäter*), although he may be obliged to accept the condemnation. On this problem, see Radbruch (2001: 85).

are a matter of individual autonomy. This is a reason for excluding that an individual ultimately weighs up the demands of rational justification and his substantive moral views. Thus, the autonomous weighing-up under the concept of substantive intersubjective reflection is not admissible as the last part of the reasoning on the validity of a norm. If one excludes this weighing-up of the strength of rational justification and individual normative conceptions, the criterion of reasonable convergence becomes decisive. Accordingly, the norms and decisions that claim to be commonly binding must be guided by standards of rationality, and this must be accepted by individual norm-addressees and norm-applying organs.

The problem of the bindingness of this norm cannot, however, be completely resolved by this approach. One might claim that from his or her moral point of view the respective norm is not binding. This autonomy right cannot be rejected.[31] From such a moral point of view, however, it will not be possible to establish a commonly binding norm. Therefore, the only way for a legal or institutionalised system to make sure that a binding norm can be established within the framework of autonomous reasoning is to call a halt to the process of weighing-up at a point where the result might be accepted as binding by all people involved.[32] This is the case if everyone considers his judgement to be of equal standing with everyone else's. The judgement can then count as being impartial and, in this sense, objective.

Objectivity in this sense is, however, not an epistemic feature but an attitude of the agent making a normative judgement. Such an attitude is required when one aims at establishing commonly binding norms. Accordingly, this attitude of objectivity is required from judges in a legal system. It can also form the basis of statements of objective morality.

## 6.5 CONCLUSION

The upshot is that normative argumentation based on balancing normative arguments implies normative claims to correctness, including the claim that every reasonable agent ought to accept the suggested normative arguments and judgements. These normative claims, together with the epistemic openness of balancing, represent the logical structure of autonomous reasoning. Furthermore, they require the coherence and universalisability of normative arguments and also the acceptance of consent as the aim of autonomous reasoning, for only consensus can establish the intersubjective validity of norms or normative judgements in substance.

Normative statements are possible only if they correspond to correct normative judgements that comply with the requirements above. Accordingly, the claim to

[31] For a similar view of the bindingness of law, see Radbruch (2001: 85).

[32] Since a gap remains between moral bindingness and legal validity, the problem of unjust laws and of the obligation, at least of law-applying organs, to apply and follow such norms might occur. However, if a norm is best justified according to the criterion of the strength of rational acceptance, one can expect that this norm is not objectively unjust.

correctness of normative statements implies respect for the moral autonomy of other agents, the claim of the universalisability of the individual normative conceptions on which they are based, and the recognition of consensus as the aim of discourse.

On this basis, a rational justification of binding norms, understood in this sense as objectively valid, would seem to be possible by appealing to the criterion of reasonable convergence, defined as a tendency to consensus on the basis of rational argumentation and intersubjective reflection. It has to be conceded, however, that individual autonomy may come into conflict with demands of rational justification, for it is not necessarily the case that rationally justified norms will be accepted as binding. The right to autonomous judgement includes that of rejecting a norm as wrong even in the case that this norm is supported by the criterion of reasonable convergence. The possibility of a conflict between claims to objective validity and individual autonomy persists. This problem can be resolved, with an eye to justifying binding norms, by means of a demand of objectivity or impartiality that restricts the use of autonomous judgement and considers all autonomous judgements to be of equal standing. Such a restriction seems to be appropriate, in particular, for legal judgements. In addition, the objective correctness of claims to objective validity must be recognised if these claims are backed by reasonable convergence and a commonly binding norm is required. In this case, autonomous agents may retain their normative view in substance but must acknowledge that the proponents of a norm backed by reasonable convergence are objectively justified in claiming the bindingness of the norm in question.

Accordingly, one can attribute objective validity to norms. On the other hand, the possibility of autonomous moral critique cannot be ruled out. Individual autonomy is compatible with the assumption that there are criteria of objective validity. Autonomous agents always have the right to individual moral judgement, even against established norms that are rationally justified. Only an autonomous agent who accepts the bindingness of a particular norm will claim the objective moral validity of this norm in the sense that everyone must accept this norm as binding. Opponents may retain their opposite view but must nevertheless concede that the claim to objective validity of the proponent is justified if it is backed by reasonable convergence and a commonly binding norm is required.

# 7

# *Rights*

A THEORY OF law or morality based on the idea of autonomous reasoning is closely related to the idea of individual rights.[1] The idea of autonomy implies the recognition of certain procedural rights in any normative system, in particular, the rights to introduce arguments and to form normative judgements as well as the right that other agents give due respect to these arguments and judgements. In addition, autonomous reasoning begins with normative claims based on individual interests and normative judgements. It is natural to present such claims in the form of rights-claims, which demand that the respective interests or normative views be respected or protected.[2] Moreover, since at least some of these interests or views are of the utmost importance to the agents concerned, individual rights will be among the most fundamental norms that autonomous reasoning establishes. Since autonomous agents will make normative claims that are based on individual interests and demand corresponding rights, the results of autonomous reasoning will reflect these rights-claims. Accordingly, individual rights and claims to the recognition of rights are of fundamental importance within an autonomy-based theory and represent an appropriate starting point for a substantive normative theory.

By contrast, sometimes norms, not rights, are the focus of normative reasoning. Rights, it is argued, are merely a 'reflex' of objective norms[3] that stem from authoritative issuance. Thus, it would follow that rights cannot be established independently of objective norms.[4] Such an assumption contradicts the conception of autonomous reasoning. Still, analysis of the role of rights in autonomous reasoning and of whether the discourse on rights presents a distinctive form of justification, compared to that of ordinary norms, is called for.

## 7.1 THE STRUCTURE OF RIGHTS

A preliminary issue is the clarification of the structure of rights. Rights can be defined as normative relations between (at least) two parties, the right-holder and the right-addressee, with a particular content (the right-content) that determines

[1] See also Richards (1981).
[2] Against the interpretation of rights as claims, however, see Martin (1993).
[3] See Kelsen (1960: 132, 134).
[4] See Kelsen (1960: 135).

the normative position of the right-holder against the right-addressee.[5] If the right-holder is an individual, the right is an individual right. The individual may be a human being or a legal person consisting of individuals, for example, a corporation.[6]

The relations of rights to other norms, obligations or duties may become clearer from the following examples:

(1) B ought to protect A against C.
(2) B has an obligation to protect A against C.
(3) B has an obligation *vis-à-vis* A to protect A against C.
(4) A has a right against B that B protect A against C.

The last two sentences express normative relations between A and B, not just simple norms, in which a normative modality is applied to a norm-content. These relations – the right of A against B and the corresponding obligation of B against A – are equivalent.[7]

Following this conception, one can distinguish rights and obligations from merely objective norms according to their relational structure. Rights and obligations include normative relations between right-holder and right-addressee. Simple or merely objective norms include normative contents but do not define normative relations between legal subjects. If, however, this were no more than a structural difference without substantive implications, one might regard the conception of rights as being of little interest. The crucial point is the meaning of the relation 'against A' (or 'against B'). According to the usual understanding of legal rights, this relation may express the idea that the obligation of the rights-addressee B is meant to protect an interest of the right-holder A, or that the right-holder can decide on how to use his right, or – as a special case of using a right – can decide to go to court with an eye to enforcing his right.[8] Although there may be exceptions, if a right exists, then in general one or another of these characteristics must be present.

These characteristics do not, however, refer to the content or structure of the right itself but to its status or function within a legal system. One might therefore argue that rights are a conjunction of merely objective norms, consisting, in the case of a fully developed right, of:

[5] Alexy (2002a: 120 ff).

[6] Rights might be attributed to other kinds of subjects, for example, collectives, but this is not taken up here.

[7] See Alexy (2002a: 132). The thesis of the equivalence of rights and obligations (or duties) might be questioned with respect to statement (2) above, since this is a simple statement of an obligation, not of a normative relation between B and A. It does not imply that A or anyone else has a right against B to be protected against C. Hence, obligations need not represent normative relations. Nevertheless, one can uphold the equivalence thesis with regard to those rights and obligations that are conceived of as normative relations.

[8] These are the features pointed out, respectively, by the interest theory and the will theory of rights. See below 7.1.2.

(1) a mandatory norm, which includes the (non-relational) obligation of someone to do something;
(2) an interest-based principle requiring the validity of this norm; and
(3) a norm stating the (non-relational) obligation on the part of the courts to enforce this norm.

The conception of rights as normative relations is, of course, compatible with this account but is not related to it.

The conception of rights as normative relations remains, therefore, unsatisfactory as long as its relational character is not linked to the above-mentioned features of rights concerning their justification and execution. The question, accordingly, is whether one can interpret the relational character of rights in a way that lends to rights a content beyond that of merely objective norms or a combination thereof. I wish to suggest that rights do indeed have a specific content that is not reducible to what is called here a simple, non-relational, or merely objective norm. The argument takes as its point of departure the notion of *rights as normatively defined normative positions* and adumbrates the idea that the structure of rights includes claims to constitutional and judicial protection, which in the case of a fully developed right will be definitively recognised by the legal system. Rights thus have a complex, multilevel structure.[9]

### 7.1.1 Descriptively and Normatively Defined Normative Positions

Rights are a type of normative position.[10] Normative positions can be defined descriptively or normatively. If one describes the normative situation of an agent that follows from legal norms, this defines a legal position descriptively. A legal right in this descriptive sense may be called a reflex of the legal order.

> For example, if there is no legislative competence to raise taxes for using the streets, the citizens have a legal position, namely, that they may use the streets without any obligation to pay for this use.

One can describe the structure of such a position as:

$$POS(A,B,N)$$

'A' designates the right-holder, 'B' the right-addressee (the state), and 'N' represents the permission to use the streets without having any obligation to pay for this use. Permission here means the absence of a prohibition. This legal position is not a simple legal norm. One cannot simplify this structure by deleting the addressee B. For example, the permission to use the streets without any obligation to pay for

[9] Also Wellman (1995: 7) emphasises the complex structure of rights, however, in a different sense, referring to the composition of rights of various Hohfeldian positions.

[10] On the theory of normative positions, see Alexy (2002a: 120 ff); Lindahl (1977).

this use might not hold against owners of private streets. Hence, legal positions *can* have a triadic structure. This structure, however, does not yet imply what is called a 'subjective right' as opposed to a right qua mere reflex of the objective legal system. It stems from a mere description of the legal system.

By contrast, the legal system may include a second-order norm granting one a right that a particular first-order norm be respected. In this case, the right is normatively defined and is not, then, a mere reflex of the legal system. Such a right has two implications. First, the right-holder can demand fulfilment of the right. That is, he will, at least in principle, have a legal remedy against the infringement of his legal position and can claim judicial protection for his right. In addition, he can claim that the legislator or some other law-creating organ must not cancel his right. One might say that his position receives constitutional protection. Accordingly, a fully developed right will command judicial as well as constitutional protection.

The formal structure of such a right includes several levels. A first-order norm states a certain normative position in relation to another individual.

> For example, one may use the street without being hindered by others and, accordingly, can demand that others not block the street.

The structure, in general, is that someone (A) can claim against another individual (B) that something ought to be done or ought not to be done. In addition, there are second-order norms that protect this normative position. These norms give one the right to demand fulfilment (FM) of the norm (N) defining the position. The resulting structure of rights is:

$$\text{RIGHT}(A,B,FM(N))$$

The addressee of the obligation to fulfil the norm N will often be the same as the addressee of the right. However, it is possible that someone is responsible for the fulfilment of a norm by another individual.

> For example, the state might be responsible for ensuring that private parties, including industrial enterprises, comply with norms protecting the health or property of citizens. In this case, citizens have a right against the state that a certain norm protecting the citizens be complied with by a third party.

On the other hand, second-order norms can demand that the normative position in question will not be altered or removed and, accordingly, will remain valid. Formally, the structure of such a normative position is:

$$\text{RIGHT}(A,B,VAL(N))$$

Again, the rights-addressee need not be identical with the addressee of the norm N.

A remarkable aspect of this analysis is that the structure of normative arguments supports both second-order structures. The concept of normative validity implies that a valid norm be applied and followed, which means that it ought to be fulfilled. That is, if A is in a position against B to the effect that B ought to do something, then there will also hold a requirement that B comply with this obligation, and it seems at least natural and coherent to assume that as long as no counter-argument is made, A has not only a first-order right with respect to B's obligation but also a second-order right that B fulfil his obligation. By contrast, the idea of a legal position that is a mere reflex of the legal system, which does not give the beneficiary a right to claim fulfilment of the respective obligation, does not conform to this structure but must be regarded as an anomaly.

Even more interesting is the second structure. According to the structure of normative arguments, any norm that is established by means of the balancing of normative arguments is backed by a higher-order requirement that demands the validity of the respective norm. This means that if someone (A) is in a normative position with the content N against someone else (B), then there will be a requirement that N be valid and, again, it is natural that this requirement for validity also be included in the normative position of A. That is, A has a right against B that N is valid.

The problem remains, however, that the judiciary and the legislature are the addressees of the right in question against B. That is, a third party is involved. In order to complete the argument that each right-holder, at least in principle, must receive judicial and constitutional protection, a further element in the structure of normative arguments is required. Normative arguments set out ideal states of affairs that ought to be realised.[11] If there is a legitimate interest on the part of an individual A that a state of affairs S be realised, this constitutes a normative argument for a corresponding requirement that S be realised. This argument has no specific addressee, but since the realisation of a state of affairs requires that someone or another realise it or, if it already exists, that no one remove it, the argument is directed against all possible addressees. That is, the requirement that an ideal state of affairs be realised implies that, in principle, everyone who is able to contribute to the fulfilment of this requirement ought to do so in whatever way he can. Such a requirement is universal as to its addressees as well as to the actions that serve to fulfil it.[12] Of course, this holds only as an argument and will not establish a definitive obligation to the effect that a particular individual is to do something. But it constitutes an argument that anyone who is able to do so ought to contribute to the fulfilment of this requirement.

From this argument, one can derive requirements of the judicial and the constitutional protection of individual rights. Such rights ought to be fulfilled and, in so far as courts can contribute to this fulfilment, a normative argument applies to the effect that they ought to do so. And since this promotes the fulfilment of an individual right, it is natural to recognise also a right to judicial protection of the first-order right.

[11] On the relation between normative arguments and the notion of 'ideal ought', see Sieckmann (1990: 76 ff; 2011).

[12] See Sieckmann (1990: 38 ff); also Borowski (2007: 176 ff).

Similarly, individual rights ought to be valid, and in so far as a legislator might remove them, this requirement for validity implies an argument to the effect that the legislator ought not to alter or remove the right in question. Since this protects individual interests, it is natural to recognise a corresponding individual right to constitutional protection – although, again, only in principle and possibly subject to constraints owing to conflicting arguments. Thus, the classical characteristics of subjective rights, being justified in serving individual interests and being linked to judicial protection, are included in the structure of rights.

Accordingly, each right must in principle be judicially and constitutionally protected. Thus, aspects of justification and enforcement are included in the structure of rights, distinguishing them from simple, non-relational norms. One might object that any valid norm and not only rights will form part of such a structure. Since, however, normative justification begins with the interest-based claims of autonomous agents, the resulting norms will be rights and not, then, any ordinary norm that might stem from legislation. It is true that one can translate rights-discourse into a discourse about obligations. Focusing on obligations would, however, obscure the point that normative justification is based on the interest-based rights-claims of autonomous agents. Rights-discourse, the balancing of normative arguments and the idea of autonomy are interrelated. Focusing on rights instead of objective norms is therefore not merely rhetorical but points to a specific justificatory framework, which again establishes a specific structure of fully developed rights.

In addition, the complex structure of rights, which integrates aspects of justification and of enforcement, shifts legal discourse from obligations to rights. Rights imply obligations of various agents, not only an obligation on the part of someone to do something but also claims against legislative and judicial organs. All of them refer to the position of the right-holder, but they are not directly related to each other. Whilst rights imply arguments for first-order obligations, constitutional and judicial protection, an obligation of someone as such, without reference to the corresponding right, does not imply arguments for constitutional or judicial protection of this normative position.[13] Therefore, notwithstanding the correspondence of obligations to rights, rights-discourse is simpler and richer than discourse about obligations.

[13] This is owing to the justificatory priority of rights against duties or obligations. According to the structure of autonomous reasoning, claims to rights will justify corresponding claims to obligations, and definitive obligations will follow from the recognition of corresponding definitive rights. Claims to rights form the reasons for the recognition of obligations and in this sense have justificatory priority. The justificatory priority of rights does not establish a conceptual priority of rights against obligations. It only means that one cannot present a plausible normative justification based on claims to obligations. Suggesting a priority of rights against obligations or duties, see MacCormick (1977: 200). Against MacCormick, Kramer (1998: 26–29).

### 7.1.2 Will Theory and Interest Theory of Rights

The account of rights as normatively defined normative positions allows one to integrate the two classical accounts of rights, that is, the will theory and the interest theory of rights.[14] The will theory suggests that a legal position is a right only if the existence or enforcement of the respective legal position is subject to the disposition of the right-holder. The interest theory of rights assumes that a right exists only if the legal position in question is meant to serve, at least in general, the interests of the right-holder.[15] This may hold true both in cases of rights that are stated explicitly and in those cases where an interpretation is required as to whether a certain legal provision includes the legal right in question.[16]

The account of rights suggested here takes up both accounts, the will theory and the interest theory, but avoids at least some of the problems associated with them. The problem of the classical will theory is that it uses the power to dispose of a right as a criterion of its existence. This might seem to be an irrelevant aspect. One must at least recognise, however, that according to an autonomy-based justification of rights, such a power on the part of the right-holder will in principle be required, although a legal system might, for certain reasons, not recognise it. In addition, one might reinterpret the will theory as suggesting that a right obtains if and only if someone lays claim to it. This corresponds to the justification based on individual autonomy. Normative justification is based on claims that autonomous agents put forward. Accordingly, if such a claim is recognised as a legal right, this right will, at least in principle, include the power to dispose of it. If not, this requires a special justification.

The interest theory suggests that the existence of a right must be recognised if the interests of individuals require it. This also corresponds to the justification based on individual autonomy, for autonomous individuals will demand rights that serve their interests. If one should accept rights that are not based on interests, this will be at most an extraordinary case. In general, autonomous justification results in interest-based rights.

Accordingly, within a theory of the justification of rights based on individual autonomy, the interests as well as the will of autonomous agents both play a role in justifying rights, and the distinction between will and interest theory appears, then, to be spurious. Any justification of a right may well refer to the will and to the interests of autonomous individuals.

[14] As to various versions of these theories, see Alexy (2002a: 115); Raz (1986: 180 ff); Kramer (1998: 1–2, 61 ff); Simmonds (1998: 195 ff); Steiner (1998: 298–301).

[15] For a somewhat different characterisation of will and interest theory of rights, see Besson (2005: 422).

[16] Still another approach is the 'status theory of rights', see Kamm (2001: 242–47; 2002: 92–93); Nagel (1995: 85), which suggests that rights express the recognition of a person's status of relatively high inviolability. This, however, does not offer a general account of rights but of a special type of fundamental rights. See also Besson (2005: 423).

### 7.1.3 Types of Rights Content

Different types of normative relations might be called rights. Following Hohfeld's analysis,[17] four types of legal position can be distinguished, in particular claim rights, privileges (or liberties), powers (or competences), and immunities. Correspondingly, there are four normative positions of rights-addressees, that of a duty, no-right, liability and disability. However, the Hohfeldian analysis is not without problems.[18] For example, one might doubt whether there are any rights other than claim rights and whether liberties, competences and immunities should be called rights at all. According to the conception of rights characterised by normative relations of second order, there is always a correspondence between rights and duties or obligations, and all rights in this strict sense are claim rights. On the other hand, one can call also permissions or competences rights, namely, those included in the content of a right in the strict sense. This casts into doubt the systematisation that places claim rights and liberties on an equal level, as well as the analogy between rights and competences. Claim rights are of primary importance, and all other normative positions must be the content of claim rights if they are to count as rights in the strict sense.

With respect to the idea of autonomy, two types of competence are of special interest. One is the argumentative competence to put forward interest-based arguments, thus establishing an obligation on the part of others to take these arguments into consideration in their balancing. The other type of competence is that of private autonomy, that is, a competence to determine one's own legal position. Since no one can determine definitive normative positions on his own, such a competence exists only in so far as it is established by general rules accepted as the result of a justificatory procedure. By contrast, what can be established on the basis of individual claims is an interest-based normative argument that such competences hold as definitively valid.

Of special importance for a theory of autonomy is one's immunity from the definition of one's own normative position by others. This is a natural correlate of the competence to decide for oneself on one's normative position, that is, the right of private autonomy. Like the competence of private autonomy, the definitive immunity against normative determination by others also exists only on the basis of general norms that are the result of a justificatory procedure. The interests of autonomous agents, however, constitute a normative argument for the recognition of such immunities and, accordingly, a normative argument that such immunities ought to exist.[19]

[17] Hohfeld (1923: 23 ff).

[18] For a general discussion, see Kramer (1998), Simmonds (1998) and Steiner (1998).

[19] This argument goes beyond private autonomy and can affect also legislative competences. See 8.3, on the notion of fundamental rights.

## 7.2 A SYSTEM OF RIGHTS

One can develop a typology of rights starting from the structure of their justification. The basis of the justification of rights includes the interests and the normative conceptions of autonomous individuals. Individual interests are what an individual wishes to be respected and protected by norms. If interest-based claims and individual normative conceptions fulfil criteria of universalisability and coherence, one must recognise demands to the effect that these interests ought to be fulfilled as valid normative arguments. Such arguments, however, might require a balancing against competing arguments. In fact, in all interesting or problematic cases there are competing arguments that render balancing necessary.

Consequently, several types of right must be distinguished: first, according to their type of validity, rights valid in principle and rights definitively valid. This distinction is not specific to rights, however, but applies to norms in general. Secondly, according to the type of interest at stake, one finds rights to do something (liberty rights) and rights that someone else act in a certain way (claim rights).[20] Thirdly, according to the stage of deliberation at which a right applies, one can distinguish procedural and substantive rights.

### 7.2.1 Liberty Rights

Liberty rights basically include a permission to do or to forbear from doing an act of a certain type. Since a mere permission or liberty is not a right in the strict sense of a claim right, attributing the character of a right to a liberty is to connect it to some form of claim right. For example, if A is in a position to do some act X, a right that B must forbear from interfering with A's doing X is a negative right. Or if A is not in a position to do X, a right that B must see to it that A is enabled to do X is a positive right to be able to make use of a liberty. Both negative as well as positive rights can refer to factual circumstances or to the normative presuppositions of making use of a liberty.

> For example, the right to use a street implies, in principle, a right to freedom from a blockade of the street (factual circumstance) or against the cancellation of its status as a public road (normative condition). It also might include a right that a street be built (factual circumstance) or a right that something be given the status of a public road (normative condition).

Accordingly, liberty rights are related to rights and duties as follows. A liberty right of A against B to do H implies:

[20] This differs from the traditional division of rights in (1) claim rights or rights to something; (2) liberties; and (3) powers. See Alexy (2002a: 120). Powers ought not to be regarded as rights, for they have the structure of criteria of validity of norms, not that of rights.

– that there is a liberty of A against B to do H;
– that there is no obligation of A against B not to do H;
– that there is no right of B against A that A forbears from doing H;
– that there is an obligation of B against A not to interfere with A's doing H;
– that there is a right of A against B that B not interfere with A's doing H.

Furthermore, if there is an interest of A that the necessary means for the use of his liberty are provided, then a liberty right will provide an argument to the effect that a right of this content be recognised. However, this will not be a definitive right but only a normative argument that states a right that is valid in principle.

Moreover, a liberty right implies, in principle, an immunity from any restriction of this normative position by means of legislative or other legal acts. Again, this holds, in the first instance, only as a normative argument that there ought not to be any restriction of a right.

Liberty rights may have as their object a competence, that is, the power to change the normative situation. However, competences or normative powers as such are not to be regarded as rights. It is appropriate here to speak of a right only if a liberty right exists to exercise such a power. The existence of a liberty right presupposes, again, a justification by some individual interest.

> Accordingly, one will not call the power to change a legal situation by means of an illegal act a right, for there is no liberty to do so. Also one will not call the power of the state to enact a law and by the same token one will not call other types of authoritative power a right either, for these cases are not meant to serve an individual interest.

In this way, one can avoid some of the unwanted consequences of the traditional distinction of liberties, claim rights and powers as species of right.

### 7.2.2 Claim Rights

Claim rights may be negative or positive rights, that is, rights to be free from the interference of others (negative rights) or rights that others do something that is in the interest of the right-holder (positive rights). Claim rights are opposed to liberty rights although there is no strict separation between them. Liberty rights imply both negative and positive rights regarding the liberty in question. Negative and positive rights may include a liberty or the protection of an interest in liberty, but they may have other types of content as well. Liberty interests include, for example, an interest in the provision of the material conditions for making use of the liberties. Other interests are aimed directly at positive action that supports or realises the interest. Such interests are, for example the protection of life, physical integrity, health or property. But they can also be directed to the promotion of certain interests, like the availability of education, transport or cultural activities.

Rights against interference, or negative rights, are a kind of right directed to certain forms of behaviour on the part of others. They are called 'negative', for they require a forbearance, not a positive act. Negative rights imply, in principle, claims to positive rights, at least against the state, to protect the individual legal sphere by positive action, for example, by action on the part of the police or the courts. Moreover, this implies that in principle the individual ought to have rights or competences to enforce his claim by legal action. One should note, however, that these implications hold only in principle, that is, the validity of a negative right supports normative arguments for the recognition of positive rights protecting or promoting the efficacy of the negative right.[21]

Rights to the effect that others ought to do something (positive rights) may be based on liberty interests or on other interests. Interests, however, do not immediately create positive rights respecting their fulfilment but only reasons that are to be taken into consideration, given that the interests are legitimate, that is, universalisable. Thus, positive rights necessarily give rise to a problem of justification, for claims against others conflict with the liberty rights that they curtail. Accordingly, justifying them requires a balancing of normative arguments.

An issue of contention is whether one can establish some sort of priority among liberties or liberty rights, negative rights and positive rights. This line of reasoning takes, in general, a critical stance on positive rights, which are regarded as difficult to justify, to interpret and to apply. In particular, the need for balancing is used as an argument against recognising positive rights.[22]

In this respect, liberties and liberty rights are special. They do not, as a matter of conceptual necessity, conflict with other interests. Consequently, it seems possible that liberty rights can be justified as definitively valid without a balancing. In this respect, they have a special status. Still, although it is possible in theory that liberty rights exist without a balancing, one cannot determine in advance which liberty rights are valid without a balancing, for the need for balancing depends on whether there is a conflict with other interests. Such conflicts cannot be excluded a priori. In addition, it would be a mistake to assume that the genetic priority of liberty rights gives them a normative priority over other normative claims in a case of conflict. As soon as a conflict arises, then liberty rights, in order that they be relevant to the argument, must be turned into normative arguments claiming that a right to a certain liberty ought to be recognised as definitively valid.

Another issue is whether negative rights are prior to positive rights. The question is whether, in a case of conflict, an interest of non-interference deserves priority, at least in general, over an interest that renders it necessary to interfere with the interest of others.

> If, for example, certain occupants of a house want to party and others want to sleep at night, is it clear that the interest in sleeping deserves priority, or is this an issue of balancing according to the strength of the competing interests?

It seems obvious that some balancing must take place, for one can hardly accept the idea that any noisy activity must be brought to a halt as soon as some-

[21] Positive rights with the function of protecting negative rights can be called defence rights or protective rights. In a wider sense, the negative right to non-interference can also be called a defence right.

[22] See, eg, Böckenförde (1991: 189 ff).

one else just wants to sleep, at whatever time this may be. Accordingly, the example above referred to nighttime, thereby implying that during the daytime some disturbances might well be permitted. Also, from a conceptual standpoint one cannot strictly hold that an interest in positive action always has to yield to an interest in non-interference. The conflict of the two interests implies that the fulfilment of one is possible only if the other is curtailed. This implies that the fulfilment of the interest of non-interference is not only a negative interest but positively demands restrictions on other interests.

A special justificatory status granted to negative rights is the result if one presupposes individual legal spheres, such as, for example, life or integrity, spheres that define a protected interest or good of someone with which others' actions must not be allowed to interfere. Without such a baseline of individual normative spheres, claims to non-interference will amount to normative arguments to be balanced against other arguments, just as in the case of claims in general. Recognition of individual legal spheres implies normative arguments to the effect that such positions ought not to be subject to balancing with other arguments, that is, that they should in principle be immune from legal change.[23]

One can elaborate on this idea by appeal to exclusionary principles.[24] These are normative arguments requiring that a balancing of certain normative positions is not to take place. As principles, they can be outweighed by competing arguments.

> For example, people in general must have the right to sleep at night, and there is no balancing of the matter with other arguments. There may, however, be special reasons that require an exception to this restriction. If these reasons are strong enough, they will supersede the exclusionary principle, and a balancing will be forthcoming.

After exclusionary principles have been overridden, the next issue arises: which arguments win the substantive balancing? This question is independent of the procedural question of whether there ought to be a balancing at all. It may well be that the exclusionary principles have been superseded owing to special circumstances that were not considered when the exclusionary principle was established. Then balancing on the substantive issue is completely open. On the other hand, it might be the case that the exclusionary principle is superseded on the strength of the competing arguments in the circumstances at hand. Then it is likely that the competing arguments will prevail on the substantive issue, too, although this is not certain, for the interests protected by the exclusionary principle may also have a relatively great weight in the circumstances at hand.

[23] However, one should not conceive these individual legal spheres as objects or territories. Such legal spheres are rather sets of legal positions that are attributed to the right-holder. They may also comprise equality rights or competences to vote or to make contracts.

[24] This takes up Raz's idea of exclusionary reasons (1999: 40 ff, 73 ff), combined, however, with the ideas of validity in principle and of balancing, which are alien to Raz's account.

### 7.2.3 Procedural and Substantive Rights

Rights may refer to the procedure of justification or to the results of such procedures. In both cases one finds the types of right outlined above. Accordingly, procedural rights, too, are only an application of liberty rights, negative and positive rights, with respect to certain acts within a justificatory procedure, be it informal or of legal character. Such rights are, for example, the liberty to put forward an argument, the right not to be hindered in taking part in an argumentation, or the right that others take into account the arguments made within their balancing.

## 7.3 THE BALANCING OF RIGHTS

The idea that rights are the appropriate form in which autonomous agents present normative claims based on their interests seems to conflict with views to the effect that rights have a special status that makes them more or less inviolable,[25] or that they are 'trumps' over political goals.[26] If rights are based on interests, it seems natural that they ought to be balanced like interests. The impression that they are somehow immune from balancing can be explained by the fact that rights, in so far as they are definitively valid, are the results of balancing, whilst the matters that are balanced are not rights but rights-claims, that is to say, claims that certain rights be recognised as definitively valid.

Closer analysis shows, however, that some rights are indeed in certain respects immune from balancing. This follows from the character of balancing as a form of autonomous decision-making. The need to look to the consent of autonomous agents stands in the way of the idea that priorities are determined simply by the relative weights of the conflicting interests in the concrete case. Autonomous agents will insist that some of their fundamental interests are to be respected in spite of the fact that they might have less relative weight then competing interests.[27] Autonomous agents understand themselves as leading their own lives, with particular relations to parents or children, to family, to friends or to other groups to which they owe a special loyality.[28] They will therefore recognise individual rights that protect these fundamental interests and personal relations.

Accordingly, what needs to be explained is, first, the thesis that what is called the balancing of rights in fact refers not to rights but to rights-claims, and, secondly, the ways in which the autonomous balancing of such rights-claims supports the idea that some rights are in some way immune from balancing.

[25] Kamm (2002).
[26] Dworkin (1978: 92).
[27] See also Rawls (1971: 27, 29) on the 'separateness of persons'.
[28] This is also relevant to the justification of human rights and fundamental rights. See 8.2, 8.3.2.

### 7.3.1 Rights and Rights-Claims

Rights have been defined as normative relations. Although rights, such as the right of free speech, are often called principles, they are not normative arguments, but the object of such arguments.[29] Rights as normative relations do not have the structure of reiterated requirements for validity. Since they are normative relations, they have the logical status of states of affairs.[30] It is true that rights as normatively defined normative positions have normative implications that require protection and enforcement. Thus, they are embedded in structures of normative arguments. Nevertheless, to speak of rights is to speak of normative relations, not normative claims.

By contrast, normative arguments demand the acceptance and hence the validity of rights as normative states of affairs. Accordingly, when one speaks of the principle of free speech, one is speaking of the requirement that a right to free speech be recognised.[31]

### 7.3.2 Rights as Trumps

What role should be assigned to individual rights in argumentation? Do rights have a special argumentative force, are they 'trumps' that cannot, in general, be overcome by policy arguments? In order to answer this question one needs to clarify the special status that rights may have in normative argumentation and especially in legal systems. Autonomous balancing might indeed result in the attribution of a special force to individual rights, though not a status of trumps over other types of argument.

The point of individual rights is that they protect the interests or goods of individuals. If this is in principle required, then when a conflict arises and a balancing of individual rights against public policies is required, a protection of rights can be achieved in either of two ways.

One might assume that rights are protected by exclusionary principles, which demand that no balancing of the right is to take place. This conception, however, does not fit for all types of right. Still, it might be adequate for establishing substantive fundamental rights, for such rights restrict legislation and are, hence, to some extent protected against being balanced within the political process. The degree to which rights count as trumps over policies depends on the weight attributed to the exclusionary principles.

[29] On this distinction, see Sieckmann (1990: 75, 87).

[30] Therefore, it is misleading to speak of the balancing of goals with rights. In fact, all normative arguments have a teleological structure, some referring to rights, some to other states of affairs.

[31] It might also refer to a principle in a descriptive sense, that is, a prima facie norm. This descriptive use of the term 'principle' should not be neglected. It does not conform, however, to the use that is being made of this term here.

Even if one cannot avoid the balancing of individual rights, a special status may nevertheless stem from the point of reference for determining the relevant factors of the balancing. The result of the balancing will depend on the abstract weights of the conflicting principles and on their respective degrees of fulfilment or non-fulfilment. The degree of fulfilment of individual rights can be determined in either of two ways. The point of reference may be the whole class of rights affected,[32] or it may be the right of one individual. The character of an individual right requires the second option. This does not exclude a balancing with respect to a whole class of rights. Individual rights, however, require a balancing that focusses on the position of the individual concerned.

The focus on the position of the individual is also relevant to the question of the abstract weight assigned to the conflicting rights or principles. A justification based on individual autonomy will assume that the position of each individual has equal weight and, moreover, that it not be given less weight then collective interests, such as, for example, the welfare of the community. What each individual can demand is that his rights are not in general or in the abstract given less weight than conflicting collective interests.

This requirement gives individuals a special position in the procedure of balancing. Their interests, contrary to what utilitarian conceptions assume, are not an element in a utility calculation, but there is a symmetrical constellation between, on the hand, the individual and his interests and, on the other hand, the collective interests of the community. In particular, if it comes to determine the extent to which an individual right is affected, the point of reference is the right of an individual, not the class of rights of all individuals. The interests of the individual, as protected by a right, and the interests of society compete at the same level. The position of the individual is not one among all the others, which inevitably would lead to subordinating it to the interests of society. Thus, individual rights have a special argumentative status which, however, is not to be confused with rights as trumps over collective goals or interests.

## 7.4. CONCLUSION

The status of rights appears to be ambivalent. On the one hand, owing to the central place of the idea of autonomy and of interest-based normative arguments, the primary normative arguments will be presented in terms of rights or, more precisely, rights-claims. In addition, the analysis of the structure of rights suggests, indeed, that a specific rights-discourse exists that cannot be reduced to argumentation about simple, non-relational norms. Rights in this specific sense concern claims to the fulfilment and protection of normative positions. Their special character becomes apparent, in particular, where the rights-addressee is distinct from

[32] In this case, one might say that the right is regarded as an objective principle, not as a subjective right. For a different interpretation of the conception of constitutional rights as objective principles, see Alexy (2002a: 352–54).

the addressee of the first-order norm. Although this second-order structure of rights may be presented just as well in terms of obligations or responsibilities respecting the fulfilment or protection of normative positions, the representation of this specific structure becomes clearer in the context of rights.

A remarkable point is that the specific second-order structure of rights includes issues of the justification and the enforcement of normative positions within the structure of the rights themselves. It also shows why it is that claim rights appear to be a distinct and primary class of rights, when compared with other legal relations.

On the other hand, the specific structure of rights does not affect the general feature of autonomous reasoning, namely, that substantive rights can only serve as the objects of normative arguments, not the starting point of argumentation. What figures as an argument in a balancing are rights-claims, not rights. The necessity of balancing shows that, beside those autonomy rights that constrain argumentation, rights cannot be the foundation but only the result of normative justification. There may, however, be rights of a more fundamental character than simply counting as the result of balancing. This is the issue of human and basic rights, which is taken up in the following chapter.

# 8

# *Autonomy Rights, Human Rights and Fundamental Rights*

IN LAW, THE idea of autonomy finds expression in the recognition of human and fundamental rights, which institutionalise moral rights protecting individual autonomy. The justification of these moral, human and fundamental rights and the relations between them are a matter of dispute, however. It is disputed, for example, how and to what extent these rights can be justified,[1] and likewise, the relations between them are disputed. Even if one can justify some moral rights, it is not clear whether this includes human rights as universal rights,[2] and whether, indeed, such rights have moral or legal character.[3] At the level of constitutional legal systems, human rights may be incorporated into constitutional law and they can then be called fundamental rights.[4] Again, however, it is a matter of dispute whether such fundamental rights are directly drawn from human rights or whether they have a distinct, non-moral foundation.[5] Beyond the issue of theoretical construction, the effects of human rights within constitutional legal systems stand in need of closer analysis, in particular respecting conflicts that arise when fundamental rights are applied by courts that have competence to review parliamentary laws on the question of their constitutionality.

As pointed out above, certain autonomy rights must be recognised by every autonomous agent and in every normative system, for their recognition is a necessary condition for the normative validity of any norm.[6] This conception of autonomy rights forms the basis of human rights and fundamental rights. The matter taken up in this chapter is an analysis of the relations between them, in particular,

[1] See, eg, Corradetti (2009); Fox-Decent and Criddle (2009).

[2] Some authors hold that a justification of rights is only possible within a certain culture, see, eg, MacIntyre (1985: 51 ff); Rorty (1993: 116 ff); Walzer (1994: 2 ff). Others deny that it is those rights recognised in Western legal culture that are justifiable; on this position, see Tugendhat (1998: 54); Honneth (2000: 274).

[3] For example, Alexy (1998) defines human rights as moral rights, and Borowski (2006: 87) suggests that what are called 'human rights' in international law, ought to be called 'international constitutional rights'.

[4] One might also speak of basic or constitutional rights. These terms might be used synonymously. One might interpret constitutional rights, however, as fundamental in a formal sense, being included in constitutional law, whilst fundamental or basic rights have a substantive justification, having a foundation in human rights or being conditions of the legitimacy of a legal or political system. As to various interpretations of the fundamental character of rights, see Bernal Pulido (2009).

[5] See Habermas (1996, orig. 1994).

[6] See 1.3.3, 4.2.3.

which human rights can be justified on the basis of autonomous reasoning and what is the character of the fundamental rights that stem from the transformation of human rights into constitutional law.

## 8.1 THE IDEA OF UNIVERSAL RIGHTS

Human rights are characterised as rights that hold universally for every human being.[7] This presupposes that human rights are justified owing to their content and moral correctness, independently of positive enactments. A central challenge to an autonomy-based theory of rights is, therefore, the justification of human rights as universally valid rights. The idea of individual autonomy itself, however, casts into doubt the claim of the universal validity of human rights. Autonomy implies the right to decide for oneself on normative issues, and there is of course no guarantee that all people will claim or recognise the same rights. The question is whether, despite this fact, at least some human rights must be recognised as universal rights.[8]

A first issue is how to understand the universal character of a right. Diverse interpretations are possible. One might refer to the content and mode of justification, describing human rights as rights that every human being has simply in virtue of being human. Or one might refer to a feature of validity, regarding human rights as valid in every legal system, quite apart from whether they have been issued as positive law. Thus, one can distinguish between universal applicability and universal validity. Universal validity means objective validity in the sense that all reasonable beings must recognise the norm in question as valid, implying, then, its validity in every legal system. Universal applicability refers to the range of application and means that a norm is applicable to all human beings.

For the theory of human rights, the interpretation in terms of universal validity seems more appropriate. It grasps the idea of human rights as objectively valid norms that hold for each and every human being. This may include rights with a restricted range of application, for example, rights of certain groups – women, children, handicapped persons or ethnic groups. Such rights are not universal in the sense that they apply to all human beings in virtue of being human. In order to protect fundamental human interests as far as possible, however, these rights ought to be included in the idea of human rights.

In addition, a problem of the justification of human rights qua rights of human beings is that the property of being human is, as a biological property, not in itself normatively relevant. An argument as to why this property serves as a foundation for human rights is required. Such an argument is, however, not at hand. By

[7] See Höffe (1998: 29); Wellman (1997: 15).

[8] This is a normative issue. The problem is whether certain rights *ought* to be recognised universally, not whether there are human rights that *are* recognised by all cultures. Accordingly, neither the fact of cultural pluralism nor the actual universal recognition of some minimal human rights is dispositive of the issue.

contrast, being reasonable or autonomous are normatively relevant features of human beings, which, however, refer to reason or autonomy, and not to the property of being human as such. Accordingly, human beings who do not count as reasonable or autonomous would not qualify as holders of human rights. Therefore, such conceptions would not succeed in justifying human rights. Thus, the idea of human rights as rights that everyone has simply in virtue of being human encounters serious objections. The notion of universal rights as rights that hold within every legal system, whether or not recognised in positive law, seems to be a more reasonable point of departure. Human rights then follow from the application of universally valid rights to human beings.

A second issue is the distinction between universal validity and universalisability. They are not the same. The requirement of universalisability may be understood semantically as the demand that concepts must be applied to all objects within their domain.[9] In normative respect, it presupposes that a norm may find the consent of every reasonable agent.[10] Universalisability in this sense is a necessary condition of validity that excludes the validity of norms not meeting this demand.[11] It does not imply that a right is or must be universally recognised. The supposed universal validity of human rights must, therefore, amount to more than universalisability.

The crucial issue here is which universal rights can be justified by means of autonomous reasoning. Various requirements of universality and universalisability in their different forms hold within this approach.

(1) Normative arguments must apply to every autonomous agent who is in the circumstances to which the argument in question applies. If not, the argument would not serve the purpose of the argumentation, consisting in establishing a commonly binding norm.
(2) Individual normative conceptions must be universalisable in the sense that every reasonable agent can accept them, that is, they must be capable of being universally valid.
(3) A competence on the part of autonomous agents to introduce arguments into a discourse and to make judgements on the basis of the balancing of such arguments must be universally recognised. This follows, in order that a rational consensus of autonomous agents be made possible. Correspondingly, an obligation on the part of other agents must be recognised, namely, to give due consideration to the respective arguments and judgements.
(4) Individual normative conceptions of autonomous agents that comport with the demand of coherence must be given equal weight, in order that a rational consensus be made possible. This requirement of equal treatment constitutes a form of universality.

[9] Hare (1963: 10 ff).
[10] See, eg, Habermas (1996).
[11] Another formal requirement is that arguments must not use indexical terms referring only to certain individuals. Accordingly, if someone claims a right for himself he must claim it for everyone else in similar circumstances, too. Even this weak claim of universality is questioned, however, by agent-relative types of reasoning. On agent-relativity, see Gesang (2000: 145 ff).

(5) With regard to the question of objectivity, autonomous individuals must, in their attempt to establish binding norms, step back from their own claims to unrestricted autonomy and consider themselves as one autonomous being among others, recognising equal rights on the part of every autonomous agent. This is necessary in order to make possible the recognition of commonly binding norms by autonomous agents.

These requirements imply certain autonomy rights. In particular, autonomy as a normative competence in the sense of (3) includes the right to form normative arguments and judgements, which, in turn, presupposes the right to take part in normative discourse. These autonomy rights are universally valid. They hold within every normative system, being necessary conditions of the existence of any system of norms that is valid in a normative sense. They apply universally to all beings who might have rights,[12] including human beings. The limitation to human beings is, however, not conceptual but contingent. As far as we know, all autonomous agents are human beings, but the concept of autonomy rights is not limited to them.

## 8.2 JUSTIFICATION OF HUMAN RIGHTS

The question remains as to which human rights one can justify on the basis of the requirements of autonomous reasoning. The core of human rights consists of autonomy rights as applied to human beings. Being necessary conditions of the justification of norms, autonomy rights can be qualified as 'a priori rights'. One need know nothing about human beings, their properties and interests, in order to justify these rights, but autonomy rights are founded directly on the structure of normative justification, which requires that every autonomous agent and every normative system recognise these rights.[13] However, human rights may include more than the autonomy rights outlined above. They may be supplemented by 'a posteriori rights', which refer to specific interests, normative attitudes or judgements of human beings. Since they refer to specific human interests, these rights can be called 'specific human rights'.

In addition, one can draw a distinction between, on the one hand, human rights that are justified on a purely moral basis, including the idea of individual autonomy, the normative claims and judgements of autonomous agents, and, on the other hand, rights that constitute necessary conditions of the legitimacy of political or legal systems. The latter may be called 'fundamental rights'.[14] What is of interest at this point is the justification of human rights on a purely moral basis, without presupposing the existence of legal authority.

[12] One ought to note, here, that autonomy rights do not presuppose autonomy as a capacity. They apply also to beings who actually are not capable of autonomous action. In these cases, interests and life plans must be assigned to them and introduced into discourse by other agents.

[13] This need not be understood as a transcendental 'a priori' in a Kantian sense, but rather that one can know something about the possible result of an argumentation before commencing with it.

[14] See below 8.3.

The purely moral justification of human rights follows from the application of autonomous reasoning to human rights claims based on individual interests. On the one hand, this justification will point out some definitively valid human rights that follow from the idea of individual autonomy of, however, only formal or procedural character. On the other hand, specific human rights can be justified on the basis of the individual interests and claims of human beings.

### 8.2.1 Individual Autonomy

The justification of human rights must begin with the idea of individual autonomy. Autonomy is conceived of here as a structure of normative decision-making or judgement. The balancing of normative arguments is the core of autonomous judgements. From the fact that these judgements are constrained by criteria of rationality but not completely determined by them, it follows that the consent of autonomous individuals must be recognised as a criterion of the validity of norms. From this, certain autonomy rights follow.

According to the conditions of justification stated above, one can distinguish rights to:

(1) equal concern, precluding arbitrary, irrational or unjustified differentiation;
(2) respect for autonomy, including participation in argumentation and due concern for the arguments put forward;
(3) a normative competence, enabling one to establish argumentative obligations for other agents;
(4) the equal value of the individual normative conceptions of autonomous agents; and
(5) the impartiality of binding norms.

ad (1): Individual autonomy requires that the validity and bindingness of norms be established according to requirements of autonomous reasoning, which apply to all autonomous agents in the same way. This implies a right to equal concern, that is, equal treatment within argumentation. In addition, the norms established as the result of autonomous reasoning must conform to these requirements. Therefore, no norm can be regarded as valid that includes an unjustified differentiation in the treatment of the agents concerned. Thus, no arbitrary distinction can be justified.

ad (2): In addition, autonomous agents must not be subject to norms that do not respect their autonomy. This implies that the consent of autonomous agents matters. This, again, has procedural and substantive implications. Procedurally, one must recognise the right of autonomous agents to participate in procedures establishing norms that are meant to be binding on them. Participation includes the right to introduce interest-based arguments as well as the right to form an individual judgement based on competing normative claims. Beyond mere participation, autonomous agents can claim substantive respect for their claims, arguments and judgements. If other agents ignore such claims and do not give them due consideration in their reasoning, one has good reason to reject the resulting norm.

ad (3): The rights to participation and to respect are not merely liberty rights but also include competences in the sense of the power intentionally to bring about a change in the normative situation of the agents concerned. Such competences apply to the argumentation itself, for autonomous agents can, by putting forward normative arguments, obligate other agents to give due consideration to these arguments. Accordingly, individual claims put forward in an argumentation must be taken into account by other agents and be treated as valid normative arguments.

ad (4): One must also recognise a right that all autonomous beings be treated as equals. Therefore, equal weight must be given to coherent normative conceptions of autonomous agents. The individual claims based on particular interests may be weighted according to their importance within normative conceptions of autonomous agents. Individual conceptions of the good life integrating the interests of an individual into a coherent life plan must, however, be given equal weight.[15] If not, then a reasonable individual might not accept the result of the argumentation on the ground that equal respect has been denied to him.

ad (5): A requirement corresponding to that of equal treatment is that one can claim a norm to be binding only if it is impartial with regard to the autonomous agents concerned.

Consequently, there are autonomy rights that are required by the model of autonomous reasoning and, hence, can claim validity as universal human rights. These rights have primarily a procedural character, for they are directed to the procedure of normative justification, but one has to bear in mind that there are at least some human rights that must be recognised as universally valid.

Moreover, as moral rights, these rights must be recognised as definitively valid, operating as constraints on balancing, without being themselves subject to balancing. It seems impossible to present a counter-argument that could justify a balancing. Where, on the other hand, legal systems are concerned, they constitute normative claims that are valid in principle. If there are valid arguments against their complete implementation, a legal system might limit such rights. It is difficult, however, to imagine what might justify such a limitation. Some rights, in particular, rights to participation, might require specification as to their application, which might include some limitation. In general, however, no justification seems to be available for a limitation of autonomy rights. Therefore, these rights must also be recognised as definitively valid legal rights.

[15] The demand of equal respect for autonomous individuals does not preclude judging individual normative conceptions according to criteria of rationality.

### 8.2.2 Specific Human Rights Principles

Human rights principles demand respect for the fundamental interests of human beings. By contrast with autonomy rights, such interests depend on what human beings actually are and want. They are based not directly on the structure of normative justification but on claims of autonomous agents, expressing their fundamental interests. Thus, they may be called 'specific' human rights principles. As principles, they include claims that ought to be fulfilled as far as possible with regard to competing principles and are capable of being balanced against other principles.

These principles apply to private as well as to public agents.[16] Since, according to the conception of rights suggested above, rights address the fulfilment and protection of beneficiary norms,[17] one might restrict the discussion of human rights to those addressed to public authorities. Directed to other autonomous agents, such claims immediately face claims on the part of those agents to liberty, which make the issue of the justification of human rights – even of human rights principles – far more complicated. By contrast, public authorities are responsible for establishing and enforcing norms. Therefore, they are the primary addressees of human rights claims. Nevertheless, the application of human rights need not be restricted to them.

The question is whether there are specific human rights principles that are universally valid, that is, that act against any public authority quite apart from the identity of the legal culture in question. If one applies a wide conception of human rights, comprising every fundamental individual interest, such as life, liberty, property, happiness, political participation, and the like, there is no reason to deny the universal validity of such principles. What is demanded is merely that those principles be taken into account and be balanced against competing claims by the legal authorities. They do not preclude the possibility, for example, that demands to protect cultural identity may be used as arguments to restrict human rights interests.

One might raise the objection that such a wide approach puts human rights in the position of demanding the correct balancing of human interests by public powers. This claim may be universal, but it seems to miss a central aspect of human rights as protection against public power, and not merely an objective of their balancing. Nevertheless, the correct balancing of the interests of autonomous agents is a fundamental demand of autonomous reasoning, which holds for every legal system. One must, therefore, recognise as a human right that to the correct balancing of interest-based claims of autonomous agents. The right to correct balancing is, in the first place, a moral right. It might suffer limitations with respect to its legal validity. A legal or even constitutional right to the correct

[16] As pointed out above, the purely moral justification of human rights does not presuppose the existence of legal or political authorities. Therefore, it may establish obligations also of private agents.

[17] See 7.1.

balancing of interest-based claims might be seen as too demanding or detrimental to the constitutional system, for example, respecting its consequences for a system of judicial review. Therefore, legal systems have to determine the extent to which they are willing to recognise such a right. However, in this decision at least they are subject to the claim of correct balancing.

Specific human rights go beyond a right to correct balancing, specifying rights with particular content. With regard to claims of a particular content, one cannot assume that every individual interest must be recognised as legally relevant in every legal system. Therefore, an individual interest as such does not suffice to constitute a human rights principle. An additional feature is necessary. This might be understood as the importance of the interest for human beings. This criterion is, however, indeterminate, leaving it to some extent up to the positive law to determine which interests are regarded as sufficiently important to constitute a human right. One might expect more from a conception of human rights. By contrast, a more specific approach is possible, using the notion of exclusionary principles.

### 8.2.3 Exclusionary Human Rights Principles

A narrow conception of human rights limits human rights principles to claims that certain individual interests are not subject to public power.

> For example, the human rights interest in one's own liberty is not only a matter of one's being able to do what one wants to do, with this interest being taken into account by public authorities, but rather, it demands that public authorities not have competence to regulate this interest. It is not an interest to be balanced but an interest that is *not* to be balanced by public authorities.

The corresponding principle can be called an exclusionary principle,[18] for it excludes the balancing of the interest in question. It grants the immunity from interference by a public power, though only in principle and not necessarily a definitive immunity. As a principle, it may be balanced and overridden by competing principles claiming that public authorities ought to have a competence to regulate certain individual interests.

Two lines of argument may lead to the recognition of a human right as an exclusionary principle. First, one might argue that a requirement to recognise an exclusionary right is objectively valid.[19]

[18] This extends the idea of exclusionary reasons, introduced by Raz (1999: 40). Raz's conception is different, however, for it suggests that exclusionary reasons exclude certain reasons or types of reasons from deliberation. The consequence is the pre-emptive character of a decision or a norm. This conception can be extended. The exclusion can refer not only to certain reasons or types of reason but to all competing reasons or means of entering into procedures of reasoning. Moreover, the exclusionary character of a reason is not sufficient to establish the peremptory character of a norm, for the distinction of definitive validity and validity in principle can be applied to exclusionary reasons as well, and the exclusionary reason may hold only in principle.

[19] As for the criterion of objective validity (reasonable convergence together with the need to have a commonly binding norm), see 6.4.

For example, one can scarcely doubt that everyone has a right not to be killed for the benefit of other people. This holds, even if one's organs would help to save lives, quite apart from whether a balancing might favour the solution that saves the greater number of lives. Such a balancing is inadmissible.

Secondly, even if objective criteria favour the public power of balancing, one can still claim that this violates individual autonomy on the ground that the individual interest in question outweighs the need to have a common norm.

For example, one might set religious freedom or freedom of conscience against legal requirements, claiming that the demands of religion or conscience are stronger than the obligation to obey the law.

One might prefer not to have a common norm if this violates interests that are of greater importance than having a legally ordered community and, hence, prefer some kind of a state of nature to a legal system that violates human rights interests.[20] This is the point of fundamental rights, which is taken up here.

### 8.2.4 Definitive Substantive Human Rights

A complete conception of human rights must not only state human rights principles but also state which substantive human rights are definitively valid, that is, are justified as a result of the balancing of human rights principles with competing normative claims. The problem here is whether there are definitive human rights that hold universally against every public power. This problem arises both for the balancing model of human rights and for the conception of exclusionary human rights as exempt from balancing.

An argument against the possibility of universally valid human rights is that rights are relative to culture. The cultural relativity of definitive human rights can stem from two situations. The balancing of human rights principles may be culturally sensitive, leading to diverse results, or particular cultural values might serve as reasons to restrict human rights. The latter approach is possible, however, only with regard to cultural values that are compatible with the idea of individual autonomy.

The balancing of principles requires value judgements on which reasonable agents may differ. It is also possible, and even likely, that different cultural backgrounds will in some respects lead to different value judgements and, accordingly, to different normative judgements. Thus, the limits of definitive human rights may differ in different legal cultures. This does not, however, rule out a universal core of definitive human rights. For example, the right to free speech rules out the case in which one's speech is met with the death penalty. This claim can be objectively justified as a definitive human right. One can easily imagine other examples of evidently unjustified interference with human rights claims.

[20] This justification of human rights would imply an argument for a right to resistance against public regulation. On the link between human rights and the right to resistance, see also Brugger (1999: 88).

A problem remains: Just how far do these rights extend? To determine the extent of definitive fundamental rights requires that one actually carry out a balancing in particular cases. If purely moral argument does not suffice to establish such definitive rights, the issue must be resolved by constitutional or international law.[21]

## 8.3 FUNDAMENTAL RIGHTS

Fundamental rights are characterised by a special constitutional status within the legal system. In a formal sense, they may be defined as constitutional rights, that is, rights recognised by constitutional law. In a substantive sense, they can be defined as rights that constitute necessary conditions of the legitimacy of a legal system. This is the notion that will be followed here.

### 8.3.1 Concept of Fundamental Rights

Without recognising fundamental rights, no system can be legitimate in its claims of authority and bindingness. As conditions necessary to constitute the legitimacy of a normative order, fundamental rights[22] may be based on human rights, but also have an independent justification. Thus, one can distinguish two sources of fundamental rights.[23] Human rights, as rights that must be recognised by every legal system, present the primary source of fundamental rights. Beyond human rights recognised by and transformed into constitutional law, the idea of fundamental rights as necessary conditions of the legitimacy of the legal system may include rights that are not human rights, such as the rights of organisations or collectivities. In general, however, also fundamental rights that present necessary conditions of legitimacy will reflect human rights claims. Hence, the central issue of fundamental rights is that of how human rights are transformed into constitutional rights.

Human rights principles require that certain rights be legally recognised. As principles, however, they cannot claim strict validity; rather, they provide for a certain though not unrestricted leeway on the question of which rights are actually to be recognised as constitutional rights. Thus, the system of fundamental rights may vary among legal systems and is to a certain extent contingent. Hence,

[21] This implies that constitutional law as well as international law is understood, not in a positivistic sense, but in a normative sense, which integrates claims of justice and morality.

[22] Two conceptions of fundamental rights can be distinguished, fundamental rights as positive constitutional rights and fundamental rights as necessary constitutional rights, which may be recognised as valid even if not recognised by positive law. Whether necessary or not, if a legal system recognises human rights as constitutional rights, it accepts the notion that the validity of these rights is required independently of the positive law.

[23] If one rejects the idea of moral justification presupposed by human rights, only the second foundation is available.

positive constitutional law has a certain autonomy vis-à-vis human rights, which implies that it is bound by human rights principles but is to a certain extent free in balancing these principles.

Still, and although the implementation of human rights in constitutional law may be regarded as the primary source of fundamental rights, it is important to note that the idea of fundamental rights is not exhausted by this approach. The human rights approach asks what rights must be recognised in every legal system. By contrast, the notion of fundamental rights is what rights must necessarily be recognised as conditions of legitimacy in a particular legal system. This approach, specific to fundamental rights, relies on the fact that fundamental rights operate within a constitutional system that not only protects and enforces rights but also establishes and legitimises public authorities. One may, therefore, ask: what are the conditions of the legitimacy of these authorities and of their regulations? Among the conditions of legitimacy, fundamental rights will have a prominent place. Thus, the definition of fundamental rights as conditions of the legitimacy of a public order follows. A suitable criterion to develop a conception of fundamental rights is, therefore, to ask which rights must be recognised by a legal system if its norms can legitimately be claimed to be binding on its addressees.[24]

Accordingly, a specific theory of fundamental rights treats them as necessary conditions of binding legal norms, that is, as conditions that must be recognised by law if legal norms are to be binding. The thesis is that certain autonomy rights and substantive rights derived from normative claims of autonomous agents must necessarily be accepted as legally valid if a legal system and its norms are to be considered as binding.

There are two features that characterise fundamental rights as conditions of the legitimacy of the law qua binding order. First, their validity is justified independently of positive enactment. Secondly, they are immune, at the very least, from ordinary legislation. The first condition points out their moral, that is, their non-relativised normative character. The second condition follows from the notion of fundamental rights as demarcating legal spheres that are, in principle, immune from exercises of political power. By contrast with the idea of individual rights as claims to be given due consideration in procedures of balancing of either moral or legal character, the conception of fundamental rights suggests that there are individual rights that are, at least in principle, not subject to public authority at all.[25] According to this conception, fundamental rights demand that public authorities not interfere with certain individual interests and that these be immune from

[24] Thus, the question arises as to whether fundamental rights might be based not only on exclusionary principles but also on simple human rights principles. This is possible to the extent that the balancing of interest-based principles is itself regarded as an object of a fundamental right.

[25] See Alexy (1997); Brugger (1999: 107), on basic rights as rights that are too important to be left to the decision of a simple parliamentary majority. However, the claim of human rights in the narrow sense is stronger, for they exclude, in principle, any authoritative interference with the right in question. Hence, one can distinguish different strengths of human rights with respect to whether they exclude, in principle, any authoritative interference, or only interference by qualified majority decisions, or only interferences that meet no standard other than that of a majority decision.

public regulation.[26] Although one must accept the existence of public power that interferes with individual interests, it would be unreasonable to accept an unrestricted political power. Hence, it is necessary to protect some fundamental interests against any interference stemming from an exercise of public power, in particular, interests that individuals deem so important that they would give up the advantages of commonly binding norms before yielding on these interests.

The immunity of fundamental rights can take various forms. A strong form is that in the event of a conflict, a fundamental right enjoys priority over positive law. A weaker form claims that in principle fundamental rights are immune from positive legislation, that is, they ought not to be subject to a balancing by the legislature or other political organs. In both of these forms, one can distinguish the case of a priority or immunity from all measures of the positive law, including constitutional law, from the case of a priority or immunity from only ordinary positive law, so that constitutional law might alter fundamental rights. The first case represents a conception of supra-positive or natural rights, the second, a conception of fundamental rights as constitutional rights prior to, or not subject to, ordinary legislation.

By combining these features, several conceptions of fundamental rights may be developed. A strong non-positivist conception will assume supra-positive validity and the comprehensive priority of fundamental rights. Where this priority is concerned, one must, moreover, distinguish between definitive priority and priority in principle. Weak non-positivist conceptions of fundamental rights hold that the validity of a fundamental right need not depend on enactments of the positive law, without, however, claiming a priority over positive law. A strong positivist conception, which corresponds to a common understanding of fundamental rights, treats them as positive rights included in the constitution that have priority over ordinary positive law.[27] A weak positivist conception will regard these rights as positive constitutional rights without priority over ordinary positive law.

It would seem that a conception of fundamental rights based on the features of independence from positive law and a priority over it that, however, holds only in principle, is the most defensible position.

First, fundamental rights ought to be recognised as valid independently of a legislative procedure or authoritative enactment. It follows, then, that fundamental rights are not simply the result of following such a procedure. Although constitutional legislation might establish fundamental rights, such legislation of fundamental rights claims at least implicitly that they are valid independently of this enactment.[28]

Secondly, the priority of fundamental rights against positive law follows from their immunity, implying that such rights ought, in principle, not to be subject to legislative balancing. Thus, they are in principle exempt from legislative power

[26] This approach employs the notion of exclusionary principles explained at 8.2.3.

[27] Again, one can distinguish between a definitive priority and a priority in principle.

[28] One might call such rights a priori rights because their existence can be established before and independently of a legislative procedure. See Nino (1991: 253).

and therefore have priority over conflicting statutes. The immunity of fundamental rights from positive law stems from their status as a presupposition of the binding character of positive law. Legal recognition of such rights is necessary, for a procedure that denies such rights does not establish valid norms. Recognition of fundamental rights is thus a condition of the validity of legal norms, understood in a normative sense.[29] This immunity, however, does not hold strictly. Overriding reasons, alone or accompanied by an explicit authorisation of the legislator, might justify an interference with a fundamental right on the part of the legislature.[30]

### 8.3.2 Justification of Fundamental Rights

A justification of fundamental rights must demarcate legal spheres that, at least in principle, are exempt from political power and, in addition, show that their recognition is a presupposition of the legitimacy of the legal system and its claim to bindingness. One should note that, by contrast with human rights, fundamental rights need not be the same in each legal system. Recognition of a certain right might be fundamental in one system but not in another.

> For example, the neutrality of the state in matters of religion may be crucial for the legitimacy of political authority in one society, but have little importance in another.

Fundamental rights may be justified in either of two ways.

First, one might demonstrate that certain human rights are objectively valid and must therefore be recognised in every legal system. Beyond the autonomy rights referred to above, however, and mere human rights principles, the problem encountered here is that a balancing is required in order to establish specific human rights as definitively valid, and that this balancing requires autonomous judgements, which might be diverse. In addition, a demonstration of universal human rights is not necessary in this respect, for fundamental rights need not be universally valid.

Secondly, one can use the difficulty of establishing objectively valid norms in order to justify exclusionary fundamental rights. The argument begins, following the definition of fundamental rights, with the question of which rights must be recognised in order that an authoritative decision be recognised as legitimate.

[29] One might also speak of legitimate validity, for positive law, if enacted legitimately, deserves to be applied and followed.

[30] This conception of fundamental rights requires rights that are more than liberty rights. Liberty rights may be fundamental rights in the weak sense of being valid independently of enactment by the positive law. Hence, they may be pre-legal rights whose existence does not depend on their legal recognition and which will exist unless and until they are removed by legal norms. Such rights can be called 'residual rights'. Such rights typically are liberty rights. For example, as a residual right, the right to physical integrity or the right to do what one wishes exist for as long as there is no legal regulation to the contrary. But this is not the sense in which fundamental rights have been defined above. Liberty rights can be established independently of legal regulation, but they have only prima facie character without normative force against positive law. This is not to say that liberties could not be the object of fundamental rights. But the concept of a fundamental right requires more than a liberty right.

The necessity of recognising rights arises when it is asked why the results of procedures of balancing established by public authorities ought to be binding on anyone. One person alone can do the balancing, but in order to be binding on anyone else, one must show that the result of this balancing must reasonably be accepted by the addressees and is, hence, intersubjectively binding.[31] If cognitive criteria were available, determining the correct decision that any reasonable agent has to accept and follow, one would not need to introduce fundamental rights in the sense defined. Autonomous reasoning does not, however, admit criteria that substantively determine the correct result of a balancing.[32] Although some formal requirements of rationality constrain the balancing, there are no substantive criteria sufficient to determine the result of the balancing.

This lack of objectivity of judgements based on balancing makes it possible for one to establish a link between the bindingness of norms and the recognition of individual rights. In so far as the bindingness of norms cannot be demonstrated objectively by reference to some normative truth that every reasonable agent must recognise, it cannot be established as binding without reference to the reasonable consent of the agents involved. Consent, however, presupposes individual normative judgements. Since the bindingness of a norm depends on the convergence of individual normative judgements,[33] it is necessary to recognise individual rights to form such judgements and to have these judgements taken into account in deciding on the legally valid norms.

Establishing a norm as legally valid and hence binding requires at least the recognition of the autonomy rights listed above. The justification of specific definitive rights, however, encounters the problem that normative arguments based on individual interests have to be balanced against each other. In some cases this will lead to a consensus among reasonable agents. One must try, at least as an ideal, to achieve such a consensus in a discursive procedure in which everyone can put forward his normative judgements and try to convince other people of his views. Many cases, however, will remain in dispute, and a consensus will not stem from free discussion alone. It then seems reasonable to introduce decision procedures that provide for authoritative decisions.[34] Such procedures are, for example, legislative enactments or court decisions. The norms established by such procedures are binding although they might not enjoy consent and, indeed, it might even be reasonable to dissent from them. They are valid on the ground that it is reasonable to accept these norms as the result of an authoritative decision.

Since the introduction of authoritative decision procedures in a legal system limits individual rights, the question arises of whether and under which conditions it is reasonable to accept such authoritative decisions as binding. These decisions, at the vey least, must realise the interest-based claims to as high a degree as possible. That is, individual autonomy must be interfered with to the least extent

[31] See Nagel (1991: 3ff).

[32] See Peczenik (1989: 84, 95 f).

[33] See 6.4.2.

[34] See Rawls (1995: 148).

possible. Furthermore, the system of decision-making must to the greatest extent possible allow the people to decide for themselves on the legally valid norms. Decision procedures must not restrict one's right to decide for oneself on the valid norms more than is required by other legally valid principles. Finally, one must take into account the possibility that authoritative decisions may fail to take account of the requirements of individual rights altogether. Therefore it will be reasonable to introduce a provision to the effect that certain fundamental interests are to be protected by fundamental rights that are not subject to authoritative determination.

Accordingly, there are two ways to justify exclusionary fundamental rights. They might be supported by objective criteria or, if this is not possible, a fundamental right can in principle be claimed on the ground that there is a need to justify public authority and a right to reject unjustified authority. The judgement as to whether such claims are justified is, of course, a matter of legal judgement, which does not depend solely on the views of the individual agent himself. But the right of any agent to make fundamental rights claims must be universally recognised.[35]

### 8.3.3 Fundamental Autonomy Rights

According to the argument outlined above, legal systems claim that their norms are binding, but for want of substantive cognitive criteria, the bindingness of norms can be justified only if the autonomy of the addressees of the norms in question is respected. A legal system that claims to be legitimate must recognise the validity of such autonomy rights and must aim to realise them. Therefore, legal systems must necessarily include certain kinds of fundamental rights required by individual autonomy. These rights are of two types: first, procedural rights that make it possible for one to justify the binding character of the results of these procedures, and, secondly, substantive rights that demarcate individual spheres that are to be respected by the outcomes of justificatory procedures.

#### *8.3.3.1 Procedural Fundamental Rights*

Autonomy rights, in the first instance, include the right to make claims based on one's own interests, the right to form one's own normative judgement, and the right not to be subject to norms if one has not given consent or at least must reasonably consent to it.[36] These rights refer to procedures of argumentation in general, but since legal systems include institutionalised procedures of decision-making, procedural rights to take part in such procedures must, in principle, be legally

[35] A consequence of this is that the guarantee of access to an independent judiciary cannot presuppose the legal existence of human rights or human rights principles. It must always remain possible that a human rights claim is brought to court and that legal restrictions are judged on the basis of whether or not they constitute a violation of a human right.

[36] See 1.3.3, 4.2.3.

recognised. That the existence of obligatory norms depends on such procedures lends a special status to those procedural rights necessary to carry out justificatory procedures in a correct way.[37] Such rights are fundamental procedural rights. They include:

(1) the right to put forward interest-based normative arguments which, as an element of personal autonomy, includes the right to form a conception of the good life;
(2) the right to form individual normative judgements on the correct compromise between competing conceptions of the good life;
(3) the right to take part in a procedure that purports to bring about an authoritative decision in those cases in which a purely rational procedure does not lead to a result.

Moreover, these procedural rights imply requirements to the effect that the diverse interests, conceptions of the good life, and individual normative judgements are respected and taken into account in procedures of legal decision-making.

Since a justificatory procedure actually has to be carried out in order to have justificatory force, the procedural rights also have to be effective in the sense that people be able to make use of them. This implies rights to the effect that people will have an opportunity to develop their interests, their conceptions of the good life, and their moral judgements, as well as an opportunity to take part in procedures of decision-making.

#### *8.3.3.2 Substantive Fundamental Rights*

Procedural rights require the recognition of legal rights to participate in legal procedures, and they also require that legal systems adopt procedures aiming at the optimal fulfilment of individual interests and normative conceptions. The latter requirement already includes substantive claims, though only in the form of principles, not definitive rights. One might ask whether these procedural autonomy rights already exhaust the idea of fundamental rights or whether, in addition, definitive substantive rights can be established as fundamental rights.

The assumption that there are substantive fundamental rights is faced with the problem of how this is possible, given the pervasive demand of justification by balancing. If a right is valid as a normative argument, it will be necessary to balance it against competing principles. If, by contrast, a right holds definitively, it seems that it can be established only as the result of a balancing and cannot restrict such a procedure. In either case, that there are substantive rights that are not only independent of positive enactments but can, indeed, impose restrictions on them, as would have to be the case with fundamental rights, seems to be impossible.

A first step towards a solution to this problem is the idea of exclusionary principles. Such principles demand that on certain issues a balancing is not to take place.

[37] See also Habermas (1996, orig.: 1994: 110 f, 135 ff, 321).

For example, the right to physical integrity contains the claim that legislation on how a living human being's organs are to be distributed in order to achieve an optimal result regarding the life and health of the whole population is precluded. It would be wrong, from the perspective of a fundamental right to physical integrity, even to begin an argument on this point.[38]

Regarding the balancing of the liberty of expression and the right to privacy or personal honour, if one were to compare the importance that the publication of certain types of information or expression has, for example, photos showing prominent figures in everyday activities, with the need to protect privacy or personal honour, one might well conclude that the latter deserves priority. The point of the right to free expression, however, might be understood as excluding such a balancing, at least in general.

Similarly, the right to private property requires that there be no legislation on the use of this property, that this decision in other words is to be left to the property holder. Even if legislation might yield better results respecting the balancing of competing interests, a right to property as a fundamental right excludes such legislation in principle.

However, principles may collide with other principles and be overridden by them. Fundamental rights principles, though exclusionary, need not be absolute. Nevertheless, the balancing, at least initially, must concern the issue of whether competence to interfere with the fundamental right exists at all. A regulation of the substantive issue will be legitimate only if this question is answered positively. And it may be the case that fundamental rights exclude such a regulation, even if it would be justifiable on substantive grounds.

How, then, do exclusionary fundamental rights principles affect the structure of a legal system? They lead to a distinction between the issues of, on the one hand, whether one may interfere with the fundamental right at all, and, on the other, whether an interference is justified in substance. The first question is answered by means of a balancing of exclusionary fundamental rights principles. The second question concerns the substantive issue of the correct balancing of competing principles. How significant this distinction will be depends on the weight that a particular legal system assigns to the exclusionary fundamental rights principles. If they are assigned very great weight, fundamental rights may become nearly absolute. If their weight is low or even zero, there will be no substantive protection of fundamental rights distinct from the issue of the substantive correctness of the legal regulation. The weight of the exclusionary fundamental rights principles indicates the extent to which a legal system protects substantive fundamental rights.

The weight of these principles will be determined by the constitution and by the practice of constitutional interpretation, based on a normative theory of fundamental rights. This practice may be evaluated according to the criteria of objective validity set out above. But it is not clear whether it will be possible to determine the weight of exclusionary fundamental rights principles independently of a constitutional practice and, hence, whether the conception of substantive

[38] See above 8.2.3.

fundamental rights based on exclusionary principles fulfils the first condition of fundamental rights, that is to say, their being independent of positive legal enactments. To answer this question, a substantive theory of fundamental rights is required. This, however, is beyond the scope of the present analysis.

## 8.4 CONCLUSION

Where the idea and existence of universal human rights are concerned, several distinctions have to be made, namely, that between:

(i) the idea of individual autonomy, which forms the basis of the justification of human rights, human rights principles and definitive human rights;
(ii) human rights principles to be balanced and exclusionary human rights principles demanding that certain interests or normative positions not be made the object of a balancing; and
(iii) fundamental rights as, on the one hand, constitutionalised human rights and, on the other, necessary conditions of the legitimacy of public authority.

At least some aspects of human rights hold universally.

(1) The idea of individual autonomy is universally valid. No normative claims can be justified that deny the right of each individual to make normative claims based on his or her interests, and to form a normative judgement regarding competing normative claims and conceptions.

(2) Human rights principles based on individual interests are universally valid.

(3) Since exclusionary human rights principles presuppose the existence of public power and must accordingly be established within a legal system, it is not obvious that such rights hold universally. Still, it seems plausible that there is a core of universally valid exclusionary human rights principles and corresponding fundamental rights. Furthermore, the right of each individual to claim a human right must be recognised as universally valid.

(4) Although definitive human rights must be established within a legal system, one can hardly deny the existence of a core of definitive human rights. Furthermore, a universal right to claim a definitive human right must be recognised, that is to say, access to the courts must be granted on the basis of alleged though not legally recognised human rights principles.

Accordingly, the thesis that there are universal human rights is, in various respects, sound. Definitively valid human rights, however, have, first of all, formal or procedural character. The justification of substantive human rights as definitively valid is only possible as the result of balancing and intersubjective reflection, and not on the basis of theoretical investigation alone. Again, this is not to say that substantive human rights cannot be justified as definitively valid.

Human rights require the recognition of fundamental rights in constitutional law. There are several ways to classify fundamental rights. With respect to their content, one can distinguish three kinds of autonomy rights:

(i) the right to moral autonomy, that is, the right to participate in discourses about morally and legally valid norms, and the right not to be subject, without sufficient justification, to norms that one does not accept as valid;
(ii) the right to personal autonomy, that is, the right to develop and live one's own life; and
(iii) the right to take part in decision procedures on questions of which norms are legally valid.

These rights must in principle be legally recognised and fulfilled as far as possible if the claim of a legal system to be binding is to be legitimate. According to their justificatory status, one can distinguish fundamental legal rights to the optimal realisation of individual interests and to participate in legal decision procedures, exclusionary fundamental rights, and substantive fundamental rights guaranteeing the acceptability of legal regulations.

# 9

# *Legal Validity*

LAW IS AN institutionalised normative order,[1] that is, a system of norms and procedures that is meant to establish binding norms for a society. Institutionalisation of law presupposes that legal norms are created and applied in organised procedures by agents who are authorised to make binding decisions on what counts as law generally or in a particular case. Accordingly, law includes a system of norms that are claimed to be binding and, in this sense, objectively valid. As a system of norms, law consists of a set of interrelated norms identified by certain criteria of validity. Relations between norms may consist of logical relations but may also stem from procedures, in particular, those procedures establishing definitively valid norms by means of the balancing of normative arguments. Since objective validity will often not result from argumentation alone, an authoritative determination is needed to establish binding norms.[2] Thus, legal validity, at least to considerable extent, will be established authoritatively. This makes its relation to autonomous reasoning a central issue of the theory of law.

The following analysis of the authoritative validity of law and its relation to the idea of autonomy will, first, outline the claims to validity and to the bindingness of law and also the way in which autonomous reasoning makes it possible to support such claims; second, point out the normative character of legal validity; thirdly, introduce the idea of formal principles as a device for establishing legal authority; and, fourthly, analyse the relation between legal validity and moral correctness.

## 9.1 LAW AS A BINDING PUBLIC ORDER

The claim of law to be authoritatively binding means that the law provides a set of commonly binding norms even if these norms are not substantively justified or, indeed, even wrong according to standards of moral correctness. On the other hand, its claim to bindingness cannot be upheld without a justification, which

[1] See also MacCormick (2005: 2).

[2] One should note, however, that this refers to the legal system, not to each legal norm. Whether legal norms can be established by purely substantive reasons and without authoritative determination remains an issue to be analysed. A foundation of legal validity on purely substantive grounds is not excluded for conceptual reasons.

must be based on principles of justice or political morality. A denial of such a justification would undermine the attempt to establish a binding legal system. For it offers a reason for not complying with the issued legal norms. Hence, the claim that legal norms are binding requires a justification of these norms, which, moreover, must match the normative claim of law.

Accordingly, law is an enterprise of establishing a justified and commonly binding public order. The issue here is the claim of law to objectivity in the sense of bindingness and the relation of this claim to the idea of individual autonomy. The problem that the idea of autonomy presents for the claim of law to be binding results from the exclusionary implications of this claim. A claim of law to be binding excludes the validity of diverging norms. Accordingly, law, as far as it is definitively valid, does not allow for competing action-guiding systems. This implies, furthermore, that legal validity cannot be ascribed on the basis of mere individual normative judgements that may compete and conflict with each other. By contrast, a model of justification based on the idea of autonomy makes validity and bindingness of norms depend on individual normative judgements. This seems to contradict the existence of binding authority. Binding authority implies heteronomous regulation, whose validity does not depend on individual acceptance. One has to acknowledge, at the very least, that individual autonomy and the authority of law conflict with each other, for the purpose of law is to restrict individual autonomy in order to establish commonly binding norms. This conflict is not a merely contingent matter but is conceptually necessary. Thus, the problem arises of how legal validity can be understood and established by means of autonomous reasoning.

In accordance with an autonomy-based conception of law, legal norms might stem from individual agreement, from reasonable convergence or from legitimate authority. Here, I will not be considering norms stemming from individual agreement, such as contracts. They presuppose objective legal norms that make such agreements legally binding.

The criterion of reasonable convergence[3] identifies norms that are objectively valid in the sense that their validity does not depend on their acceptance by each individual agent. These norms can be claimed to be binding if there is a need to have a commonly binding norm. Norms that are supported by reasonable convergence and that respond, in addition, to the need to have a commonly binding norm, might be regarded as valid legal norms, whether positively issued or not. In so far as this is possible, no conflict between autonomy and authority arises; autonomous agents must recognise authoritative norms that fulfil these criteria. Two problems remain: that of establishing reasonable convergence and hence objective validity of norms,[4] and the conflict of autonomy with positivist conceptions of law that do not grant the possibility that the legal validity of norms can be

[3] See 6.4.2.

[4] On this issue, see 4.3.3, 6.4.

established directly by means of the criterion of reasonable convergence without appeal to the authoritative issuance of a norm.[5]

Another issue to be discussed is the criterion of legitimate authority. The concept of legal validity must integrate the seemingly conflicting ideas of autonomy and authority. It must not only determine whether legal validity can be established directly on criteria referring to moral correctness, like that of reasonable convergence, but also present an account of how legitimate authority is possible and law's claim to authority can be justified in the framework of a theory based on autonomy. I will argue the following theses:

(1) The concept of legal validity must be normative in the sense that the legal validity of a norm implies a requirement to apply and follow this norm.
(2) Legal authority must be constructed by means of formal principles.
(3) One cannot exclude the possibility that a legal system includes principles owing to their moral correctness.
(4) Definitively valid legal norms can be identified formally or empirically, as the result of legal procedures of the balancing of normative arguments, but they can be established only by normative judgements.

The upshot of this is that, within a framework of autonomous reasoning, an adequate conception of legal validity must include normative elements and cannot be defined on the basis of positivist, that is, empirical and analytical criteria alone.

## 9.2 CONCEPTIONS OF LEGAL VALIDITY

Conceptions of the validity of norms may be normative or non-normative, depending on whether the validity of a norm implies a requirement that this norm be applied and followed or whether the obligation to comply with norms is seen as separate from the issue of their validity. The claim of law that its norms are binding requires a normative conception of legal validity. This assumption is, to be sure, controversial. Positivist theories of law that claim to be descriptive (for example, HLA Hart's theory)[6] apply a conception of legal validity that is not normative.

### 9.2.1 Empirical, Criterial and Applicative Conceptions of Validity

Three conceptions of legal validity should be distinguished. A conception of legal validity may focus on the empirical existence of law, on the criteria of membership of norms in a legal system, or on the requirement that legal organs apply and follow a norm.

[5] One might ask whether reasonable convergence should not be seen as a positivist criterion, for it refers to actual judgements of the agents involved. These judgements, however, claim normative correctness, not empirical correctness. Therefore, the criterion of reasonable convergence requires the application of normative criteria, orientated towards moral correctness.

[6] Hart (1994: v).

The first option is taken by conceptions of legal realism that try to reduce legal statements to statements of empirical fact, be they sociological or psychological in nature. This way, law is seen in terms of rules that are reducible to the behaviour of legal organs or its addressees, or of patterns of mental attitudes. Statements of law are interpreted as statements of what rules are followed or accepted in the practice of law-applying organs. Such conceptions, however, are inadequate for analysing legal validity, for they cannot give legal guidance to law-applying organs. Thus, they miss the central feature of the normativity of law.

The second option is that of legal positivism. Legal validity is defined by criteria of membership of norms in a legal system. The criterial approach is followed, for example, by Hans Kelsen, who identifies legal norms by criteria that ultimately refer to the historically first constitution, and by HLA Hart, who offers as a criterion of identification a rule of recognition, which is constituted by the practice of legal officials and which defines the criteria according to which legal validity is determined. The criterial approach allows one to identify the norms belonging to a legal system and the claim to validity connected with these norms, but leaves open the normative issue of whether these norms ought actually to be applied and followed.

The third option defines legal validity by reference to the normative issue that legal norms ought to be applied and followed, at least by the organs of the legal system. Accordingly, the legal validity of a norm implies that the law-applying organs, at least in principle, must apply this norm, if they are confronted with a case to which this norm applies. Ronald Dworkin's conception of law presents a theory of legal validity of this type.[7] The point of law, according to Dworkin, is the justification of the enforcement of legal rules.[8] Although one might distinguish between an obligation to apply a norm and the justification for applying it,[9] Dworkin's conception certainly is a normative conception of legal validity, that is, a conception suggesting a criterion that purports to be relevant to the issue of which norms are to be applied as law.

Although what is of interest here is a normative conception of legal validity, one should not discard the alternative conceptions.[10] Each of them grasps an important aspect of law. The empirical approach focuses on the character of law as a social fact, the criterial approach elaborates the systemic character of law, and the applicative approach is orientated towards the normative function of law. Still, without disputing the relevance of other approaches to law, any conception of the binding-

[7] Dworkin's conception of law is, however, more complicated, distinguishing semantic, jurisprudential, doctrinal and adjudicative stages. See Dworkin (2006: 9 ff). He does not focus on the adjudicative stage (18).

[8] Dworkin (1986: 190): '. . . the concept of law . . . connects law with the justification of official coercion. A conception of law must explain how what it takes to be law provides a justification for the exercise of coercive power by the state'.

[9] A justification in a weak sense might only show that it is permitted to apply a norm. The justification of an obligation to apply a norm requires a justification in a stronger sense.

[10] Raz (1999: 127 f) defines validity in a normative sense but distinguishes legal validity from validity, as it may either mean systemic validity or normative validity.

ness and legitimate authority of law must be normative and from the perspective of a normative theory of law it is the application of law that is of primary interest. Empirical and systemic issues are certainly relevant to a normative theory of the application of law. But if one asks what law as a normative phenomenon means, the answer requires a definition of which norms ought to be applied and followed as law.

Accordingly, law must be understood as a normative system and the concept of legal validity must be normative. That is, the legal validity of a norm must imply a requirement that this norm be applied and followed. Thus, legal validity consists not merely in social facts or in the membership of a norm in a system of norms but has normative implications. Without these implications legal norms could not fulfil the function of law, that is, to guide and order the behaviour of people. A legislator cannot issue a norm by saying 'We hereby issue the norm N as valid law. The citizens may or may not elect to follow this law'. Courts cannot base their decisions on norms by claiming 'It is valid law that N. We may apply N or not. In this case we decide to apply it'. Obviously, law has normative implications, and a conception of legal validity that denies this fails to provide an adequate account of law.

Consequently, the concept of legal validity ($VAL_L$ . . .) must be defined in accordance with a normative concept of validity. Thus, it must include the following relation regarding the validity as a legal norm:

(VL1) If a norm N is valid in a legal system L, then also valid in this system is a requirement to apply N.

$$VAL_L N \rightarrow VAL_L \; O \; APPL \; N$$

In short, legal validity must be normative.

### 9.2.2 Absolute and System-relative Validity

Still, the normative character of legal validity leaves open the issue of whether the concept of legal validity must include validity in an absolute, not merely system-relative sense. Legal validity must be normative, but the law's claim to normativity is, in the first place, a system-relative claim, which forms part of the legal system itself. The issue is whether an implication holds between the validity of a norm in a particular legal system L and the non-relativised, absolute validity of this norm. More precisely, definitive validity and validity as an argument, or in principle, must be distinguished. In order to make this distinction, one can express definitive legal validity by an indexed predicate of validity $VAL_{LDEF}N$ and legal validity in principle accordingly as $VAL_{LARG}N$.

With respect to the implications of definitive validity, the issue is whether definitive validity in a legal system L implies absolute definitive validity, that is, demands actually to apply and follow the law. What is of interest is the transition from system-relative validity to non system-relative validity. Should this be possible, it means that the statement of definitive validity implies a direct normative statement and, hence, the ascription of validity in an absolute sense.

As has been pointed out above, however, within a model of autonomous reasoning one must distinguish a procedural and a substantive sense of definitive validity.[11] In a procedural sense, a norm is definitively valid if it is the result of a complete justificatory procedure. In a substantive sense, definitive validity implies bindingness, that is, that the norm ought actually to be applied and followed. As one might put it, bindingness is real normative validity. It is not clear that legal validity must be understood as substantive definitive validity. Just as autonomous individuals may make definitive normative judgements in the sense that these judgements are the final result of their autonomous reasoning, although not binding on other agents, legal systems might establish norms as definitively valid in a procedural sense, thus claiming but not establishing the binding character of the legal norms in question. Just as autonomous individuals cannot establish bindingness, individual legal systems are not able to do so either. Legal systems must, in so far as they are rational, recognise this. Therefore, they cannot assume substantive definitive validity for their norms.

Nevertheless, legal systems must *claim* that the norms they qualify as definitively valid be binding on their addressees. This claim is not merely system-relative but absolute. That is, the claim is not that, according to the perspective of the legal system in question, a certain norm be binding; rather it is that the norm be binding simpliciter, without reservation or restriction to the perspective of the system itself. Each autonomous agent must therefore, according to the claim of the legal system, consider this claim within his reasoning at least as a valid normative argument. Accordingly, each legal system includes the relation:

> (VL2) If a norm N is definitively valid in the legal system L, then, according to this system, there is a valid normative argument in L for the absolute, non system-relative validity of the norm N.

$$|\,VAL_{LDEF}N \rightarrow |\,VAL_{LARG}\,VAL_{DEF}\,N$$

Thus, legal validity in a normative sense will pragmatically imply claims to absolute definitive validity, that is, bindingness of legal norms.

In addition, if the legal system is legitimate, that is, its claim to normativity is justified, the legal claim to bindingness of legal norms will constitute a normative argument that these norms be recognised as definitively valid and hence binding. This argument holds in case that the claim in question conflicts with contrary claims of competing normative systems. In this situation, no system can claim its superiority over the other systems, but the competing normative claims must all be considered as valid arguments in a non system-relative discourse. Thus, the

[11] See 4.3.2.3.

situation of conflicting legal systems is analogous to that of competing normative judgements of autonomous individuals. None of them can claim supremacy, but the claims of each of them must be respected as normative arguments.

Accordingly, for all legitimate legal systems the following relation holds:

(VL3) The claim of the legal system L for the absolute, non system-relative validity of its norms constitutes normative arguments that these norms be recognised as definitively valid.

$$|VAL_{LARG}\ VAL_{DEF}\ N \rightarrow |VAL_{ARG}\ VAL_{DEF}\ N$$

As a consequence, the claim to definitive legal validity of a norm implies the claim that there is a non system-relative argument for the non system-relative definitive validity of the norm in question, that is, the legal system claims in principle absolute normative validity.

## 9.3 AUTHORITATIVE CHARACTER OF LAW

An adequate model of law must accommodate the authoritative structures of law. In order to do this, the conception of 'formal principles' is needed.[12] This conception suggests, first, that the authority of law must be justified by means of balancing and, secondly, that this balancing establishes formal principles that attribute authoritative powers, although again only in principle. Definitive authoritative powers must be justified by means of a balancing that includes those formal principles.

Thus, the hierarchical ordering of the legal system, the so-called '*Stufenbau der Rechtsordnung*',[13] is replaced by a structure consisting of principles, which may be substantive or formal, and definitive norms stemming from the balancing of these principles. The hierarchical ordering of legal sources and norms must be established on the basis of these principles. A strict hierarchy may, but need not, result from this reasoning.

### 9.3.1 Formal Principles

A central thesis is that in order to construct legal authority, a legal system must include, not merely substantive or material principles but also formal principles establishing such an authority. Since the formal criteria of validity, such as that of the authority of democratic legislation, must be respected, material criteria of justice or political morality cannot automatically define the legal validity of norms. The structure of the legal system is characterised by an interplay of principles,

[12] As to this conception, see Alexy (2002a: 58, 82, 414 ff; 1987: 416 f); Sieckmann (1990: 148); Raabe (1998: 208 ff); Afonso da Silva (2003: 144 ff).

[13] As to this idea, see, in particular, Merkl (1931) and Kelsen (1960). See also Koller (2005: 106 ff).

optimising requirements and definitive norms in procedures of balancing and, in addition, by formal principles that constitute normative relations between different procedures within a legal system by making the results of an earlier procedure binding on subsequent procedures.

An example of a formal principle is that of democracy, demanding that the decisions of a democratically elected legislative body be binding quite apart from their correctness. Thus, it creates authoritative structures within a legal system. It includes a requirement that the norms established by the legislator be followed. This principle, again, is supported by further principles, such as the political autonomy of the people, the representative function of parliament, or the prevention of arbitrary decisions by general statutory rules. Another example is that of the separation of powers. This principle includes a requirement that the decisions of the legislator be followed. This requirement is backed by arguments in favour of the separation of powers, such as the mutual control of public powers and the protection against abuses of power.

Another formal principle is that of the bindingness of precedents. In this case, a formal principle requires that one follow the norms established by a previous court's decision. The conditions under which this authority holds require specification and may differ in different legal systems. Nevertheless, one may argue that each legal system will accept some normative force of precedents.[14] Again, the formal principle demanding the bindingness of precedent is supported by further principles, such as that of equal treatment, the protection of expectations created by a court decision, or the creation of a unified legal system.

It is also possible that there are arguments for the exclusion of deliberation on certain issues, for example, preventing a legislative body from deliberating on issues outside the scope of its jurisdiction, or preventing courts from questioning the result of prior authoritative decisions. The effect is the same as that of principles that require positively that certain decisions be followed. However, the structure of the balancing is different. Positive formal principles are to be included in a first-order deliberation. Principles excluding deliberation (that is, negative formal principles) apply within a balancing on whether one ought to engage in a first-order deliberation. In any case, if the formal principle prevails, the decision it demands will be binding quite apart from whether it is correct or substantively justified and, hence, the decision will be authoritative.

Binding authority and the exclusion of deliberation themselves require a justification by means of the balancing of principles, and they may turn out to be unjustified. For example, there may be arguments against a statutory norm that are sufficiently important to give rise to doubts as to the bindingness of this law.[15] The authoritative character of law exists to the extent that the formal principles supporting authoritative decision-making prevail over substantive principles that conflict with the law's claim to bindingness.

[14] See Sieckmann (1990: 158 f).
[15] See Günther (1988: 274).

Thus, authoritative structures stem from formal principles that constitute the bindingness of normative decisions or their immunity against deliberation. These decisions must be based on balancing. The first order arguments relevant to the issue in question are still valid, and are to be included in this balancing. No relevant argument can be excluded from balancing. However, the balancing can be structured in such a way that some arguments are relevant only at certain earlier stages of a balancing but not at subsequent stages.

Raz has suggested a different explication of authority, based on the idea of pre-emptive or exclusionary reasons (1979: 16 ff; 1999: 100 f, 191 ff). The conception of exclusionary reasons assumes that authoritative bindingness results from the exclusion of substantive arguments referring to the merits of the case. This, too, stands in need of a justification, which, according to Raz, normally follows from the fact that the decision of the authority is likely to offer a better judgement based on the balancing of the interests and arguments at stake than a balancing on the part of the individual agents on their own ('normal justification thesis'). Consequently, the authoritative decision determines the normative situation. However, both the binding character of the decision as well as the exclusion of competing arguments requires justification, which, again, must be based on balancing. Even though it should be true that the point and purpose of authorities is to pre-empt individual judgements on the merits of the case (Raz 1986: 47 f),[16] and to the extent that legitimate authority exists, acting on individual judgement is excluded, the crucial point is whether legitimate authority exists, that is, whether it is justified, and to what extent.

Since this justification requires balancing and, in order to be rational, this must include all relevant arguments,[17] it is an illusion that the conception of exclusionary reasons can avoid a balancing of first-order arguments. If someone accepts the idea that the balancing of a legal organ will probably lead to a better judgement than his own balancing, but on a certain issue holds a view contrary to the official judgement, a conflict occurs between the argument for following the official judgement and his own judgement. The presumption that the official judgement will in general be better does not imply that one has thereby waived the claim to the correctness of one's own judgement in a particular case. Therefore, a conflict arises between the argument to follow the official judgement and the claim to correctness of one's own judgement in a particular case. One might decide to follow the official judgement, but this is not necessary. One might just as well decide to uphold one's own judgement, thus rejecting the authoritative claim of the official judgement.

[16] See also Stavropoulos (2009: 342, 345). However, this characterisation of authority seems to be mistaken. The point of authority is not to exclude individual judgement, but to establish binding directives notwithstanding their substantive correctness. Anyone may criticise authoritative decisions from the standpoint of his individual judgement as long as he follows them.

[17] One should note, again, that balancing may be structured. One need not consider all relevant arguments at the same time. There may be reasons to exclude arguments from consideration at earlier or later stages of the balancing. But at some point each argument must have been taken into account.

> For example, the law of the European Union claims priority over the legal systems of the Member States. Thus, it claims to be exclusionary. Whether courts of national legal systems accept this claim depends, however, on a balancing, which might include substantive principles. Such a substantive principle is the protection of fundamental rights, which forms part of the German legal system as well as of other systems of EU Member States. This principle might be regarded, under certain circumstances, as so important that the claim of EU law to priority is rejected. How important it is depends on the degree to which EU law provides protection of fundamental rights that is comparable to what is provided by the legal system of the Member State in question. Thus, a balancing of an exclusionary claim to validity with substantive first-order principles is required.

Accordingly, exclusionary reasons cannot exclude the first-order issue of balancing; rather, they enter into conflict with first-order arguments. They can only provide a certain structure to the balancing. As far as they receive priority, the result of an overall balancing will be the recognition of the bindingness of the authoritative decision in question, and as long as this normative situation persists, balancing on the substantive issue is excluded and replaced by the bindingness of the authoritative decision. Accordingly, authority based on exclusionary reasons is only a special case of the justification of authority by means of balancing.

### 9.3.2 Types of Authority

Several types of authority should be distinguished, namely, in terms of its strength, its substantive or procedural character, and its coordinating or repressive function.

First, according to the strength of the authority, one can distinguish whether a normative decision has authority only if arguments of regular weight are at stake or also if important principles are to be respected, in particular, fundamental rights.

Secondly, the justification of authority may be substantive or procedural. An example of a procedural justification is the argument of public autonomy, which suggests that a democratic legislator has authority owing to the fact that its decisions are autonomous decisions of a political collective and therefore deserve respect. Another example is the justification of an authority owing to the fact that a regulation is needed and the organ to which authority is attributed is in the best position to issue and enforce it. By contrast, a substantive justification might suggest that the decisions of a democratic legislature be respected because the legislature best represents the interests of reasonable people. Examples of substantive justification are also arguments to the effect that one ought to respect precedent owing to the requirements of equal treatment or the protection of legitimate expectations.

Thirdly, there is a difference between coordinating and repressive authority. Coordinating authority solves problems of coordination, for example, on which side of the road one drives. There are no substantive arguments for one or the other solution, but there must be a solution. Repressive authority restricts substantive interests by binding regulation. Hence, repressive authority must be justified against substantive normative claims, whilst this is not necessary for purely coordinating authority.

A special case of the need for authority is the dispute between competing normative positions for want of objective criteria as to which position is right. In this case, one might argue that any of the possible positions is equally acceptable and, hence, there is only a coordination problem. This, however, would be too simple, for even if there are no objective criteria of priority, there are competing normative claims, and these claims may well be upheld without being objectively justified. Only if one accepts that objective criteria are required for making normative decisions, would a lack of objective criteria convert a normative dispute into a pure coordination problem. This is not, however, the usual way to handle these problems. Competing normative claims remain relevant to the argument, although that cannot be stated as objectively valid. Consequently, a clear separation of first-order normative claims and second-order criteria for deciding disputes between competing normative positions[18] will not work.

## 9.4 LEGAL AND MORAL VALIDITY

A central issue of a theory of legal validity is the relevance of moral correctness for legal validity. By moral correctness, I understand absolute, non-relative normative correctness, as stated in a direct normative judgement or statement. No specific interpretation of morality is implied here. Its characteristic is normativity in the sense that it implies a requirement that it be applied and followed. Positivists in general deny this dimension of the law, claiming the separation of law from morality.[19] Non-positivist theories claim a conceptual connection between law and morality.

For example, Ronald Dworkin claims that it is impossible to state the criteria of legal validity in the form of a rule of recognition.[20] One cannot separate a set of legal norms from principles of political morality, for, at least in hard cases, judges must refer to principles of morality in justifying their decisions.[21] This is a denial of the positivist thesis of the separation between law and morality. It is a matter of dispute, however, whether this attack on positivism succeeds,[22] or whether the determination of legal validity can be restricted to positivist criteria.[23]

[18] This is suggested in Jansen (1998b).

[19] However, some authors, for example, Raz (2007), accept some conceptual connection between law and morality, although not regarding the criteria of legal validity.

[20] In Dworkin (1978: 22 ff, 46 ff), owing to the existence of principles in law; later in his interpretive theory of law (1986), rejecting the criterial (in Dworkin's terms 'taxonomic') approach to law (2006).

[21] Dworkin concedes, however, that these principles must be consistent with the vast bulk of established rules and the principles underlying them, see Dworkin (1985: 17).

[22] Defending legal positivism, for example, Kramer (1999); Marmor (2001, 71 ff); Rodriguez (2002). On the debate between Dworkin and Hart, see Watkins-Bienz (2004).

[23] This problem is addressed by the 'incorporation thesis' of Dreier (1991: 107), suggesting that constitutional democratic states have incorporated in their constitutions the principles of the law of reason.

### 9.4.1 Theses about Law and Morality

The separation thesis and the connection thesis offer differing statements on the relation of law and morality. Various versions of these theses need to be distinguished. In the first place, these theses may refer to the criteria of legal validity. There are, however, other aspects in which one might find a conceptual connection between law and morality, in particular, the claim to the normativity of law and the corresponding need to justify legal norms.[24] Here I shall discuss only the criteria of legal validity. With respect to the criteria of validity, one must distinguish strong and weak conceptions of positivism and non-positivism. Strong conceptions include general, that is, positive theses about the relation of legal validity and moral correctness, weak conceptions include merely negative claims that follow from the negation of one of the positive theses, sustaining the point that there are cases to which the general thesis does not apply.[25] The four resulting positions are as follows:

> (1) Strong non-positivism: for all legal systems, the criteria of legal validity include that of the moral correctness of a norm.

This is a strong non-positivist thesis, for it includes moral correctness as a feature of a concept of law. It offers a general thesis about the criteria of legal validity.[26]

> (2) Weak non-positivism: the criteria of legal validity of a system may include that of the moral correctness of a norm.

This thesis negates a strong positivist thesis that the criteria of legal validity never refer to normative correctness, but it does not include a general thesis as to these criteria.

> (3) Strong positivism: for all legal systems, the criteria of legal validity do not include that of the moral correctness of a norm.

This thesis purports to state a general feature of law, which might form part of a concept of law.[27]

> (4) Weak positivism: the criteria of legal validity of a system need not include that of the moral correctness of a norm.

The standard formulation of the separation thesis, which claims that there is no necessary conceptual connection between law and morality,[28] amounts to the weak

[24] See Sieckmann (2009a: 225 ff). See also Coleman (2009: 383 ff); Perry (2009: 312 f), on problems with the separability thesis.

[25] Accordingly, one may distinguish positive and negative positivism. See also Coleman (1982).

[26] For example, Alexy (2002b; 2010).

[27] Examples are the social fact thesis (or sources thesis) of Joseph Raz (see 1.2), the conventionalism of Andrei Marmor (2001: 19 ff), and Scott Shapiro's 'planning theory of law' (2009: 326, 329 ff). Against this view Greenberg (2004: 157).

[28] See Hart (1994: 203).

positivist thesis. It denies a general connection between legal validity and moral correctness as a feature of the concept of law. On the other hand, it does not preclude the possibility that in some legal systems, criteria of moral correctness are used as conditions of legal validity. It insists, however, that this connection is a contingent matter, not a conceptual one.

Strong positivism may also be called 'exclusive positivism', for it precludes moral correctness as a criterion of legal validity. This position is usually confronted with 'inclusive positivism',[29] which rejects the exclusionary thesis (3) of strong positivism as well as the thesis (1) of the necessary inclusion of moral correctness among the criteria of legal validity, thus embracing the theses of weak positivism (4) and of weak non-positivism (2). Since 'inclusive positivism' includes an non-positivist element, one may well ask why it should count as positivism. An additional feature is needed in order to render 'inclusive positivism' positivistic. This feature is the need of a positive inclusion of moral correctness as a criterion of legal validity. That is, according to inclusive positivism moral correctness is granted as a criterion of legal validity only if this is established by positive law.[30]

This 'inclusion thesis' allows for two distinct interpretations, following from legal conventionalism or from what might be called the 'incorporation thesis'. On a conventionalist reading, law has a conventional character; hence, the criteria of legal validity are whatever legal conventions determine, and if it is conventionally accepted in a legal system that moral correctness be used as a criterion of legal validity, this criterion forms part of the law. On an incorporativist reading, moral correctness can figure as a criterion of legal validity if and only if it is incorporated into law by positive legal norms.[31]

The non-positivist analogue to 'inclusive positivism' consists in the thesis that the inclusion of moral correctness as a criterion of legal validity depends on reasons of political morality, which is to reject strong non-positivism (1) and embrace a weak non-positivism (2). Accordingly, a normative conception of law might claim that in some legal systems only positively issued norms may be regarded as legally valid, whilst in other systems legal judgements may be based directly on criteria of moral correctness.[32]

The above theses on the relation of law and morality do not specify how moral correctness affects legal validity. Moral correctness might figure as a sufficient condition of legal validity, or at least as one part of a sufficient condition of validity. By contrast, it might only figure as a necessary condition of legal validity, so

[29] This term was introduced by Waluchow (1994). The distinction is also made in terms of 'hard' and 'soft' positivism. See also Coleman (2009: 368); Greenberg (2004: 158); Soper (1996). On 'inclusive positivism', see also Székessy (2003).

[30] One might call it a 'weak positive positivism', for it suggests a general thesis about law, but it is weaker than the strong or 'exclusive' positivism that restricts law to social or institutional facts. By contrast, weak positivism in the sense of negative positivism does not suggest a conception of law at all.

[31] On this distinction, see Sieckmann (1990: 192 f). Conventionalism grants moral correctness as a supreme criterion of legal validity, whilst incorporativism grants it only as a dependent criterion, derived from positive criteria of legal validity.

[32] See Sieckmann (2009: 233 f).

that norms that are immoral, grossly immoral or evidently immoral, cannot be legally valid. At least with regard to developed legal systems, moral correctness alone cannot be regarded as a sufficient condition for legal validity. Legal validity presupposes reference to some institutional fact, which is made relevant by a formal principle. Besides this reservation, neither of these types of relation can be excluded straightaway and without further consideration.

According to the conception of autonomous reasoning, normative correctness is determined by autonomous judgements and objective validity can only be established by the reasonable convergence of autonomous agents. Such a convergence constitutes a social or institutional fact. However, it also has normative content, for it requires judgements on the part of the agents involved on the normative issue of which norms ought to be regarded as binding in their society or legal system. Consequently, one might ask whether one can assert or deny legal validity by way of an autonomous judgement, be it an individual judgement only or one that is objectively valid. More precisely, the issue is whether statements of the following types are, at least under certain conditions, admissible:

(1) N is morally correct. Therefore, it is legally valid.

(2) N is morally incorrect. Therefore, it is not legally valid.

Accepting one of these theses implies rejecting strong legal positivism, which, by contrast, maintains that criteria of legal validity are exclusively of formal or empirical character.

### 9.4.2 Moral Correctness as a Criterion of Legal Validity

The primary issue to be discussed here is, accordingly, whether it is admissible or indeed obligatory to state or to deny the legal validity of a norm owing to its moral correctness or incorrectness. A subsequent issue is whether legal validity can depend on criteria of moral correctness only if positive law says so.

The problem of the applicability of criteria of moral correctness within law may be illustrated by the following examples:

(1) Let us assume that it is required by morality that the rights of animals be recognised, but the legal system does not lend support to such rights by authoritative decisions backed by formal principles. Is it obligatory or at least admissible to recognise legal rights of animals?

(2) Is it admissible or obligatory to deny the legal validity of norms prescribing racial discrimination on the ground that it is morally wrong?

In order to discuss these issues, several distinctions must be made: first, that between individual normative judgements and judgements claiming objective validity; secondly, that between direct normative judgements and normative statements of legal validity; and, thirdly, that between validity in principle and definitive validity.

#### *9.4.2.1 Objective Validity and Individual Normative Judgements*

A first problem is that law claims to be objectively valid in the sense of being commonly binding, and an objective validity such as this cannot be claimed for mere individual normative judgements. Objective validity can only be asserted as the result of a process of intersubjective reflection. Moreover, in order to establish the objective validity of a norm directly, not by means of authoritative decision, this process must lead to a convergence of reasonable judgements. This convergence cannot be established by the autonomous judgement of a single individual agent, even if based on intersubjective reflection, but can only be the result of a discursive process.[33] However, objective validity may be claimed by individual normative judgements if they can be justified by objectively valid norms together with formal criteria of rationality showing that competing views respecting the interpretation of these norms are mistaken and only the suggested individual judgement is correct. Therefore, objective validity of a normative judgement does not presuppose consent or general support of the judgement in question.

> For example, let us assume that the constitutional right to free association is interpreted by the courts as applying solely to associations of private law and not to those of public law, for, so the argument goes, only private law associations are founded on the exercise of freedom, whereas the membership in public law associations is obligatory by law and freedom of association does not apply. Now, a common feature of liberty rights is that they include a positive and a negative dimension, that is, the right to make use of the liberty in question and the right not to make use of it. This applies also to the freedom of association. The negative dimension of the freedom of association is, however, affected by the obligatory membership in a public law association. This follows clearly from already established norms and their interpretation, and there is no reason not to apply this line of reasoning in the case of public law associations. Thus, an individual normative judgement that acknowledges this right can claim to be objectively valid.

A normative statement of objective validity refers to the fact of the convergence of the normative judgements of the agents involved that stems from an argumentative procedure or from a more complex fact, namely, that the result is derived from an objectively valid legal norm together with criteria of rational argumentation, such as, for example, coherence arguments. Such arguments show the possibility of an internal rational critique of established legal norms. Rational critique is always possible. If it is based on principles not recognised by the legal system in question, it is merely an external critique and cannot show that an alternative norm is legally valid. By contrast, if recognised legal norms support another norm that mistakenly has not been recognised within the system itself, one can state the legal validity of the latter norm on the basis of the recognised norms along with the fact that there is no alternative interpretation that could be claimed to be valid.

In cases where an established interpretation of a norm is rejected owing to arguments of rationality, a convergence of reasonable judgements arises, for the

[33] See 4.3.3, 6.3, 6.4.

competing judgements are qualified as mistaken on objective grounds.[34] Disputed legal issues, however, will not always be decidable on objectively valid grounds. In the case of a reasonable dispute, where both sides are rationally justified and neither can prove the other to be mistaken, the question arises as to whether it is legitimate to claim legal validity for either of them. Such judgements include claims as to what ought to be recognised as objectively valid. Accordingly, the issue is whether legal validity may be stated in autonomous reflective judgements or whether it can only be stated in the case of a convergence of reasonable judgements.[35] In the first case, an individual may introduce moral arguments into his legal reasoning. In the second case, morality can enter into a legal judgement only if a moral norm can be established as objectively valid.

> Let us assume, for example, that in the case of the protection of animals there is no objectively valid norm on the ground that there is no convergence of reasonable judgements. By contrast, someone might argue, after balancing the relevant principles and reflecting upon the various normative positions on the issue, that the protection of animals is morally required. According to the first position, he might in this situation claim that the principle of the protection of animals is legally valid. By contrast, according to the second position this principle lacks objective validity and cannot be considered valid law.

The second alternative creates a problem if one takes up the point of view of a judge who has to make a decision in a controversial case. He must claim that his judgement is correct in the sense that it is required by the prevailing principle and on the basis of intersubjective reflection. This must suffice to attribute legal validity to the respective norm. However, if reasonable agents disagree, the norm in question is not objectively valid. If objective validity is a necessary condition for the justification of legal judgements, the normative situation of a judge in a disputed issue is as follows.

(1) There is no objective law on a certain issue, but the judge believes that one ought to recognise as law a particular norm, for the principles supporting it are of greater importance in the case to be decided than are the competing principles.
(2) Accordingly, the judge recognises the norm in question as valid. He makes a corresponding normative judgement and states the legal validity of this norm.
(3) Thus, the judge is required to make a legal statement that is in fact not justified, for the norm stated is not objectively valid and, hence, not legally valid.

[34] This will not always lead to a unique result, however, for the possibility remains that a positively established norm is qualified as invalid but a reasonable dispute exists as to which alternative is legally valid. For example, norms instituting a dictatorship may be declared invalid, but the question remains which type of political system ought to be chosen. One cannot assume that all such problems can be decided on rational grounds.

[35] One might find this issue as well in the dispute between Dworkin and MacCormick on 'interpretive' and 'institutional' conceptions of law. See MacCormick (2005).

The problem arises from the assumption that judicial statements of legal norms must be objectively justified. Therefore, one must give up the assumption that statements of legal validity must necessarily be objectively justified. By contrast, normative legal judgements may be autonomous judgements on the basis of intersubjective reflection. They do not require or presuppose the objective validity of a norm.[36]

However, this assumption encounters the problem that law seems to have objective validity and cannot be determined by mere individual judgements. It would be odd if, on a disputed legal issue on which there is no reasonable convergence, an individual agent declared his normative view to be valid law. He can legitimately make a normative judgement as to which norm is to be recognised as definitively valid law and offer his view as an interpretation of law. The further step, however, of stating this norm to be definitively valid law requires a competence to establish this norm as valid or at least a competence to make a normative statement as to this effect. Accordingly, a court that has to take a decision may declare a norm to be valid law based on its intersubjectively reflected normative judgement. In fact, it cannot avoid the step from the judgement that, as result of the balancing of legal principles, a certain norm ought to be recognised as valid law to the statement that this norm is valid law. By contrast, an individual citizen is not in the position of a court and cannot correctly declare his interpretation of law as definitively valid law. The crucial point in this argument is the distinction between legal judgements and legal statements, which corresponds to the more general distinction between normative judgements and statements.

### *9.4.2.2 Legal Judgements and Legal Statements*

Normative judgements are distinct from normative statements. The former express a requirement that a particular norm *be* valid, the latter state that a particular norm *is* valid. Although these two types of expression are interrelated, they are not equivalent.[37] The normative statement that a norm N is definitively valid complies with the demand made in a normative judgement that the norm N ought to be recognised as definitively valid. Correspondingly, legal judgements and legal statements must be distinguished.

The conceptual distinction goes hand in hand with a difference in the mode of justification and the conditions of correctness of making legal judgements or statements. Legal judgements can be made by every autonomous agents on the basis of the balancing of legal principles. By contrast, legal statements can correctly be made only under certain additional conditions. Conditions that allow one to correctly make a legal statement based on balancing are:

[36] In a certain sense, this might support Dworkin's view to leave aside the issue of objectivity in legal reasoning. However, the conclusion that the quest for objectivity does not make sense in general, is not justified. Against Dworkin, see Rodriguez-Blanco (2004: 10 ff, 65); Pavlakos (2008: 67). Following the line of Dworkin, Stavropoulos (1996) and Iglesias Vila (2001).

[37] See 2.2.

(i) the objective validity of the statement, based on the criterion of reasonable convergence and the need to have a commonly binding norm;
(ii) the link of the statement to the creation of the stated norm, that is, the statement is made by one who has a legislative competence to create such a legal norm, and the statement expresses this legislative act;
(iii) a competence to make a legal statement following a legal judgement based on balancing.

The first case applies to every autonomous agent, the second to legislative organs. The third case is of interest here. It responds to the need that courts make statements as to the definitively valid law even in cases in which no objectively valid solution can be established and although they do not have a legislative competence to render the norm on which they found their decision valid law.

In contrast to legal statements, legal judgements claim correctly to state the law but do not claim to state objectively valid norms. Legal judgements are understood here as normative judgements as to what is valid law, and normative judgements are autonomous judgements resulting from the balancing of normative arguments. Nevertheless, they are not simple individual judgements but must be based on a process of intersubjective reflection, including all legally relevant arguments. Moreover, a normative judgement of definitive validity will claim that the validity holds independently of whether an agent recognises its validity in his judgement.

For example, someone claiming the legal validity of a requirement of the protection of animals implies that this solution is correct independently of his own judgement.

Nevertheless, a legal judgement that a particular norm be definitively recognised as legally valid does not amount to a statement of its definitive legal validity. It includes a requirement as to which norm ought to be recognised as law, which any autonomous agent may legitimately make.

In this respect, there is a crucial difference between legal judgements of judges presented in their authoritative decisions, and those of ordinary citizens. Autonomous agents, following their own normative judgement, might claim the legal validity of the respective norm in the sense that this norm be recognised as valid law. This, however, will only be their interpretation of law. It is not a statement of definitive legal validity. Legal statements need an objective justification, according to the criteria of reasonable convergence, owing to a legislative competence, or owing to a legal competence to make such statements based on normative judgements. Since judges have the competence to take decisions based on their legal judgements, they can make legal statements as to the definitively valid norm even though this statement is merely based on their normative judgement. Thus, the objective character of law is not an objection against using criteria of normative or moral correctness not only in legal judgements but also in judicial statements of what is definitively valid law.

*9.4.2.3 Definitive Validity and Validity in Principle*

The discussion of legal judgements and statements has not distinguished between principles and definitively valid norms. One can make judgements and statements of the legal validity of both definitive norms and principles. The justification of a legal judgement will be based on formal principles of law, requiring respect for authoritatively enacted law, but may also consider substantive principles of political morality and will ultimately consist of a normative judgement of an autonomous individual. Accordingly, normative correctness may come into play in two respects: respecting the selection of the principles to be considered and respecting the judgement based on the balancing of these principles. The question of whether moral correctness is or can be a criterion of legal validity requires different answers with regard to principles and to definitively valid norms resulting from the balancing of principles.

With regard to definitively valid norms, legal judgements are justified by means of the balancing of normative arguments, and legal statements refer to the results of such balancing. This implies that one can always state a positive fact on which definitive legal validity is based (the same holds for definitive moral validity). This fact, however, cannot be used within the justification of definitive validity, for it only states the result of this justification. The justification itself must claim normative correctness. It must be based on the relevant legal material, but it is a normative judgement that cannot be derived from pre-established premises. Instead, it is based on the balancing of normative arguments. Accordingly, it claims absolute, non-relativised validity. It expresses the actual normative view of the respective agent, rather than merely the content of a normative system defined by certain criteria of membership. It is not merely descriptive or system-relative. Since normativity in this absolute sense is seen here as the characteristic feature of moral validity, ascribing legal validity by balancing of normative arguments includes a claim to moral correctness. The legal judgement based on the balancing of principles claims to be the morally correct decision with regard to the relevant material. It does not matter whether this material also includes substantive principles or only formal legal principles and the authoritatively issued norms supported by them.

This claim to normative correctness does not imply, however, that the norms established as definitively valid are just or morally correct. The result of the balancing depends on the principles that figure as arguments in this balancing. If a legal system includes unjust principles, the result may be unjust, too. The claim of the judgement based on balancing is still normative in an absolute sense, in that it claims to be the correct solution on the basis of the relevant principles. But the established norm may be morally wrong. The only way to avoid this result is to forbear from a balancing on the basis of unjust principles. If, for moral reasons, one wishes to declare invalid a certain result, one needs an alternative basis for the balancing that includes morally correct principles. The balancing of principles as such does not guarantee morally correct or acceptable results. Nevertheless, it rules out the possibility that legal judgements might be founded on formal criteria of legal validity alone.

The justification of the legal validity of principles is different from that of definitive norms. Principles are valid on the ground that they express normative claims of autonomous individuals. In so far as these claims refer to the formation of the legal system, they form normative arguments for recognising certain legal principles. Such arguments do not directly establish the legal validity of the principles in question. There may be reasons against assuming their legal validity. For example, not just any content will be suitable for a legal principle; not just any claim might be sufficiently important to establish an obligation on the part of legal organs to consider it. Or the claim might conflict with other agents' claims against recognising such a principle as legally valid. If, however, there are no sufficient reasons that count against following the normative claims made by autonomous agents, these claims will constitute legal principles.

Accordingly, legal principles based on individual autonomy have an empirical basis. Since they are based on autonomous claims, no further justification is necessary to establish their legal validity in the sense that legal organs have to take them into account within their legal reasoning, at least regarding the legal validity of principles demanding the realisation of such claims. All autonomy-based principles with legal content, that is, with a content that refers to the formation of a legal system, are legally valid if this is not precluded by the legal system itself. Their legal validity does not depend on positive recognition. Positive law would only serve to exclude their legal validity.

A legal system might restrict the set of legally valid principles by requiring that a legal principle be identified by formal criteria, such as authoritative enactment, support by judicial decisions, or social acceptance within the legal community. The legal validity of principles may thus depend on further conditions.

> For example, moral arguments might claim validity in principle within legal systems, but reasons of legal certainty might justify one's not taking into account purely moral arguments within legal reasoning.

Whilst in the field of morality a valid normative argument will automatically be definitively valid as an argument, with respect to law or other institutionalised normative systems one can distinguish between normative arguments that are definitively to be applied as principles of law and those which merely claim to be applicable but are excluded from the balancing of legal principles by overriding reasons. However, the restriction of the set of legally valid principles by a legal system must itself be justified. Therefore, it may turn out that the exclusion of morally valid principles from the legal order is itself unjustified and hence invalid.

There are two arguments suggesting that the exclusion of morally valid principles from the legal system will not hold strictly.[38] First, the formal criteria of legal validity have different weights. Direct enactment by the democratic legislator will

[38] Another line of argument against the closure of the legal system is suggested by Atria (2001: 218 ff), relying on the idea of 'images of law'.

have great weight. Indirect, slight support stemming from a judicial decision will have little weight. Since the formal support of legal principles may have very little weight, it is implausible to suppose that autonomy-based moral principles never have sufficient weight to prevail over the formal legal indices that would exclude these principles from the legal system. Secondly, a legal principle might be affected to a very low degree, whereas an autonomy-based moral principle might be of great importance and, moreover, affected to a very high degree. Accordingly, the moral principle may be of great importance in the concrete case. Again, it is implausible to assume that legal principles will always override autonomy-based moral principles.

Nevertheless, it is possible that the exclusion of merely moral principles by a legal system is justified, given the features of the particular system in question. For example, a legal system might incorporate all the relevant moral principles, so that a conflict between the law and important moral principles can actually be excluded. This may well be the case in constitutional systems that recognise human rights, democracy and the rule of law. In this case, one can correctly state that only those principles formally recognised as law are legally valid. However, the conceptual possibility that mere moral principles can override legal principles cannot be excluded.

The introduction of principles based on moral correctness makes it possible to declare authoritatively established norms to be legally invalid for moral reasons. This may be done in either of two ways. First, the legal validity of an authoritatively issued norm may be denied owing to a conflict with principles of justice.

> For example, one might deny that racial discrimination is valid law. From this, it does not follow that a right to racial equality is valid on grounds of positive law. It does follow that there is no valid positive law on this point and, as a legal decision is required, this must be taken on moral grounds. Thus, moral principles enter into the legal system.

Secondly, one might make a positive statement on the legal validity of a norm that contravenes an authoritatively issued norm.

> With respect to the example of racial discrimination, this means that racial equality is stated as legally valid despite the authoritative regulation to the contrary.

In practice, the two accounts come to the same thing. Morally valid principles constitute legal arguments unless the legal system legitimately excludes them.

## 9.5 CONCLUSION

A characteristic of autonomous reasoning is that the legal validity of norms must be completely justified by the balancing of normative arguments. This balancing includes not only substantive principles but also formal principles, which require respect for authoritative decisions without regard to their correctness. Formal principles allow for the reconstruction of the authoritative structures of a legal system. Autonomous reasoning is therefore compatible with the fact that legal systems contain norms that can be applied without a balancing. Such norms may be valid in certain circumstances at a certain time. One cannot, however, exclude balancing when the legal validity of norms needs to be determined, and one cannot, therefore, evade the requirement of rational justification in law and legal argumentation.

As a consequence, legal positivism appears to be unacceptable as a general theory of law. On the other hand, if a system fulfils requirements of justice or moral correctness adequately, it might legitimately exclude those merely moral arguments that have no institutional backing from legal argument. Thus, in so far as principles are concerned, a general non-positivist thesis is also not correct with respect to the criteria of validity of a legal system.

In addition, if law is understood in a more comprehensive sense, including legal reasoning or the processes of creating a legal system, neither legal norms nor legal judgements resulting from these procedures can be restricted to those identifiable by formal or empirical criteria.

An interesting result of the above analysis is that legal validity need not be objective validity in the sense that every reasonable agent must accept the norm that purports to be legally valid as actually valid and binding. Although legal judgements cannot be mere individual normative judgements, all that can be required of judges and other law-applying organs are intersubjectively reflected judgements claiming to present a correct solution to legal problems.

# 10

# *Legal Interpretation and Autonomous Reasoning*

AUTONOMOUS REASONING STANDS in sharp contrast to conceptions of legal interpretation that claim to determine the existing content of the law. Interpretation in this narrow sense claims to make explicit what is already included in existing law, whilst autonomous reasoning concerns the justification of norms or normative decisions that has not been determined by given norms.[1] The narrow understanding of legal interpretation is presupposed by traditional legal methodology, which gives expression to the claim that one is discovering the content of existing law, not creating it.[2] Conceptions of legal interpretation are not, however, restricted to this narrow view,[3] and nowadays it is widely acknowledged that legal interpretation includes creative elements. If, however, legal interpretation is not about discovering the meaning of legal norms, the question remains: what is the point of legal interpretation and which role does authoritative determination and autonomous judgement play in it?[4]

Legal interpretation cannot consist of pure autonomous reasoning, for it takes place within an authoritatively established legal framework. Therefore, the relation between autonomous reasoning and legal interpretation requires clarification. This is of particular importance with respect to the competences and powers conferred on courts within constitutional systems. By contrast to their traditional role as mere interpreters of the law and owing to the primacy and openness of constitutional law, courts act as creative organs exercising great power within the legal system.[5] Such judicial activity requires a theoretical framework that makes it possible to impose control over the decisions of courts and makes it possible, too, to determine their competences in a rationally justified manner. An analysis of what interpretation means within a conception of autonomous reasoning will be of help in developing such a framework.

[1] This contrast was emphasised above, distinguishing autonomous balancing from interpretation.

[2] See, eg, Larenz (1983: 299). Against the traditional view, see Kelsen (1960: 240). As to Kelsen's view, see Paulson (1990).

[3] By contrast, Marmor (1992: 13) defines interpretation as the imposition of meaning on an object, and contrasts with it the explanation of the meaning of an expression (23). On this reading, there is no tension between interpretation and autonomous justification.

[4] Authoritative determinations must have at least some determinate meaning, as expressed by linguistic means. Accordingly, semantic arguments will be used to give effect to these determinations. On semantic argument in legal interpretation, see in particular Klatt (2004).

[5] On the extensive discussion of constitutional review, see, for eg, Riecken (2003). On the limits of judicial competence in general, see Neuner (2005).

## 10.1 BALANCING, INTERPRETATION AND THE AUTHORITATIVE STRUCTURE OF LAW

An initial issue this. In what respect does autonomous judgement occur in the interpretation of law? If interpretation consisted merely in deriving the legal consequences of norms by means of semantic rules, no room would be left for autonomous judgement. Legal reasoning, however, can very often not be completely presented in the form of a deduction.[6] In many cases legal interpretation will include judgements based on the balancing of competing legal principles. Thus, it includes autonomous judgements by the law-applying organs. The idea of autonomous judgement seems, however, to contradict the idea of law as an authoritative standard, that is to say, a standard that is binding and must be respected by the addressees of law even if wrong. Where the content of law is determined by an autonomous judgement, it turns on a judgement taken by the addressee of the law. Hence, it is not clear how the law could be authoritatively binding on such a judgement. In short, this underscores the necessity of defining the relation between the authority of law and autonomous judgements in the interpretation or application of the law.

Moreover, the relations between different legal organs interpreting the law stand in need of clarification, in particular, those between legislative and judicial organs. According to a common view, the application of law consists of a sequential process, where legal norms have been established by law-creating organs, more concrete norms have been established by inferior organs, and finally the courts or other law-applying organs determine the legal situation with respect to a particular case.[7]

> For example, parliamentary statute is legally valid because it was enacted in accordance with a procedure defined by the constitution. Perhaps a decree of the government supplements it with more specific regulations. The law or its regulation is then applied by administrative or judicial organs. Thus, the hierarchical structure of the legal system is manifested ('*Stufenbau der Rechtsordnung*').

This structure characterises positivist legal thinking and is, indeed, adequate in standard cases of the application of law in those legal systems that have developed a ranking of law-creating organs and their competences.

By contrast, within a framework of autonomous reasoning the application of the law does not proceed strictly sequentially but includes independent and parallel procedures of the application of law.

> For example, principles of constitutional law are binding on the parliamentary legislature when enacting a law, but they are also binding on a court when applying this law

[6] This is not meant to deny that a legal argument might be represented in the form of a deductive inference. In cases of balancing, however, this would not be a complete representation of the reasoning that is necessary to justify the conclusion.

[7] See Kelsen (1960: 240 f).

> and, in particular, if the constitutionality of the law is cast into doubt. Both organs decide on the basis of the same principles, although the decision procedures may vary in other respects. One cannot presuppose that the constitutional interpretation of a court, even a constitutional court, is automatically superior to what the legislator at least implicitly adopts when enacting a law.[8]

Accordingly, autonomous reasoning implies that the structure of the application of law diverges from the standard conception of a hierarchically and sequentially ordered process of law application, supplanting it with a model of competing conceptions of law of different legal organs, and this makes crucial the issue of priority among these conceptions.

## 10.2 CONCEPT OF INTERPRETATION

In so far as the role of interpretation in a model of autonomous reasoning is concerned, one needs to clarify what is to be understood by interpretation and what types of interpretation are to be distinguished in order to analyse their relations with autonomous reasoning.

The concept of legal interpretation is ambiguous.[9] Interpretation is concerned with the determination of the meaning of a certain object, but this may be understood in various ways:

(1) the determination of the content of the legal system by means of attributing legal validity to certain general norms;
(2) the determination of the meaning of individual legal norms; and
(3) the determination of the meaning of legal norms for particular cases.

The second alternative presents the core of legal interpretation. Indeterminate terms are interpreted by general semantic rules.[10] Thus, one determines the sense (or intension) of the norm in question. In this respect, one must distinguish between semantic interpretation, that is, the determination of the terms that are used in a norm-sentence by semantic rules that refer to an existing usage of language, and normative or constructive interpretation, that is, the determination of interpretive rules by any form of legal reasoning.[11]

In a wider sense, one may regard as interpretation also the application of legal norms to particular cases. Such an application determines whether a case belongs

[8] On this model of competing conceptions of law, see Sieckmann (2009a: 200 ff).

[9] See Raz (1996); Alexy (1995: 72). On different conceptions of legal interpretation, see also Spaak (2007).

[10] Semantic rules are understood here in a wider sense, as rules attributing a specific meaning to linguistic expressions, such as terms or sentences. In a narrow sense, one might regard as semantic rules only those that determine the meaning of linguistic expressions according to the existing use of these expressions. It is important to note this distinction, in particular, because the following distinction between semantic and constructive interpretation understands the former as restricted to the narrow conception of semantic rules.

[11] The constructive character of interpretation is emphasised in particular by Dworkin (1986; 2006).

to the reference (or extension) of the respective norm.[12] In this sense, the application of a norm concerns the determination of its meaning.

In addition, any determination of a norm as legally valid by means of legal reasoning constitutes a form of legal interpretation, for it determines the meaning of law. If one chooses to call this an interpretation of the law, any case of balancing counts as a case of legal interpretation.

This distinction of various senses of interpretation is relevant for the question in which respect legal interpretation includes balancing and autonomous reasoning. The relevance of balancing is most obvious in the third case, the interpretation of law or the legal system as a whole.

> For example, the issue of the balancing of the rights to free speech and of personal honour in a particular case is the content of the legal system in this case. This determination will not present a semantic rule about the meaning of the norms in question, but is nevertheless a determination of the content of the legal system. Therefore, it qualifies as a form of legal interpretation in a larger sense. A central aspect of this type of interpretation is the balancing of competing constitutional arguments.

By contrast, interpretation in the strict sense of determining the meaning of individual norms, either in general or in a particular case, has a syllogistic structure. It includes a normative statement as a basic premise, an interpretive premise and an inference leading to a conclusion. The crucial point is that the basic premise and the conclusion have the same type of validity, for example, definitive validity. This makes it possible to present the argument in a syllogistic form.[13] However, one can collapse the structural difference between balancing and syllogistic reasoning by replacing the colliding normative arguments by abstract norms of definitive validity, which then are interpreted in the form of syllogistic reasoning.

> For example, instead of a right to free speech, one begins the argument with the premise that everyone has a right to an adequate degree of free speech. The problem then is what counts as 'adequate'. This requires a balancing of the underlying normative arguments. The surface structure of the argument, however, has been converted into syllogistic reasoning.

[12] On the distinction between sense and reference, or intension and extension, see Koch and Rüssmann (1982).

[13] In the case of interpretation by general semantic rules, one can represent this structure as:

Interpreted norm: $(x)(Cx \rightarrow Rx)$

Interpretive rule: $(x)(C_1x \rightarrow Cx)$

Conclusion: $(x)(C_1x \rightarrow Rx)$.

In the case of the application to particular cases, one can distinguish

Applied norm: $(x)(Cx \rightarrow Rx)$

Application: $Ca \rightarrow Ra$

Subsumption: $Ca$

Conclusion: $Ra$

The transformation into syllogistic reasoning does not remove the problem of balancing. Nevertheless, in order to distinguish between balancing and interpretation one cannot refer merely to the surface structure of the argument. The difference rather is that in some cases a balancing is already required by the structure or the formulation of the norms involved, whilst in other cases the necessity to balance is a contingent matter, depending on whether a conflict of arguments is actually at hand.

Accordingly, problems of balancing might occur in any form of legal interpretation. In its basic form, legal interpretation can be represented by means of a deductive inference, whose premises are statements of legal norms, semantic rules and eventually premises of empirical facts.[14] Even if, on its surface, it does not include the balancing of normative arguments, problems of balancing occur within the interpretation of law whenever competing premises have to be taken into consideration. This may be the case not only at the level of norms but also with respect to semantic rules.

> An example of balancing with regard to an interpretation of a legal term is the problem of whether in a certain context 'law' (*Gesetz*) means a law of parliament or any general norm. This is relevant for the obligation of courts to submit a case to the constitutional court in order to obtain a decision on the issue of the constitutionality of a law.[15] In this case, the issue is the meaning of the term 'law' as used in a particular constitutional provision. The competing arguments suggest incompatible semantic interpretations of this term, based on conflicting normative arguments. Hence, a balancing is required.

And it may also be the case with respect to empirical premises relevant to the interpretation of a legal norm.

> For example, the issue of what is the ordinary meaning of a term like that of 'weapon' within current linguistic practice is an empirical one. There may be arguments both in favour and against the existence of a certain linguistic practice. Again, a balancing will be necessary.

Also, the application of the law to a particular case may involve problems of balancing, problems that may concern the justification of norms, semantic rules or empirical facts. The problems are basically the same as those of interpretation in the strict sense.

However, it is not clear that balancing with respect to semantic rules or empirical premises is a type of autonomous balancing. With regard to semantic rules and empirical premises one might doubt that there is room for autonomous choice.

> For example, there might be diferring arguments for or against the noxious character of a particular substance and the legal decision might depend on the resolution of this empirical issue. In this case, the empirical premise on which the legal decision is finally

[14] See Alexy (1989a); Koch and Rüssmann (1982); Atienza (2006).

[15] Such an obligation is stated in Art 100 s 1 of the German Basic Law. The Federal Constitutional Courts interprets this provision as applying only to laws enacted by parliament.

based will depend on the balancing of arguments with an eye to the question of which empirical premise should be accepted.

Or one might ask whether calling someone a 'cripple' is actually used to humilliate the addressee. This requires determining an existing semantic rule, and there may be arguments for and against the assumption that such a rule exists.

Although a balancing may be necessary with regard to empirical issues or the existence of semantic rules, this will not be autonomous balancing. By contrast with the balancing of normative arguments, individuals cannot claim to decide on empirical or semantic issues by themselves. Semantic rules and empirical premises must be justified according to standards that are independent of autonomous decisions. Even if a balancing of competing arguments is required, which in its structure resembles that on normative issues, the resulting judgement must claim to be objective in the sense that it states a fact that does not depend on the judgement itself. It is therefore not a case of autonomous judgement.

## 10.3 STRUCTURE OF LEGAL INTERPRETATION

Legal interpretation is understood here in a comprehensive sense that includes not only the determination of the meaning of legal provisions but also the determination of the content of the law as such and in the application of the law to particular cases. In all of these modes of interpretation, the balancing of normative arguments may be required. These arguments will take the form of legal principles, understood as norms whose application requires a balancing in which they figure as arguments to be recognised to as high a degree as possible.[16] One can term interpretation by means of balancing a constructive interpretation, for it includes the justification of a norm that has not yet been established as valid.

### 10.3.1 Constructive and Semantic Interpretation

Accordingly, one must distinguish between, on the one hand, the interpretation of legal norms in a narrow sense, that is, semantic interpretation, and, on the other, the constructive interpretation of law by establishing the legal validity of a norm by means of balancing. Semantic interpretation makes explicit the meaning of a given norm, that is, an implication of this norm according to its linguistic meaning and the relevant rules of argumentation.[17] By contrast, constructive interpretation does not claim that the normative judgements stemming from balancing express the semantic meaning of another norm.

[16] This adopts the interpretation of principles as requirements of optimisation, see Alexy (2002a: 47), however, only as a characteristic of the application of normative arguments, not as a structural feature of the arguments themselves.

[17] In the case of a systematic interpretation it may also refer to other norms of a legal system that necessitate a particular interpretation or at least exclude some interpretive options.

This is obvious where substantive legal principles are involved, for example, in the case in which one must determine the extent of the freedom of speech where this is in conflict with the protection of the right to personal honour. But methodological arguments, too, can collide and hence require a balancing of normative arguments. This may occur in the case of arguments regarding the literal meaning, the intentions of the legislator, the reasonable purpose of a regulation or general principles of law. Therefore, conflicts of methodological arguments require autonomous judgement if the conflict cannot be resolved by appeal to a pre-established rule.[18]

Accordingly, the relation between legal interpretation and autonomous judgement is that legal interpretation includes not only interpretation in a strict, semantic sense but also constructive interpretation by means of the balancing of normative arguments in order to establish the legal validity of a norm. In so far as the interpretation of law requires a balancing, it includes an autonomous judgement of the law-applying organ.

### 10.3.2 Types of Constructive Interpretation

Several types of constructive interpretation should be distinguished. First, the application of normative arguments in a balancing may be merely procedural or also substantive. Secondly, the decision may be completely or incompletely bound by normative arguments. Thirdly, one must distinguish between open and closed balancing, according to whether the balancing establishes a new preference or interprets an already established norm or preference relation.

#### *10.3.2.1 Procedural and Substantive Application of Legal Principles*

The distinction between a procedural and a substantive application of legal principles refers to the difference between the mere consideration of a principle in a balancing and its having an actual effect on the result of the balancing. One might regard balancing as a form of the application of law already if a legal principle is involved in the balancing, or only if a legal principle receives priority. The first case is that of a mere procedural application, the second case, a substantive application of a principle.

Speaking of the application of law by means of the balancing of principles presupposes that at least one of the arguments to be considered in the balancing is based on a legal principle, that is, a principle identified by criteria of legal validity – and not, then, merely owing to its substantive correctness and its relevance to the case. If no principle involved in the balancing has legal character, one would not speak of an application of the law. By contrast, if one of the principles involved

[18] In fact, the resolution of conflicts always requires autonomous judgement. Even if an established rule applies, one might ask whether this rule is to be followed or not. Rejecting an established rule is an issue, however, of legal validity and may well be kept apart from issues of legal interpretation.

in the balancing is legally valid, one can regard the balancing as an application of law in a procedural sense.

On the other hand, one might understand the application of law more narrowly. In a case in which legal as well as extra-legal principles are involved, one might speak of the application of law only if the legal principle receives priority and determines the result of the balancing. For if the extra-legal principle receives priority, the decision would be a case in which the established law is not applied. Against this narrow view, one might argue that a legal principle may be acknowledged in general although it is superseded in exceptional cases by extra-legal principles. In a certain sense, one cannot deny that the argumentation in such a case is an application of law, although the positive legal norms do not determine the decision. Nevertheless, positive norms figure as reasons in the balancing and are thus relevant to the determination of the scope of definitively valid law. Consequently, it is a case of the interpretation of law.

Accordingly, one must distinguish between the application of law in a procedural sense, which only requires that a legal principle be involved in the argument, and in a substantive sense, which requires that a legal principle determine the decision. It seems to be appropriate to use the term in the procedural sense.

### *10.3.2.2 Completely and Incompletely Bound Balancing*

Within the scope of balancing in a procedural sense, one can distinguish between pure political decisions, where no legal principle is involved, and the application of law, where at least one legal principle is involved that must be taken into account in the balancing. Regarding the application of law, one can again determine whether the balancing is bound by law completely or incompletely. In the case of a completely bound balancing, all principles that must be taken into account have to be legal principles and no extra-legal principle may be considered. According to a normative conception of law, legal principles ought to be applied by legal organs in their reasoning.[19] Thus, if only legal principles apply to it, the set of principles relevant for the balancing is fixed, and the decision is completely bound by these principles. By contrast, a balancing is bound only incompletely by law if the law-applying organ may also take into account principles that it deems to be valid according to its autonomous judgement or may even pursue self-established political goals that it does not regard as obligatory.

According to a traditional though disputed view, judicial decisions represent the paradigm case of completely bound legal decisions, for judges are not allowed to introduce their own moral or political convictions as such but only arguments

[19] One might ask whether principles may count as legal already if legal organs are permitted to apply them. Within a procedural conception, this must be denied. A mere permission to consider a principle does not constitute its legal validity. Legal organs may ask with respect to any extra-legal principle whether it is relevant to their reasoning. On the other hand, the substantive notion of the application of law allows for legal principles that one may apply, although this is not obligatory.

supported by legal norms.[20] If, however, judges have the competence to decide upon their own judgement as to what is the law, although this judgement cannot claim to be objectively valid, the traditional view needs to be modified: judges must present their judgements as completely bound by law, even though they should not be justified on the grounds of objectively valid law. Objectively, judicial decisions may be incompletely bound by law. Still, judicial decisions must always be presented as completely bound by law. By contrast, administrative discretion includes the balancing of legal principles but also of administrative goals, and legislation is bound by constitutional principles but may be based on self-chosen policies as well. Although administrative or legislative balancing may occasionally be completely bound by legal principles, these cases will be rather exceptional. The paradigm case of administrative and legislative discretion is that of a decision only incompletely bound by law, in objective as well as in subjective perspective.

#### *10.3.2.3 Open and Closed Balancing*

Open balancing must be distinguished from another type of balancing that serves to interpret an already established norm or preference that limits the decision substantively. The latter may be called 'closed balancing', for a balancing takes place within the scope of a norm that establishes conditions and legal consequences and thus already has some descriptive content. Such norms do not merely refer to or cover up the need for a balancing of normative arguments, for example, by demanding an optimal, reasonable or adequate result. A consequential problem is how to relate this descriptive content to the need to balance competing arguments. Two types of closed balancing can be distinguished, namely, balancing with respect to the interpretation of legal norms and with respect to the interpretation of preference relations.

Regarding the balancing aimed at the interpretation of an already established legal norm, the typical case is the interpretation of concepts given expression by the norm to be interpreted. Nevertheless, this interpretation is not merely semantic, but constructive, determining the content of the norm in question by means of balancing.

> An example is that of the right to free development of one's personality according to Article 2 section 1 of the German Basic Law (Grundgesetz, GG).[21] The scope of this right is disputed. One interpretation, established by the German Federal Constitutional Court, is that this provision includes the right to do whatever one wishes, though subject to the constraint referred to in Article 2 section 1 GG. Another interpretation is

[20] For example, Dworkin's conception of law as integrity claims that judicial decisions are completely bound, with which Dworkin contrasts 'pragmatism'. See Dworkin (1986; 2006).

[21] Article 2 s 1 GG: everyone has the right to the free development of his personality as far as he does not violate the rights of others or acts against the constitutional order or the moral law ('Jeder hat das Recht auf die freie Entfaltung seiner Persönlichkeit, soweit er nicht die Rechte anderer verletzt und nicht gegen die verfassungsmäßige Ordnung oder das Sittengesetz verstößt').

that only activities of some importance to the individual or of some value are protected as part of this fundamental right.

The arguments relevant to this interpretation begin from traditional rules of legal interpretation. The literal meaning rather favours the second position, that is, a narrow interpretation. However, the original intention of the framers of the constitution supports the first interpretation, for the materials of the process of the formation of the constitution show that the first interpretation was intended and the formulation was only changed to make the provision appear more weighty. A systematic argument in favour of the first interpretation is that the restricting clauses in the second part of Article 2 section 1 GG would not make sense, at least in part, if the extension of the right to liberty were already restricted. Finally, there are arguments respecting the consequences of the alternative interpretations for other principles or values, of law or of political morality. The first interpretation extends the protection of individual interests and makes possible a nearly complete judicial control of state action that interferes with individual rights. It will, however, also enhance the judicial power to interfere with the decisions of political institutions that can claim to have a stronger democratic legitimacy. Moreover, the idea of fundamental rights might suggest that not just any individual interest deserves constitutional protection but only important and valuable interests. Hence, there are competing principles and normative conceptions that make necessary autonomous judgement for a decision between them. Moreover, the choice between different conceptions of fundamental rights, democracy and judicial review is not determined by the constitution itself but depends on issues of political morality.

The upshot of all this is that the interpretation of the concept of developing one's personality is concerned with a great deal more than the semantics of this concept and the intentions of the legislature. Although linguistic arguments and legislative intentions form an essential part of a closed balancing, this balancing may and usually will include a number of additional normative arguments. The semantic interpretation as well as the intentions of the framers of the constitution count as considerations in this balancing, for their legal relevance can be supported by normative arguments, such as, for example, the publicity and reliability of legal provisions, or the democratic legitimacy of the enactment of the legal provision. But the search for the semantic meaning of a legal provision or the subjective intention of a legislature will be no more than a part of the argument and, especially in constitutional interpretation, often not even a decisive part.

Another case of closed balancing concerns the interpretation of an established preference relation. When preference relations between competing principles have already been established for some cases, the question arises of whether these rules of preference can also be applied to other cases where the principles in question collide. This depends on whether there are relevant differences in the cases and whether such differences require a different solution. Relevant differences exist if the weight of a principle in the case at hand differs from that in the decided case, or if there are further principles applicable to the case at hand that were not relevant in the case for which the preference relation had been established.

> For example, the German Federal Constitutional Court has decided that a call for the boycott of films of a former Nazi director must be permitted, and could not be regarded as an illegitimate interference with the competing rights of those affected by the boycott.[22] A decisive argument was the importance of the right to free speech in public debate in a democracy, which again is recognised by the German constitution. This rule applies also in other cases where offensive speech is meant to be a contribution to the public debate on a disputed issue and is therefore not without legitimacy. In another case, however, the issue was whether a powerful media enterprise would be permitted to call for a boycott against the products of competing media enterprises that published the television programmes of the former German Democratic Republic in TV guides. It threatened not to deliver its own products to newsagents who sold products of the latter enterprises. In this case, the Federal Constitutional Court declared the call for a boycott not to be justified; rather, it was deemed to be a violation of the rights of the enterprises against which the boycott was directed.[23] What are the differences in this case? The call for a boycott was motivated not only out of concern for the public good, in particular, the damage that the re-emergence of a former Nazi director might cause for the image of post-war Germany, but also by economic interests. Moreover, the call for a boycott was enforced by a threat of boycott against non-complying newsagents. The first point affects the weight assigned to the right to free speech, the second point casts into doubt whether the protection of the right to free speech is applicable at all, for the use of economic power contradicts the purpose of public discourse, that is, a free exchange of arguments. In any case, an application of the formerly established preference was not justified. And even if one were to adopt this view, it could not stem from an application of the established preference rule but would require a new balancing, which would have to take into account all the relevant facts and normative arguments.

What effect can formerly established preference rules then have for the decision of new cases? If the new case corresponds in all relevant respects to the one decided, the preference rule determines the result. This follows from the lack of any new arguments. Hence, the following rule holds:

> ($I_1$) If a preference rule establishes the priority of a principle $P_1$ over a principle $P_2$ under a condition C, and a new case corresponds to the decided one in all relevant respects, then one ought to follow this rule.

This presupposes that the preference rule is actually established as definitively valid. It is, of course, possible that the validity of this rule is disputed, and that a revision of its justification is required.

On the other hand, if the new case exhibits new features that appear to be relevant to the solution, the established preference rule cannot be applied directly. Nevertheless, it can count as a reason for adhering to the established rule, although not a decisive reason. This leads to the following principle (or prima facie rule) of interpretation:

[22] BVerfGE 7,198 – Lüth.

[23] BVerfGE 25, 256 – Blinkfüer.

($I_2$) If a preference rule establishes the priority of a principle $P_1$ over a principle $P_2$ under a condition C, then prima facie one ought to follow this rule in any case of conflict between $P_1$ and $P_2$ where C obtains, whatever other features the case at hand may have.

This argument may, again, be based on concerns over stability, equality and the certainty of the law. Moreover, a decision may have authority derived from formal principles, which establish the legitimate authority of the deciding organ and make its decisions bind, at least in principle, whether they are substantively justified or not. The addressees of these formal principles, usually other organs of the respective legal system, are in principle bound to follow the decisions of the authority established by the formal principle independently of their correctness. Thus, introducing formal principles shifts the focus from interpretation to the competence to make binding legal decisions.

## 10.4 COMPETENCE AND LEGAL INTERPRETATION

Competence comes into play in legal interpretation in various respects. One aspect is the power to establish binding interpretations in the strict sense, as already explained. Another is the competence to balance, that is, first, to make such a decision at all and, secondly, to make a normative judgement that is binding on others.

The need for balancing normative arguments in legal interpretation leads to the question of which legal organs ought to have the competence to make such decisions and, in addition, in which respect such decisions are binding on other organs. According to the traditional view, which regards legal interpretation as merely the determination of the meaning of established law, the competence of the courts to apply the law includes that of interpreting it, with the consequence that all organs bound by law have to submit to the interpretations of the courts. However, the structural similarity of autonomous judgement and completely bound legislative decisions contradicts the traditional view. Both include the balancing of normative arguments. Therefore, in problematic cases, too, judicial decisions have to establish a new rule, rather than simply applying an existing one. Hence, they create new law, although they must at the same time claim their judgment to be required by the prevailing legal principles. And legislative decisions, if completely bound by constitutional principles, display the same characteristics. They create new law, claiming that the new law is required by constitutional principles.

This creative character of judicial decisions might raise doubts as to whether, and to what extent, courts ought to have the competence to establish law by means of balancing. Moreover, other legal organs, too, must and can claim to be applying the law. The problem then is how to relate the competences of various legal organs to legal interpretation based on balancing.[24]

[24] See also Riehm (2006: 193 ff).

### 10.4.1 Competence as to Open and Closed Balancing

The question of competence arises, on the one hand, in the case of closed balancing within the interpretation of a particular norm or preference relation and, on the other, in the case of open balancing that establishes a definitively valid norm directly on the basis of legal principles. Whilst the closed balancing forms part of the traditional judicial task of interpretation, it is not clear whether judicial competence to interpret the law also includes open balancing. This problem is not without relevance, although most of the judicial decisions of balancing are interpretive. There are, however, examples of open balancing, and in these cases judicial competence is called into question.

> An example of open balancing is the decision of the German Federal Constitutional Court on limits of the taxation of investment income, which held that owing to the constitutional protection of property rights, taxation must not go beyond around 50 per cent of investment income.[25] Although the court claimed to base this decision on a semantic interpretation of Article 14 GG, there is no plausible semantic argument; the judgment could only be justified on the basis of an open balancing of, on the one hand, the principle of the protection of property rights and, on the other hand, the public interest in taxation. Was it within the scope of constitutional review to establish the 50 per cent limit on taxation, or did the court reach beyond its competence?[26]

According to the analysis suggested here, open balancing that is completely bound by legal principles is not only a form of the application of law but also a type of judicial decision-making; hence, it belongs to the competence of the courts. Moreover, the structure of legal principles makes it necessary that anyone who holds that such a principle receive priority over competing principles must claim that this judgement is required by the prevailing principle itself and, hence, is required by the law. Someone making a normative judgement of this nature must claim that their decision is the legally correct one. From the perspective of an observer, one might have to say that another decision might have been possible and could have been regarded as correct, too. However, from the internal point of view of the agent forming a normative judgement, a claim to the normative correctness of the decision must be made that excludes other options.[27]

[25] BVerfGE 93, 121.

[26] One might object that the problem of the limits of taxation was not completely bound by constitutional principles; the reasons for taxation are political in nature, and not derived from constitutional law. One can meet this objection by distinguishing between the judicial review of the power to tax and the review of particular taxes. A review of a particular tax might require that the reasons for it be evaluated, which calls for a review of political arguments. By contrast, a review of the limits of the power of taxation need not inquire into whether the reasons for a particular tax are sound and what weight ought to be assigned to them, but will presuppose the legitimacy and importance of those reasons according to the view of the legislator. With this presupposition one can analyse the problem as one of completely bound balancing, a balancing that is not taking into account political arguments.

[27] Consequently, even in the case of the 50 per cent limit on taxation on the basis of constitutional principles of the protection of property rights and the legitimacy of taxation, the court's decision was within the judicial competence of constitutional review.

### 10.4.2 Competence as to Incompletely Bound Balancing

A greater problem is presented by the issue of the competence of courts as to a balancing that is not completely bound by law. This would attribute to the courts the power to set aside legal principles in favour of extra-legal principles. Although, at first glance, one might regard this as being incompatible with the character of a court, one cannot exclude this possibility, for the reason that a legal system might confer this power on its courts in defining the limits of jurisdiction.

However, the problem needs to be formulated more precisely. Two interpretations of the juxtaposition of legal and extra-legal principles are possible:

(1) legal principles are principles that legal organs are bound to apply in their legal reasoning, and extra-legal principles are principles that legal organs are not bound to apply;
(2) legal principles in the sense of principles of positive law are identified by means of empirical-analytical criteria, and extra-legal principles are non-positive principles, identified by their moral correctness.

According to the first interpretation, the issue is whether legal organs may limit the application of legal principles by giving preference to principles they have no obligation to apply. In this respect, one must again distinguish as to whether there is no obligation to apply a principle from an objective or from a subjective perspective. From a subjective perspective of the law-applying organ, no obligation to apply means that it is permitted either to apply a principle or forbear from applying it. This, however, can hardly be the case, for the structure of normative arguments implies that one ought to apply them. An agent who regards a principle as legally relevant cannot be indifferent to its application.

For example, if someone believes that in principle one ought to protect animals even though no such obligation is recognised by law, he cannot regard the application of this requirement as merely permitted but must regard it as obligatory.

In an objective perspective, the difference between an obligation to apply a principle and no obligation to apply it might be understood as the difference between an objectively valid obligation and one that holds only according to the individual normative judgement of an agent. As argued above, legal organs have competence to make claims to legal validity based on their individual normative judgements, by contrast with ordinary citizens.[28] The problem here, however, is different, for the issue is not a matter of making a claim to legal validity without objective foundation, but rather a matter of limiting an objective legal obligation to apply a principle owing to a principle that is claimed to be legally valid but for which there is not sufficient support to state an objectively valid obligation to apply it. In this case, it is not clear that the competence of legal organs to make statements of legal validity based on mere individual normative judgements must

[28] See 9.4.2.1.

be recognised. A legal system might recognise this competence, but it might just as well deny it and limit the set of legal principles to those that one can show to be objectively valid.

According to the second interpretation, the issue is a dispute between positivist and non-positivist conceptions of law, in this instance respecting the application of principles. Some theoretical arguments suggest that a legal system cannot completely exclude the power of courts to take decisions based on a balancing that includes non-positive but objectively valid principles.

First, legal principles can either be complied with or not complied with to one degree or another, and if a legal principle is complied with nearly completely, one cannot exclude the possibility that a court will give priority to arguments of political morality that are not supported by legal principles, thereby justifying a marginal interference with a legal principle.

Secondly, the formal or positive criteria of a legal system for identifying legal norms cannot close the system and exclude the possibility that non-positive principles may be applied, for the weight of these criteria might differ in particular cases to such a degree that no general precedence can be established. Formal criteria might have so little weight that merely substantive principles can override the formal principles.

> For example, principles can be introduced explicitly, inferred by induction from more specific rules, embedded in jurisdiction, or presupposed in a single judicial decision. In addition, the support stemming from these formal factors may be more or less clear.

Even among competing principles with positive support, stronger formal support does not strictly determine the priority among them. An explicitly introduced principle might, in certain circumstances, be superseded by a principle developed through jurisdiction, and a principle stemming from long-standing jurisdiction may be superseded by one inferred from a single decision. In the same line of argument, one cannot exclude the possibility that a principle with only weak formal support is superseded by a competing principle with no formal support at all but considerable substantive appeal. This is owing to the fact that the strength of the formal support varies and might be weak or without any weight at all.

In addition, the strength of a formal principle, together with the principle it supports, will also depend on the importance of the supported principle in the abstract as well as in the particular case.

> For example, if a legal system does not, on the one hand, recognise a constitutional principle for the protection of animals but, on the other, includes an unqualified right to scientific research, a limitation on this right, prohibiting experiments with animals in cases of very low scientific relevance, might be justified.

It may be difficult to find a clear example of a non-positive principle superseding a legal principle, for legal systems usually provide instruments to cope with such problems within the legal system itself. Nevertheless, the theoretical argument stands as follows: a legal system cannot be closed by positive criteria of validity, but judicial decisions might be based on principles that are valid for substantive reasons and independently of their formal legal support.

### 10.4.3 Competing Competences with respect to Legal Interpretation

In so far as balancing is involved in legal interpretation, it is not only the courts that will have to interpret the law but, indeed, all legal organs to which the law is addressed. Accordingly, they have to claim the legal correctness and bindingness of their interpretation. If these interpretations differ, the question arises as to which interpretation ought to be decisive.[29] The structure of the legal system, where the courts are in a position to monitor the acts of other legal organs, suggests that the courts will have the final word. This, however, might lead to an overwhelming judicial power, for courts could in theory replace virtually any decision taken by another legal organ. This consequence is often criticised and rejected as being incompatible with a constitutional democracy, for the parliament is regarded as the legal organ with the greatest and most direct democratic legitimacy, which therefore ought to have supreme power where the creation of law is involved.[30]

Whether such claims are justified will not be taken up here, for these claims can only be assessed with respect to particular constitutional systems. What does need elaboration, however, is the way in which the conception of autonomous reasoning may help in analysing the problem of conflicting competences with respect to interpretation, that is, in which way an adequate allocation of the competence of courts and of other legal organs, especially legislatures, can be made with respect to the interpretation of the constitution and the law in general. The focus will be on the issue of constitutional interpretation, for this is the area where the problem of interpretive competence is most acute.

#### *10.4.3.1 Problem of Interpretive Competence*

Basically, the courts cannot claim to have all the power that might, in theory, be based on the interpretation of constitutional law, and parliament cannot claim to be immune from constitutional review where balancing is taken up in the course of an interpretive judgement. Constitutional practices ought to follow an intermediate course, and, at least in some cases, indeed do so. This becomes obvious when courts restrict their control to clearly or obviously mistaken evaluations of the legislature or other organs.

> For example, according to Article 14 section 3 GG, expropriation is constitutional only for reasons of the public good. The German Federal Constitutional Court assumes that

[29] This description of the problem might not always be adequate. If it is clear who will have the final word, other organs will not develop such conceptions. On this problem, see Kaufmann (1997).

[30] See, in particular, Böckenförde (1991); Habermas (1996).

this requirement is subject to judicial review, also in the case of expropriation by statutes. If, however, evaluations or assumptions of the legislator have to be reviewed, a court may replace them only if they are clearly refutable or obviously mistaken, or if they contradict the scheme of values (*Wertordnung*) of the Basic Law.[31] Thus, cases in which courts accept results that appear to be contrary to constitutional law remain.

Another example is the constitutional control of decisions of ordinary courts that apply constitutional principles in the course of applying ordinary, non-constitutional law. The German Federal Constitutional Court differentiates the intensity of its control according to the intensity of the infringement of fundamental rights interests. The greater the interference with an interest protected by a fundamental right, the more intensive the control of the constitutional court. If the interference is not very intensive, the control will be limited to the question of whether or not the court of ordinary jurisdiction has acted upon a fundamentally mistaken interpretation of the meaning of a fundamental right.[32] Again, the restricted control may well mean that some unconstitutional results remain unchallenged.

In addition, the intensity of the control of the requirement of equal treatment (Article 3 section 1 GG) differs. If fundamental rights are affected or groups of people are treated differently, the constitutional court may review, in detail, the question of whether there are, according to their weight and quality, sufficient reasons for the differentiation. In other cases, it is only the arbitrariness of the differentiation that counts. One might suggest that in these cases different substantive constitutional criteria exist. However, the constitutional court explicitly declares that not only the substantive limits of legislative action are different, but also the intensity of constitutional control.[33]

It seems that courts tolerate normative decisions that on closer analysis might turn out to be unconstitutional. In certain circumstances, however, the courts avoid this closer analysis. The acceptance of unconstitutional decisions by the courts requires, however, a constitutional justification.

The most plausible justification is that the courts respect acts of other legal organs based on a competing interpretation of the constitution by those organs.[34] Thus, various organs may hold competing conceptions of the interpretation of the law, and the conception, for example, of the legislature respecting the constitutionality of a statute may be relevant when a court has to make a judgement as to whether or not this statute is constitutional.

[31] BVerfGE 24, 367, 406.

[32] BVerfGE 61, 1, 6.

[33] BVerfGE 88, 87, 96.

[34] Raabe (1998: 271) objects that this is incompatible with the idea of an objectively valid law that exists independently of the agent making legal judgements. This consequence, however, should not come as a surprise within a conception of law based on individual autonomy. The issue of whether there exists objectively valid law on a certain matter can only be addressed within this model; it cannot be presupposed. Another objection addresses a violation of the independence of the judiciary. Judicial independence, however, only exists with respect to the application of legal standards and is not affected by a legal obligation to consider, within their reasoning, the constitutional interpretations of other organs. In addition, and by contrast with what Jestaedt (1999: 223 n 73) argues, such an obligation may well be justified by the principle of democracy.

*10.4.3.2 Demarcation of Interpretive Competence*

The idea of competing competences to interpret the constitution and, accordingly, of competing interpretations offered by various organs of the legal system does not imply that there is no constitutional review of the interpretations of other organs. Competing interpretations, however, create the problem of whose interpretation ought to be decisive. Then, the issue is how the interpretive competences of various organs can be demarcated. Guidelines for a demarcation of competences can be found in the structure of normative justification according to the model of balancing and, in particular, in the structure of fundamental rights.

One cannot seriously doubt that the courts must have the power to correct mistakes in the legislative process that contravene conditions of a correct balancing of constitutional principles. Furthermore, where a particular result of a balancing can be justified as objectively valid, the courts must have the power to enforce this result. An additional point is that courts must also control the procedural rules that are meant to guarantee that the political process leads to results acceptable to all autonomous agents. This includes, in particular, the protection of the right to participation in the political process.

Moreover, judicial review can be justified with respect to fundamental or basic rights that are in principle immune from legislative interference. If there are no sufficient reasons to override this immunity, the legislature does not have the power to subject fundamental rights to any balancing with other principles or political goals. If, however, the legislature interferes in in principle forbidden territory, it seems natural that it is not for the legislature itself to determine the legitimacy of this interference and it belongs to the power of the courts to make this judgement, even if the judgement necessitates an open balancing.

If, on the other hand, none of the listed reasons applies, then one must ask which organ is best qualified to take the decision in question. This cannot be assessed on merely theoretical grounds. In particular, the demarcation of the competence of final decision-making will depend on the features that concern the reliability or expected correctness of their decisions. Accordingly, what matters is the quality of argument on the part of the courts as well as within the political process. Finally, the assignment and distribution of the competence of authoritative decision-making respecting constitutional interpretation is a question of positive law.

## 10.5 CONCLUSION

Although law claims to be an authoritative order, the application of law leaves room for autonomous judgement in various respects. In so far as the application of law cannot proceed without the balancing of legal arguments, it must include autonomous judgements. This may be the case not only with respect to problems of open balancing of legal principles beyond the scope of established legal rules but also within the interpretation of established legal rules whenever and wherever they do not determine, beyond a reasonable doubt, a unique solution. And even if they do, the acceptance of this solution can still be regarded as an act of autonomous judgement – although not within legal interpretation but respecting the validity of law.

The need for autonomous judgement in legal application has implications for the model of legal application. A view of the judiciary as merely applying law and, accordingly, enforcing the authority of the law appears to be inadequate. There may be different legal organs with competing interpretations or conceptions of law, and all claim to be right in their interpretation and all compete for the competence to make a binding decision on the issue in dispute. Hence, the focus shifts from legal interpretation to the issue of the competence in the field of interpretation.

One must define the respective competences of various organs, establishing who will have the final word and which role the interpretive determinations of other organs is to have. This demarcation of competences must begin from a set of formal principles that support the particular interpretive claims. Moreover, it is not only legal organs who can suggest interpretations of law: any citizen can do so as well. There is no reason to exclude, from the outset, individuals' conceptions of law in the course of deliberation, although the task of finding a final, authoritative solution is left to the legal organs.

The competition of diverse interpretive competences means that legal interpretation does not have a hierarchical structure, where a legislature creates norms to be applied by courts and to be followed by the citizens. Rather, the procedure is complex with various inputs, where the final judgement, even though still the task of the courts or of other legal organs, is based on a process of intersubjective deliberation.

# 11

# *The Autonomy of Legal Systems*

THE PARADIGM CASE of a legal system is the law of the state, which is sovereign and hence independent of other legal systems. This suggests that legal systems determine their own content and are not subject to the claims of other legal systems. This assumption, however, is faced with various problems. First, legal systems may conflict with requirements of morality. Secondly, they may conflict with other legal systems. The latter problem may concern other national legal systems or, in particular, their relation to supranational systems, such as the European Union, or the system of international law.

The problem of law and morality has already been discussed under the heading of legal validity.[1] Legal positivism claims that legal systems are conceptually independent of morality. This is also cast as the thesis of the 'autonomy' of law, a terminology, however, that must be sharply distinguished from the understanding of autonomy suggested here.[2]

By contrast, autonomy in the sense of self-legislation combines the binding character of normative arguments with the indeterminacy of and, hence, the freedom of choice involved in the balancing of these arguments. In this sense, legal systems are autonomous, for they can balance claims of morality in order to determine which norms are definitively legally valid. Legal decisions must, however, take into account moral arguments as long as these arguments have not been legitimately excluded as legal arguments by the law itself.

With respect to conflicts between legal systems, the traditional solution in the law of states consists in the model of the federal state, which establishes a hierarchy of legal systems, retaining the sovereignty of the superior system. Also with respect to international law, the dispute among monistic and dualistic theories focusses on the issue of hierarchy. However, this solution may be inadequate, for law consists of a plurality of systems without a determined hierarchical ordering among them.[3] Legal systems may be interrelated in various ways, not only by means of priorities. The conception of autonomy introduces a new instrument for

[1] The positivist claim has been refuted, at least for a theory of law from the internal point of view of those who make legal judgments. See 9.4.

[2] The positivist interpretation of 'autonomy' should, moreover, be rejected because it defines autonomy as mere independence. See Postema (1996: 80 ff), with a critique of this conception (88). Still another use contrasts autonomous or constitutive institutions, which regulate behaviour in order to create the possibility of institutional facts to be brought about, to regulative institutions, which regulate behaviour in order to create a certain effect, see Atria (2001: 30, 43).

[3] This is emphasised also by Christensen and Fischer-Lescano (2007: 21).

analysing possible conceptual relations between legal systems. In particular, it allows one to introduce normative requirements between legal systems that may either be accepted or rejected by the addressed systems.

My basic thesis is that law is a complex structure of interrelated systems of norms, which includes, as autonomous subsystems, normative conceptions of law defined by law-applying organs. The analysis will begin with an outline of inter-systemic relations in general and then address the problem of the autonomy of legal systems.

## 11.1 CONCEPT OF A LEGAL SYSTEM

A first issue is how to define a legal system. The paradigm case of a legal system is the law of a national state. In addition, however, the law of supranational organisations such as the European Union, international law and regional systems of international law need to be considered.

### 11.1.1 Definition

A legal system includes a set of interrelated norms that is defined and identified by particular criteria of legal validity.[4] Criteria of legal validity may define the norms belonging to the system or the existence of the system as a whole. The existence of a legal system requires, in addition to the definition of a set of norms, the existence of legal institutions and procedures. Here, however, I will focus on legal systems as systems of norms. In this sense, a legal system is constituted by the criteria of validity that determine the membership of its norms together with the facts or circumstances that meet these criteria, thus establishing the legally valid norms of that particular system. Such criteria are positive, that is, they include conditions sufficient for legal validity. Furthermore, there are norms whose legal validity is derived from other norms of the particular legal system. Accordingly, one may characterise a legal system, conceived of as a system of norms, as follows:

> $DF_{LS}$ A legal system is a set of norms that meet the criteria of validity in the system in question or are established as valid on the basis of norms identified by these criteria.

The definition of a legal system presupposes the existence of criteria of legal validity. This might appear to be circular, for the criteria of validity refer to the legal system that is to be defined. At this point it is necessary to distinguish between the existence of a legal system and the delimitation of a legal system, that is, the determination of what belongs to one system or another. The definition stated above does not purport to determine when a legal system exists; it is concerned with the delimitation of legal systems. The existence of legal systems is presupposed. Legal systems are established by social and institutional practices. Accordingly, there will

[4] See, eg, Raz (1983); Alchourrón and Bulygin (1971).

be a legal practice that acknowledges and employs certain criteria of validity: which criteria, is a matter of the interpretation of the legal practice. On the basis of these criteria, one can reconstruct the legal practice as a legal system defined by these criteria. Hence, the suggested definition is not circular.

### 11.1.2 Systemic Legal Validity

According to the above definition of a legal system, the legal validity of a norm can be defined as follows:

> $DF_{LV}$ A norm is legally valid according to a legal system $S_i$ if and only if it meets at least one of the criteria of validity of the system $S_i$.

In this definition, criteria of validity are understood as positive and, moreover, sufficient conditions of validity, not as negative or partial criteria. The criteria of legal validity may be defined in three ways. They can focus:

(i) on the position of a law-applying organ by asking which norms this organ ought to apply and follow in making its legal decisions;
(ii) on norms of legislative competence and, correspondingly, legislative acts; or
(iii) on the legal practice of a particular society, that is, on the question of which norms are actually applied and followed by the organs of a particular legal system or the citizens of a particular society.

In order to delimit a legal system as a system of norms, the focus on norms of legislative competence seems most appropriate. This may be called a criterial approach to law. One may call a legal system, as defined by the criterial approach, a C-system of law. However, the definition of legal systems by means of criteria of validity does not encompass the complexity of law completely. A criterial approach to law does not necessarily imply that the norms identified as law ought actually to be applied and followed. This would hold only if the selected criteria of validity guaranteed the bindingness of legal norms. Such a definition would lose, however, the advantage of the criterial approach, namely, providing for a fairly clear and easy identification of the norms of a legal system. Perhaps one could combine the criterial approach with a defeasible or prima facie claim to the bindingness of the identified norms. If, however, definitive validity or bindingness is claimed for a legal norm, then the criteria of validity have to be justified on the basis of a normative theory, and this is to confront all the problems of balancing, of diverging opinions and of indeterminacy that are typical of normative theories. Therefore, although the criterial approach to law comes closest to the paradigm of understanding the law as a legal system, it does not provide an adequate account of law as a set of norms that is actually to be applied and followed by the organs and addressees of a legal system.

Since one cannot apply the law without making claims to definitive validity, a conception of a system of legal norms is needed that includes those norms that are claimed to be definitively binding law. Since these norms are established only on the basis of the application of legal norms, I will call such a system an A-system. The focus on the position of law-applying organs is adequate for a normative conception of law. Such a conception, however, will not identify a set of norms that resembles the paradigm case of a state legal system. A judge will not necessarily have to apply all of the norms of a particular system, rather only a subset of them. Moreover, he might have to apply norms of other legal systems or principles of political morality as well.

Besides the C-system and the A-system of law, a third way to define a legal system is by means of the identification of legal norms and criteria of validity according to their empirical existence. As empirical phenomena, legal norms and criteria of validity are conceived of as institutional facts. This type of system can be called an E-system. It is not fully adequate as a conception of a legal system, however. A definition of law in terms of those norms that are actually applied within a particular legal system encounters a problem of circularity, for there is a reference to the very legal system that is supposed to be defined. Moreover, the criterion of actual acceptance is to some extent indeterminate and fuzzy. The acceptance of a particular norm does not, by itself, determine which norms are accepted as general norms. What is more, various acts of acceptance may conflict. Still, if one understands law as a social fact, this conception is, then, necessary.

### 11.1.3 The ACE Theory of Law

Law appears to be a complex structure that comprises of A-, C- and E-systems. These are interrelated in various respects. The C-system and the E-system are relevant to an A-system in so far as a formal principle of law renders certain criteria of validity and institutional acts normatively relevant. Such a principle requires that the norms identified by the C- and E-system ought to be applied and followed in legal decisions. The A-system and the E-system are relevant for the C-system of law, for they determine which criteria of legal validity ought to be applied or, indeed, which are actually applied by the organs of a legal system. The resulting C-systems of law are, or may be, distinct, however, for normative and descriptive conceptions of law may well identify different sets of norms. The C-system and the A-system of law are relevant for the E-system in so far as the actual legal practice follows the criteria of validity of the C-system and takes up the internal perspective of law-applying organs who are attempting to establish legally binding norms.

Hence, a theory of law must include several conceptions of law. At the level of the application of law, normative conceptions of law are required that determine which norms actually ought to be applied and followed. These again are based on criteria of legal validity. Thus, a conception of law as a system of norms identified by certain criteria of validity is needed. Moreover, a conception of law as an empirical phenomenon is needed, for the criteria of legal validity and the application of law in individual normative conceptions must have an empirical basis. One may call this the ACE theory of law, where 'A' stands for the applicative conception of law, 'C' for the criterial approach, and 'E' for the empirical approach to law.

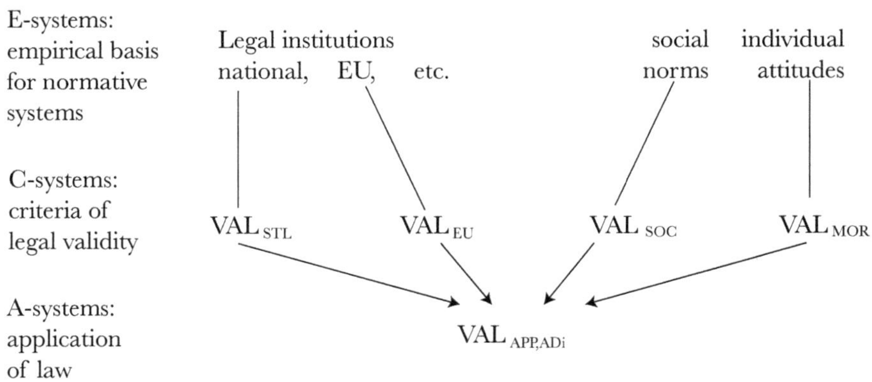


**Figure 11.1: ACE-theory of law**

The relations of different legal systems illustrated in Figure 11.1 are as follows. A theory of law comprises of conceptions of law as empirical systems (E-systems), systems defined by criteria of validity (C-systems), and systems of normative applications of law (A-systems). E-systems determine which C-systems in fact exist. C-systems contain requirements on the A-systems that have an influence on but cannot determine the content of the A-systems. There are several A-systems. Actually, each addressee of a C-system must develop, at least in a rudimentary form, an A-system, that is to say, must determine which norms actually ought to be applied and followed as law. The A-systems of law-applying organs have a special status, since their judgments will have binding character, at least for the case being decided, or at least will constitute arguments to be considered by other law-applying organs. But ordinary citizens, too, will have to develop A-systems. These A-systems will, again, form part of the empirical basis of the law as a complex legal system. Law, therefore, is a complex phenomenon that comprises various systems, each of them defined in a particular aspect.

### 11.1.4 Structure of Criteria of Systemic Legal Validity

For the analysis of a legal system as a set of norms, the criterial approach to law seems to be most appropriate. The structure of a criterion of validity is that of a conditional general statement of validity of a norm in a particular system:

(CV) $(n)\ Cn \rightarrow VAL_{Si}n$

Here, n is a variable representing norms (in a semantic sense, without assigning validity to them); (. . .) is the universal quantifier; (n) means, accordingly: 'for all n holds that . . .'; VAL is a predicate attributing validity to norms according to a particular system $S_i$; C defines a condition sufficient for the validity of a norm in $S_i$; $VAL_{Si}n$ represents a proposition that n is valid in $S_i$; and Cn that n fulfils condition C.

For reasons of simplicity I will refer not to a general statement but to a particular statement of validity concerning an individual norm represented by N:

(CV') $C(N) \rightarrow VAL_{Si}(N)$

The most important type of criterion of legal validity in contemporary legal systems is that of legislative enactments. The legal validity of a norm N follows from its issuance by a legislature L. The structure of a corresponding criterion of validity hence is:

(CVE) $ISS(N,L,S_i) \rightarrow VAL_{Si}N$

The issuance of a norm is an act A of someone (the legislature L), performed (DO(A,L)) with the intention (INT) of establishing the validity of a norm N in a particular system by means of this act ($VALS_iN,A$):

(LEG) $ISS(N,L,S_i) \leftrightarrow DO(A,L) \ \& \ INT(VAL_{Si}N,A)$

In order to be able to legislate, that is, to issue a valid norm, one must have a legislative competence. Competence is a normative position that enables one to bring about the validity of a norm by an act intending to establish the validity of this norm. Hence, the structure of competence is:

(COMP) $DO(A,L) \ \& \ INT(VAL_{Si}N,A) \rightarrow VAL_{Si}N$

The point of a norm establishing legislative competence is, accordingly, to transform an intention to create a legally valid norm into the fact that the intended norm be legally valid. This norm, of course, must define conditions under which someone has the respective legislative competence.

At least some of the criteria of validity of a legal system will be norms that confer legislative competences. Criteria of validity can, however, have other types of conditions, and, in addition, not every legal norm that establishes competence is a criterion of legal validity. For example:

(1) General and longstanding acceptance and employment of a norm as legally valid is usually regarded as a criterion of legal validity, establishing customary law.
(2) Judicial decisions establish the legal validity of a norm for the case at hand, but they may have general force. A judicial decision is not, however, a legislative act

in a strong sense; rather, it is the application of law. That is, the court does not intend to establish the validity of a norm independently of the existing legal situation but claims that its decision is backed and justified by already existing legal norms. This distinguishes judicial decisions from legislative acts, notwithstanding the fact a judicial decision might create a new norm and that the norm established by a judicial decision is legally valid even if it does not conform to existing law.

(3) Competence to enter into a private contract is not regarded as legislative competence, although private transactions are performed by intentional acts aimed at creating a legal relation, and they establish a legal obligation of the law-applying organs of the legal system to acknowledge and enforce such a contract. However, the competence to make private contracts is not granted as an instrument to establish intentionally legal norms that courts have to apply. The obligation of courts follows from a different norm, a norm that acknowledges the interest of private parties in defining their legal situation.

Furthermore, a legal system may attribute validity to norms owing to their validity in another legal system. For example, international private law may demand the application of a foreign state's law in a divorce case where the marriage was performed according to the law of that state. Such problems of reference to another system are an issue of intersystemic relations.

## 11.2 TYPES OF INTERSYSTEMIC RELATION

Intersystemic relations between legal systems arise in various circumstances.

(i) With respect to legal systems of national states, problems arise if, for example, a system makes applicable a norm of another system, or in cases of conflict law, where it must be determined which legal system rules the case.

(ii) In federal states there are relations between the legal system of the federal level and the systems of the member states or provinces. Moreover, the logical relations between legal systems represent a central problem with respect to state legal systems, international law and supranational law.

(iii) With respect to the relation between national and international law, monistic and dualistic conceptions are in dispute as to the question of whether national law can be derived from international law or vice versa, or whether they are independent of each other. However, even a dualist position must acknowledge that there are some relations between them.

For example, some or all norms of international law may be valid in some sense in a state legal system as well; it is not clear, however, whether they are valid as international law or whether there exist parallel norms in the state system.

The European Convention on Human Rights (ECHR) creates rights of citizens against states, but do these rights hold within a state without an act of transposition? This was a problem in the case of Krenz and other former officials of the former

German Democratic Republic. The European Court of Human Rights applied the Convention without showing that it had been transposed into the law of the GDR,[5] whereas in the German discussion the direct applicability of the ECHR was disputed.[6]

With regard to the European Union, some EU regulations are directly valid in the Member States, whereas others only constitute guidelines, but even if a mere guideline is not respected by a Member State, EU law requires that state law under certain conditions provides compensation to a citizen who has suffered damage owing to the state's failure to transpose a guideline.[7] Is this a claim of EU law or of the legal system of one of the Member States that is required by and necessary according to EU law?

What are the relations of the different legal systems involved in these cases? Issues raised here are the delimitation of legal systems, their interdependence, and the relations of priority among them.

### 11.2.1 Case of the Primacy of EU Law

I will take up an example in order to get a clearer view on the logical relations between legal systems. The example refers to the relation of EU law to state legal systems. EU law prohibits national regulation that hinders transnational commerce within the EU (Article 34 of the Treaty on the Functioning of the EU,[8] formerly Article 28 of the EC Treaty). The structure of the EU norm prohibiting certain national regulation can be formulated as:

> If a norm $N_1$ is valid according to EU law and another norm $N_2$ is incompatible with $N_1$, then it is valid in EU law that the legislature of a Member State shall not issue $N_2$.

However, the consequent of the regulation states the validity of a norm according to EU law, not according to a state legal system. What, then, is the relation between EU law and the state legal systems? One might formulate this as a relation of direct validation or direct invalidation.

Direct validation means, in the case of the EU, that the norm of the EU system is also valid in the state legal system:

> If a norm $N_1$ is valid according to EU law, then it is valid according to the law of the EU Member States.

This, however, is not the case, for the priority of EU law does not mean that EU norms are norms of the legal systems of Member States as well.

Direct invalidation means that the conflict of a norm of the state legal system with a norm of the EU system leads to the invalidity of the state norm within the state legal system:

[5] ECHR, 22 March 2001, EuGRZ 2001, 210–18; 219–24.

[6] See Alexy (1993).

[7] *Francovich*, ECJ, 19 November 1991, Slg. I 1991, 5357.

[8] 'Quantitative restrictions on exports, and all measures having equivalent effect, shall be prohibited between Member States.'

> If a norm $N_1$ is valid according to EU law and a norm $N_2$ is issued by the legislature of a Member State that is incompatible with $N_1$, then $N_2$ is not valid in the law of the Member State.

This also implies that the issuance of a norm in the state legal system does not result in the validity of this norm and, thus, restricts the competence of the legislature of the state. This relation of direct invalidation does not, however, adequately represent the primacy of EU law. For EU law, at least according to the ruling doctrine in Germany, is recognised as having a priority, not respecting the validity of norms but only respecting their application. Accordingly, EU law does not purport to invalidate state legal norms directly. And even if it did, it does not follow that state regulation is actually invalidated. The content of the EU law is only a prohibition. That is, it should be stated:

> If a norm $N_1$ is valid according to EU law and a norm $N_2$ is incompatible with $N_1$, then it is valid in EU law that $N_2$ shall not be valid in state law.

Hence, we have a second-order norm of EU law containing a prohibition regarding the validity of a first-order norm contained in state law. This shows that if we wish to analyse the relations between EU law and the state legal systems, we must consider norms of a higher order.[9] The analysis of the primacy of EU law shows, moreover, that one must distinguish two kinds of intersystemic relation, those of validating or invalidating a norm of a different system and those consisting of normative requirements in one system that are directed to another system.

### 11.2.2 Intersystemic Validation or Invalidation

With respect to the relations of validation and invalidation, one must distinguish between direct and indirect validation, and these relations must, in turn, be distinguished from that of the incorporation of norms within a legal system.

#### *11.2.2.1 Direct Validation or Invalidation*

Direct validation means that a normative system itself establishes the validity of a norm in another system; direct invalidation that it determines the invalidity of a norm in another system.

> An example of direct validation can be found in monistic theories of state and international law. According to these theories, the validity of international law ($S_2$) depends on the recognition by state law ($S_1$) or, conversely, the validity of state law ($S_2$) is based on international law ($S_1$). Hence, the former system determines the content of the latter.
>
> Another example is found in the requirement of homogeneity of article 28 section 1 of the German Basic Law (GG), claiming that the constitutional systems of the particu-

[9] As far as this priority in application is recognised by the Member States, there is a corresponding state norm.

lar states must be in accordance with the fundamental constitutional principles of the federal constitution.[10] One can interpret this as stating that the federal constitution establishes the validity of these principles within the constitutional systems of the states.[11]

Still another example is found in the law of autonomous legal bodies, such as municipalities, universities or private associations. Their legislative competence follows from state or federal law, but the norms they issue will not belong to the state or federal law but form a separate system.

Direct validation constitutes the validity of a norm in one system by legislative acts carried out within another system. As the examples show, however, some interpretation might be necessary in order to establish a case of direct validation. In addition, direct validation might be limited to norms of competence, so that norms established in the exercise of such competences are validated only indirectly.

By contrast with direct validation, direct invalidation means that one system might exclude or remove the validity of certain norms in another system.

For example, in German law, direct invalidation would be the consequence of German federal law with respect to conflicting state law.[12]

In general, direct validation or invalidation is not possible among different legal systems. It is only in certain exceptional cases that these relations might exist.

For example, though German federal law can invalidate the law of a state, it cannot in general validate a norm qua norm of a state. The validity of a federal law implies that the organs of the particular states must apply this law. It remains, however, federal law and does not create a corresponding norm in the legal system of the particular states.

If a legal system could in general validate norms in another system, this would establish a closer relation between the systems than is the case with a federal state. Still, one can distinguish the system so long as it is not the case that all the norms of one system are established as valid by another system.

There are two ways in which a direct validation may result. One possibility is that of inference:

(VD1) If a norm $N_1$ is valid in system $S_1$, then it is valid in system $S_2$.

$$VAL_{S1}N_1 \rightarrow VAL_{S2}N_1$$

[10] Article 28(I)(1) GG: The constitutional order in the states must conform to the principles of the republican, democratic and social government based on the rule of law, as defined by this Basic Law (Die verfassungsmäßige Ordnung in den Ländern muß den Grundsätzen des republikanischen, demokratischen und sozialen Rechtsstaats im Sinne dieses Grundgesetzes entsprechen).

[11] Another interpretation is possible, however, as well. The federal norm might only be seen as a requirement that must be fulfilled by the law of the particular states. Thus, a legislative act of the particular state would be required, and this would not be a case of direct validation. On the other hand, if a particular state did not comply with this requirement, one would nevertheless assume the validity of the principles required by the federal constitution in the constitutional law of the particular state. Thus, the homogeneity clause constitutes a case of direct validation.

[12] See Art 31 GG: Federal law has priority over the law of the states (Bundesrecht bricht Landesrecht).

For example, a morally valid norm might be immediately valid in a legal system. In this case, one might say that $S_1$ (the system of moral norms) forms part of $S_2$ (the legal system).

On the other hand, the inference may hold under some additional condition C:

(VD2) If, given certain conditions, a norm $N_1$ is valid in system $S_1$, then it is valid in system $S_2$.

$$VAL_{S1}N_1 \& C \rightarrow VAL_{S2}N_1$$

In this case, the content of system $S_2$ depends in some respects on another, dominating system $S_1$, and the validated norms form part of the dominated or dependent system S2. However, only some norms of $S_1$, not all of its norms, will form part of $S_2$. If, by contrast, all the norms of a system $S_2$ are valid because they are valid in $S_1$, that is, if $S_1$ completely dominates $S_2$, then $S_2$ forms part of $S_1$.

A second possibility of validating a norm in another system is that a system $S_1$ includes a criterion of validity that establishes the validity of a particular norm N in a system $S_2$, either unconditionally or under certain circumstances C. The validity according to system $S_1$ may be represented as:

(VD3) In system $S_1$ it is valid (perhaps under certain condition C) that the norm N is valid in system $S_2$.

$$VAL_{S1}(VAL_{S2}N) \text{ or}$$

$$VAL_{S1}(C \rightarrow VAL_{S2}N)$$

However, this relation does not suffice for a validation, for it does not follow that N is actually valid in $S_2$. It is only an intended domination of $S_1$ over $S_2$, which might not result in the validity of N in $S_2$. A validation requires a rule such as this:

(VD4) If in system $S_1$ it is valid (perhaps under condition C) that the norm N is valid in system $S_2$, then (under condition C) N is valid in system S2.

$$VAL_{S1}(VAL_{S2}N) \rightarrow VAL_{S2}N \text{ or}$$

$$VAL_{S1}(C \rightarrow VAL_{S2}N) \& C \rightarrow VAL_{S2}N$$

That is, system $S_1$ orders (unconditionally or conditionally) the validity of a norm N in system $S_2$ and, as a consequence, this norm is actually valid in $S_2$ (in case of a conditional validation, if the condition in question obtains).

Such a criterion may be called a system-transgressing criterion of validity.[13] The difference from the first form of validation is that norm N is not valid in the

[13] The validation of norms in a different system follows from conditionals that are not attributed to any particular legal system. Since they constitute legal relations, however, one should assume that they

dominating system $S_1$ but only in the dependent system $S_2$. Therefore, the validated norm does not belong to $S_1$, and the criterion of validity of $S_1$ does not belong to $S_2$. In this case, one can speak of $S_2$ as being a subsystem of $S_1$, but not a part or subset of it.

For example, the law of a federal state might establish norms valid in its member states that are not valid at the federal level.

A point that needs clarification is the relation between the dependence and the autonomy of legal systems. With respect to the example of autonomous legal bodies, one may doubt that the autonomous character of these subsystems fits with the characterisation as a dependent system, one that is dominated by another system. If one nevertheless wants to assume that the relation of validation exists (for example, between state and international law), one may interpret the autonomy of a legal system in a weaker sense, namely, as merely excluding that another system determines which norms are valid in the legal system while granting that its authority is derived from another system. In this case one can speak of a formal dominance of a legal system over an autonomous subsystem.

#### *11.2.2.2 Incorporation*

The structures of inferring or establishing validity by a dominating system must be distinguished from that of incorporation. In the case of incorporation, a norm of one legal system establishes for this system that a norm of another system is valid in it.

For example, the German constitution incorporates the general rules of international law as part of the federal law. That is, if a norm is valid as international law and it is generally accepted in the community of states, then it is valid as federal law.[14] Other examples include constitutions that incorporate all or some of the norms of international law.

The structure of incorporation is:

(VD5) It is valid in system $S_2$ that if the norm $N_1$ is valid in system $S_1$ (perhaps under condition C), then $N_1$ is valid in system $S_2$.

$$VAL_{S2}(VAL_{S1}N_1 \rightarrow VAL_{S2}N_1) \text{ or}$$

$$VAL_{S2}(VAL_{S1}N_1 \ \& \ C \rightarrow VAL_{S2}N_1)$$

belong to some legal system. It will at least be possible to define a legal system that includes them. This system need not be a normative system; it can be a system of norms identified by empirical criteria. In any case, if an intersystemic relation does not belong to one of the legal systems to which the conditional refers in its antecedent and consequent, one must assume that there is a third legal system which comprises the relations between particular legal systems. Moreover, one can define a comprehensive legal system including all particular legal systems and the intersystemic relations between them.

[14] See Art 25 GG: 'The general rules of international law shall be an integral part of federal law'.

Incorporation is not a case of the validation of a norm in another system, for it is based on a criterion of validity of the same system ($S_2$).

### 11.2.3 Competing Requirements of Application

Validation, invalidation and incorporation are not the only forms of intersystemic relation. In fact, according to a normative conception of validity, which links the validity of a norm to the requirement that the norm be applied and followed, legal systems and the relations between them ought to be analysed not as criteria of validity but as competing requirements of application.

#### *11.2.3.1 Systems of Application*

The need to consider requirements of application, and different systems thereof, becomes obvious in the case of EU law. An important point regarding the relations of EU law to the state legal systems of the Member States is that EU law does not have, and does not claim to have, the power to validate or invalidate norms of a state legal system. It is assumed to have priority in application (*Anwendungsvorrang*), not priority regarding the validity of the competing norms. That is, incompatible state norms remain valid within the state legal system but the norm-applying organs of the state systems are bound to apply the EU law and not the state law.

In order to construe this relation, it seems appropriate to use the notion of validity in the sense that a valid norm is to be applied and followed by its addressees. This notion of validity is not specific to the problem of EU law; it can be understood as defining validity in a genuinely normative sense.

This notion of normative validity, defined as the obligation to apply a norm ($VAL_{APP}$), together with the definition of a particular class of addressees of norms (AD) can be used to define a legal system as a normative system. It contains those norms that refer to a particular class of addressees of a system, for example, the norm-applying organs defined by a legal system, and demands that they apply these norms in making and justifying their decisions. Such a system has been called an 'A-system'. Validity in this system will be denoted, according to the type of validity and its scope (here the law of the Member States STL of the EU) by '$VAL_{APP,STL}$'.

Such a system is different from systems that are defined by criteria of validity of norms that do not imply an obligation to apply and follow the respective norms. This is the case with systems of norms defined by their origin, for example, being issued on the basis of legislative competence. The difference is the normative character of the A-system, owing to the correlation of validity and bindingness in this system. Hence, an A-system can be called not only a system of norms but also a normative system.

The distinctness of these systems does not imply, however, that there are no relations between them, that is, relations between a genuinely normative system and other systems of norms. Any legal system will include requirements directed to its law-applying organs to apply the norms of the particular system, and also requirements directed to its subjects or citizens to follow the norms of the particular system. These demands do not necessarily result, however, in an actual obligation to apply and follow the norms of the respective system, as the discussion on extremly unjust positive law shows. The relation between both systems is that the C-system, that is, a system defined by criteria of validity, claims to have as a subsystem the system of norms that its addressees ought to apply and follow.

The problem regarding priority in the application of the EU law, then, is that both systems, EU law and the state legal system, include a claim to the effect that its norms be applied by the courts or other norm-applying organs of state legal systems. This conflict must be resolved – not in these systems but in the system that consists of the norms that are actually to be applied and followed by the organs of the state legal system (that is, the respective A-system). That is, the validity in the A-system ($VAL_{APP,STL}$) is defined by a norm of the A-system. The normative claims that the competing systems $VAL_{EU}$ and $VAL_{STL}$ make are integrated by the A-system. The intersystemic relations of the systems involved thus become internal relations within the integrating A-system.

### *11.2.3.2 Intersystemic Normative Requirements*

This analysis suggests that there are normative claims of legal systems regarding each other, and in particular regarding the A-systems of the type $VAL_{APP,STL}$, that is, a normative system addressing the organs of a state legal system. None of the systems making these claims has, however, the power to determine the relation of priority that holds in the respective A-system. They can only make claims as to which norm *ought to be* valid in the A-system. That is, the EU law contains a requirement that in the normative system to be applied by the organs of a state legal system, there ought not to be a valid norm $N_2$ that conflicts with an EU norm $N_1$.

An analogous claim might be made by a state legal system. In fact, however, the relation between EU law and the state legal system is not symmetrical; the legal systems of the Member States acknowledge, at least in principle, the priority of EU law in the application of law.

One might suggest that EU law claiming priority together with a state legal system that acknowledges this claim will determine the content of the A-system ($VAL_{APP,STL}$). This suggestion, however, fails to take account of the fact that, even if state law accepts the primacy of EU law, it is not clear that the courts will follow this rule.

> For example, in Germany it was initially the Constitutional Court that restricted the claim to the primacy of EU law, and it was only later that the legislature included the jurisdictional reservations in the constitution.

As the example shows, even if the competing legal systems converge on the question of primacy, they do not have the power to determine the content of the A-system ($VAL_{APP,STL}$).

One might object that a legal system orders its norm-applying organs to apply the norms of the system. Hence, a legal system includes a subsystem of norms regarding the application of its norms. This, however, only amounts to a requirement that is valid in the state legal system $VAL_{STL}$. It holds, for example, a requirement that the organs of the system STL ought to apply a norm $N_1$:

$$VAL_{STL}\ O\ APPL(N_1,STL)$$

This does not necessarily result in a corresponding requirement in the A-system that the respective organs actually ought to apply the norm $N_1$, that is:

$$VAL_{APP,STL}N_1$$

Should this consequence hold generally, the system $VAL_{APP,STL}$ would be a subsystem of $VAL_{STL}$. If the state legal system set down this requirement it would be claiming that $VAL_{APP,STL}$ is a subsystem of its own, that is, it would be trying to dominate it. In fact, this is what legal systems are doing: demanding obedience from its organs to the established norms. From this claim alone, however, it does not follow that $VAL_{APP,STL}$ actually is a subsystem of the state system. It is a subsystem only in so far as the state system succeeds in determining the content of the system being applied. This will often be the case, for the law-applying organs are instituted by the state legal system, and they will recognise their duty to apply the state law. But it is not necessary.

Accordingly, the A-system must be autonomous to the extent that there are other systems that also legitimately claim the application of their norms.

For example, courts must take into account EU law or international law as legitimate sources of law; they cannot refer solely to the law of their own state.

This problem exists, too, with respect to the norms of political morality. Although in principle a legal system may exclude non-positive sources of law from application by its organs, this exclusion is possible only within certain limits, not for example in cases of extremely unjust law. Hence, if various legal systems compete for application, the decision on which norm actually ought to be applied must be an autonomous decision on the part of the organ of the A-system. Within the A-system the competing requirements of application can only be regarded as arguments for certain decisions which should in principle be followed but must be balanced against competing arguments. Such relations can be expressed as follows:

($VR_{STL}$) If a norm N is valid in the system of a Member State STL, there is an argument for the law-applying organs of STL to apply N.

$$VAL_{STL}N \rightarrow ARG_{APP,STL}N$$

($VR_{EU}$) If a norm N is valid in the system of the European Union EU, there is an argument for the law-applying organs of a system STL to apply N.

$$VAL_{EU}N \rightarrow ARG_{APP,STL}N$$

($VR_{INT}$) If a norm N is valid in the system of international law INT, there is an argument for the law-applying organs of STL to apply N.

$$VAL_{INT}N \rightarrow ARG_{APP,STL}N$$

($VR_{MOR}$) If a norm N is valid in a system of moral norms MOR, there is an argument for the law-applying organs of STL to apply N.

$$VAL_{MOR}N \rightarrow ARG_{APP,STL}N$$

The upshot of this is that there are normative requirements of legal systems respecting the A-systems of the organs of that particular system, but there are also requirements directed to other systems, such as the requirements of EU law to state legal systems, or vice versa. Such intersystemic normative requirements cannot create definitively valid norms in another system. If the requirement is legitimate, however, it creates a normative argument that must be taken into account and balanced with competing requirements by the organs of the system being addressed.

A problem remains as to the legal status of the arguments that follow from requirements made by other systems. One might understand them as legal arguments, to which the organs of the particular legal system in question are bound to give due consideration within their own legal reasoning. Whether or not to recognise such an obligation is, however, a legal issue determined within the system itself. It might reject the legal relevance of certain requirements made by other legal systems, thereby denying an obligation of legal organs to consider them within their own reasoning. This implies that one has to distinguish three levels within the A-systems developed by law-applying organs:

(i) the level of general normative arguments;
(ii) the level of legal normative arguments; and
(iii) the level of definitive legal norms.

Requirements from alien systems constitute arguments at the first level. They will also constitute legal normative arguments if this is not legitimately excluded by normative determinations of the system to which they are addressed. This confirms that the application of law, as found in A-systems, is open to a general practical discourse,[15] and boundaries can only be drawn within the legal system itself.

## 11.3 DEFINITIONS AND GENERAL THESES

On the basis of the above analysis, one can formulate some general theses regarding the relations between legal systems as defined here.

[15] For the thesis that legal discourse is a special case of a general practical discourse ('special case thesis'), see Alexy (1989a: 212 ff).

### 11.3.1 Independence

(IND1) A legal system $S_1$ is independent of another system $S_2$ if, and in so far as, $S_2$ has no impact on the content of $S_1$.

The independence of a system is a matter of degree in so far as some parts of a system can be independent of another system in some respects while being influenced by it in other respects. In addition, the independence of a legal system can hold with regard to a particular legal system, with regard to some, or with regard to all other legal systems. The independence of a system has the following implications:

(IND2) The norms belonging to an independent legal system are defined exclusively by the criteria of this system.

(IND3) A legal system cannot validate or invalidate norms of another legal system that is independent of it.

### 11.3.2 Dominance and Superiority

(DO1) If a legal system $S_1$ can validate a norm in another legal system $S_2$, then $S_1$ dominates $S_2$.

There are two forms of domination: inferring the validity of the norms of one system from another system and establishing validity by system-transgressing criteria of validity. This leads to the following relations:

(DO2) If a system $S_1$ completely dominates a system $S_2$ through inferences of validity, then $S_2$ forms part of $S_1$.

(DO3) If a system $S_1$ completely dominates a system $S_2$ by system-transgressing criteria of validity, then $S_2$ is a subsystem of $S_1$ but not part of it.

(SUP) If a system $S_1$ can invalidate any norm whatever in another legal system $S_2$, then S1 is superior to $S_2$.

Superiority does not imply dominance; it refers solely to the invalidation of norms. By contrast, dominance implies superiority as far as it goes and with respect to definitively valid norms. On the other hand, this implication does not hold with regard to legal principles, since the validation of legal principles does not invalidate conflicting norms.

### 11.3.3 Autonomy of a Legal System

DFAS A legal system is autonomous if it can determine its own content.

Autonomy of a legal system means, accordingly, that its organs can determine the content of the system. It is taken for granted that the legal system in question is a normative system, that is, that it is at least claimed that its norms ought to be applied and followed. Without such normative content, one could not speak of autonomy.

In so far as a normative system is not dominated by another system, it is autonomous. The autonomy of a system implies that the definitive validity of a norm in this system does not depend on the criteria of validity of a different system. However, autonomy does not exclude the possibility that one system is influenced by another system. Legal systems can and will make normative demands against each other and, hence, one system can and, to the extent that these requirements are accepted by the addressed system, will influence another system.

What has been called 'A-systems' are autonomous legal systems. They are at least autonomous subsystems of a legal system, not dominated subsystems. That is, their content is not determined directly by other legal systems.

> For example, in so far as competing requirements are imposed on the law-applying organs, the application of state laws results from an autonomous judgement of the law-applying organ that the law in question ought to be applied.

Hence, A-systems are autonomous. Autonomy, on the other hand, does not imply independence. Those norms in the system that are actually to be applied and followed by the organs of the system must reflect the fact that its organs are bound to apply the norms of the legal system. Therefore, these norms must have an impact on their decisions, constituting normative arguments to be balanced against competing requirements

### 11.3.4 A-Systems and the Concept of Law

Can one define the concept of law by reference to the A-system in the sense outlined above? Such a definition might well suggest that legal norms are those that law applying-organs ought to apply and follow in the course of taking their legal decisions. This definition states the reverse relation to the one characterising the normative conception of law. A normative conception of law requires that legal norms be applied and followed at least by the law-applying organs. By contrast, the conception of law as an A-system assumes that if a norm ought to be applied and followed by the law applying-organs in their legal reasoning, it counts as a legally valid norm.

Such a definition of law is faced with various objections, however. Its adequacy is cast into doubt with respect to non-positive moral norms, but also with respect to the application of norms of alien legal systems and with respect to standards of logic or practical rationality. It seems that not all the norms that law-applying organs have to apply within their legal decisions qualify as legal norms.

However, these objections can be met. With respect to moral norms, the problem is not well formulated, for, according to the conception of law as an A-system, a law-applying organ who believes that a norm ought to be applied in his legal reasoning will not regard this norm as purely moral but also as a legal norm. The problem that his view might not be objectively valid can be overcome, for as a legal organ he has the competence to make legal statements based on his normative judgements.[16]

With regard to the issue that a system may authorise or demand the application of norms of alien legal systems, the norm that is directly applied is this authorisation or requirement. The application of an alien norm complies with this norm. This makes it possible to draw a distinction between the application of norms of one's own system and those of other systems, defining more precisely what application of a norm means with regard to an A-system. Norms of such a system are those related to the balancing of legal principles. These norms are the legal principles balanced against each other, requirements of rationality applied in this balancing, and the resulting definitive legal norms. Norms of an alien legal system do not figure among these norms. Therefore, one can exclude them from an A-system for systematic reasons, and not simply by stipulation.

With respect to standards of rationality, logic or mathematics, first of all, the same holds as with alien norms. They belong to an A-system only if they figure as norms in procedures of balancing legal principles. Now, some of these formal requirements do indeed apply in balancing procedures. Consequently, the respective requirements have to count as norms of the respective A-system. This is not as odd as it might seem. These norms are not identical with logical or mathematical relations, but are rules formulated on the basis of these relations. The norm that a legal organ ought to follow rules of logic does not, therefore, refer to a norm of another system, which, according to the definition of an A-system, should be regarded as a legal norm. As a norm to be applied by legal organs, it belongs to the A-system in question. The fact that these norms are not identical with standards of rationality, logic, etc., is, in addition, proven by the possibility that a legal system might qualify the obligation to apply such rules.

> For example, the criterion of Pareto-optimality, which is a requirement of rational decision-making, can be found in part in the criterion of necessity as applied within the principle of proportionality. An interference with an individual right must be necessary, that is, it is not allowed that there be an alternative that is less intrusive but equally effective with respect to the objectives underlying the intervention. The criterion of Pareto-optimality applies also to the realisation of these objectives. However, if these objectives are mere policies, a court will not determine whether there is an alternative with equal effect for individual rights but that is better for the realisation of this policy. Bad policy, as such, is not a concern of the courts. Thus, the law itself defines the scope of application of a criterion of rationality.

Accordingly, one may well regard requirements to apply formal standards like those of rationality, logic, or mathematics, as far as they apply to legal organs, as legal norms.

[16] See 9.4.2.1.

In sum, a definition of law corresponding to that of an A-system seems possible, limiting the ascription of legal validity to norms related to the balancing of legal principles. A corresponding definition of the validity of legal norms for A-systems is:

> DF$_{LNA}$ Legal norms are those that law-applying organs ought to apply and follow within their balancing of legal principles and as the results of such balancing.

One should note that this definition aims at identifying the norms that are qualified as valid law from the internal perspective of someone making legal judgments. It is not the case that all law-applying organs will necessarily qualify the same norms as valid law. Although this will in general be true, there may be diverse and contested views as to which norms are valid law. From the perspective of the law-applying organs, the idea of the unity of the legal system, which presents law as a single set of consistent and objectively valid norms, can be no more than a regulative idea that guides the attempt to develop a coherent legal practice.

The objections to this view seem to be founded on a different understanding of law, namely, one as a C-system defined by certain criteria of validity. However, merely taking a different perspective on law does not constitute an objection to a definition of law from the perspective of the requirements to apply the law. It may well be true that the usual understanding of law follows the conception of a C-system. For an analysis of law within the framework of autonomous reasoning, however, the conception of A-systems is of primary interest. Nevertheless, one ought also to note that no definition of law under a particular aspect, such as the application of law, the criteria of legal validity or the existing legal practice, can claim to give a comprehensive account of the complex phenomen of law.

# 12

# *Conclusion*

THE OBJECTIVE OF this study is an analysis of autonomous reasoning and its consequences for law and morality. The analysis is founded on the idea of autonomy as the balancing of competing normative arguments, which requires a peculiar conception of normative arguments as reiterated requirements for validity along with the distinction between normative arguments, judgements and statements. Normative arguments figure as reasons for balancing precisely in the situation of conflict with other arguments. Normative judgements and statements present the results of such a balancing, the former being judgements that every autonomous agent has the right to make, the latter being statements of objectively valid and hence binding norms that no autonomous agent can determine solely by means of his own judgement.

These elements determine the structure of autonomous reasoning, and its relation to moral realism, cognitivism and the conception of normative objectivity. They have a crucial role also in the theory of rights, of legal systems, of legal validity and of legal interpretation.

(1) Autonomy as self-legislation seems to have a paradoxical structure. How can individuals be bound by norms that are valid only because they recognise these norms as valid? In addition, autonomy seems to be incompatible with authority, in particular, the authority of law. If the validity of norms depends on their recognition by autonomous agents, how is an authoritative determination possible? The solution to these problems suggested here is that of normative justification by means of autonomous reasoning. Autonomous reasoning begins with agents making interest-based claims that constitute normative arguments, and forming normative judgements as to which norm ought to be accepted as definitively valid with respect to these claims. Autonomy is defined as the balancing of conflicting normative arguments (autonomy thesis). Such a balancing establishes a norm as valid; it is not determined, however, by pre-established criteria. Accordingly, it is at the same time free but also lays claim to the normative validity of the established norm and, therefore, exercises autonomy in the sense of self-legislation.

(2) The semantic foundation of this conception is the distinction between normative arguments, judgements and statements, with different logical structures and following different logical rules (fragmentation thesis). Normative arguments are claims that autonomous agents put forward. Being used as arguments in a balancing, they do not have the structure of propositions, although one can

describe their definitive content by means of normative propositions, making explicit the character of validity of a normative argument. Normative judgements result from the balancing of normative arguments. They are individual judgements of autonomous agents, claiming definitive validity in a procedural sense, after all relevant arguments have been considered. Normative statements claim to state objectively valid and hence binding norms. They are possible only after all the problems posed by conflicts of arguments and divergence of judgements have been resolved.

(3) The central analytical instrument is the conception of normative arguments, which conceives them as reiterated requirements for validity (reiteration thesis), and distinguishes them from normative propositions, judgements and statements (non-propositionality thesis). Since normative arguments include claims of the validity of a certain norm, they are capable of figuring as arguments for a normative judgement based on balancing exactly in the situation of conflict with other arguments and, thus, make it possible for one to introduce normative claims without realist or cognitivist presuppositions. Five central arguments support the reiteration thesis: the structure of balancing, the structure of normativity, the structure of interest-based arguments, the structure of autonomy and the possibility to present a complete model for the justification of norms, thus avoiding the trilemma of deductive justification.

(4) A crucial feature of the resulting conception of normative argumentation is that of an oscillating process in which different types of validity are attributed to norms that are included in normative arguments, individual normative judgements and statements of definitive validity. The ultimate aim is to establish norms as definitively valid and hence binding, which requires that one proceed from claims of a weaker type of validity to claims of stronger types of validity, a process which, however, is reversible, for any result may again be challenged by still other normative arguments and judgements (reflexivity thesis).

(5) A central critical thesis is that one cannot begin an argument with cognitive or realist claims on normative issues. If norms existed independently of individual judgements on their validity or if such judgements were cognitively determined, then no room would be left for autonomy in the sense of self-legislation. Accordingly, morality cannot be derived from nature, rationality or reason, but consists in applying requirements of rational justification to normative claims made by autonomous agents. This is not meant to preclude the possibility that cognitivist or realist theses are correct in some respects. However, without clearly distinguishing between normative arguments, judgements and statements, a discussion of cognitivism and moral realism makes little sense.

(6) The core of normative justification is the balancing of conflicting normative arguments, based on the claims and normative judgements of autonomous agents. The result of the balancing is bound by these arguments though not completely determined by deductively applicable criteria. Therefore, balancing includes an autonomous decision or judgment (autonomous balancing). The resulting structure of the justification of norms or normative decisions reveals the structure of

autonomous reasoning, which begins with normative arguments and ends with normative judgments or statements. Two issues of the justification of norms must be distinguished. The first problem is how, beginning with normative claims and arguments, one arrives at normative judgments. This concerns the structure of the balancing of normative arguments yielding autonomous judgments. The second problem is how to get from autonomous judgments to statements of the objective validity of norms, that is, to norms that must or can be regarded as binding for norm addressees. To these procedures, various criteria of correct balancing apply. These criteria follow from requirements of formal rationality that any reasonable agent must accept whatever his normative attitudes may be. Thus, criteria of rationality are applied within a procedure of argumentation that does not presuppose cognitive claims as to the validity of substantive norms (thesis of non-cognitive rationalism).

(7) Autonomous reasoning can establish the objective validity of norms in the sense that every reasonable agent must, under certain conditions, accept the idea that statements of the validity and bindingness of norms are correct and, thus, objectively valid (objectivity thesis). This requires a reasonable convergence of autonomous agents, based on intersubjective reflection of their diverse normative views, and the need to have a commonly binding norm. Objective validity of norms therefore presupposes some form of empirical support for the validity of the respective normative claims, which, however, does not turn normative statements of objective validity into an empirical issue. On the other hand, objectivity as truth or as correspondence with reality seem to be inappropriate for reasoning by means of the balancing of normative arguments, for balancing is not about discovering a normative reality but about constructing it.

The model of autonomous reasoning leads to specific theses regarding the structure of law and morality.

(8) A theory of law or morality based on the idea of autonomous reasoning is particularly close to the idea of individual rights. Normative claims of autonomous agents are presented in terms of claims respecting individual rights, owing to the fact that such claims are based on individual interests. The rights terminology makes explicit this justificatory basis. This is confronted, however, by the view that norms, not rights, are the focus of normative reasoning, rendering rights redundant. By contrast, the conception of autonomous reasoning implies that the primary normative arguments will be presented in terms of rights or, more precisely, rights-claims. In addition, the analysis of the structure of rights shows that a specific rights-discourse exists that cannot be reduced to arguments about ordinary norms. Rights in this specific sense concern claims respecting the realisation and protection of normative positions. Although this second-order structure of rights may be presented just as well in terms of obligations or responsibilities regarding the realisation or protection of normative positions, it becomes clearer in terms of rights.

(9) Certain autonomy rights, specific human rights protecting interests of human beings and fundamental rights as conditions of the legitimacy of the

authority of law or legal organs must be recognised. Autonomy rights include, in the first place, the normative power or competence to put forward interest-based claims, which constitute normative arguments and create argumentative obligations of autonomous agents. Autonomy rights follow, as necessary conditions of normative justification, directly from the structure of autonomous reasoning. In addition, specific human rights can be established on the basis of the claims to protect fundamental interests or goods of human beings. Human rights principles may be principles to be balanced with other arguments or exclusionary principles demanding that some interest, good or right ought not to be subject to balancing. Moreover, fundamental rights are founded as necessary conditions of the legitimacy of legal or political systems. Fundamental rights shift the focus from a general balancing to one concerning the limits of what may legitimately be demanded from individual autonomous agents.

(10) In a theory of law based on the idea of autonomy, legal validity is to be understood as normative validity in an absolute, not merely system-relative sense. Authority of law is established by means of formal principles, which demand that authoritative decisions be binding without regard to their substantive correctness. Different types of authority can be distinguished. However, legal systems based on principles will not be closed in the sense that for conceptual reasons they admit only of empirical or formal criteria of validity. Moral principles can be excluded from application in legal judgments only by a legal system itself – if, indeed, such an exclusion is legitimate.

(11) With regard to legal methodology, the model of autonomous reasoning implies that the focus shifts from the interpretation of law as a determination of the existing content of the law to the balancing of legal principles. Thus, the creative function of judicial decisions is emphasised but also limited by criteria of correct balancing. A further consequence is that the application of law must deal not only with the interpretation of the law, but also with competing interpretive conceptions of legal organs and the demarcation of interpretive competences.

(12) Autonomy of legal systems is explained in accordance with the general concept of autonomy, that is, taking a decision bound but not determined by normative arguments. Thus, the interpretation of the autonomy of law as separating it from morality is rejected. With respect to the relations between competing normative systems, conflicts between them can be analysed in terms of problems of balancing where several systems make incompatible claims in the treatment of particular cases. This conception applies to conflicts within one legal system as well as to conflicts between different legal systems.

The analysis of autonomous reasoning presented here remains incomplete. Many issues require further investigation. In particular, the semantic and logical foundations of this account need elaboration in various respects, as well as the application of this account to law and morality. Thus, rather than a conclusive theory, the present analysis offers a starting point for further investigation. Its aim is to present a coherent conception of autonomous reasoning, not a refutation of competing philosophical accounts. Although some of these are rejected as being incompatible with the account of autonomy as self-legislation defended here, such as, for example, Kantian conceptions of autonomy, moral realism or cognitivism, they are not discussed and critised from the standpoint of the plausibility of their own premises. However, it is argued that discussion of issues like moral realism or cognitivism makes little sense without a clear understanding of the notion of autonomy, and whoever understands oneself as autonomous will accept such accounts only within the framework of autonomous reasoning.

# Appendix

## *Symbols, Key Notions and Rules of Argumentation*

### Logical Symbols

'O': the deontic operator 'ought to'

'$VAL_{DEF}$': a predicate '. . . is definitively valid'

'$VAL_{ARG}$': a predicate: '. . . is valid as a normative argument'

'N': a term denoting a particular norm (a norm individual)

'n': a term denoting a variable for norms

'|': assertion-sign, indicating that the following sentence is used to make a statement or an assertion

'. . .': argument-sign, indicating that the norm presents a normative argument, which the speaker is ready to support by normative arguments of ever-higher order

'¬': negation 'not . . .'

'→': conditional 'if . . ., then . . .'

'↔': biconditional 'if and only if . . ., then . . .'

'&': conjunction '. . . and . . .'

'(. . .). . .': universal quantifier 'for all . . . , . . .'

'->': pragmatic inference, defining argumentative steps that are required and that must be accepted as correct

### Key Notions

*Autonomy*

$DF_{A}$ 'Autonomy' means establishing the definitive validity of norms by means of the normative judgments of the norm-addressees themselves.

$DF_{AI}$ 'Individual autonomy' means establishing the definitive validity of a norm by one's own individual normative judgment.

$DF_{AP}$ 'Political autonomy' means establishing norms to be definitively valid and binding by the normative judgments of the norm-addressees themselves.

$DF_{AA}$ An agent has autonomy if he is in a position to take a normative decision that is bound by normative arguments.

$DF_{AB}$ Autonomy exists if a normative decision is to be taken by means of the balancing of normative arguments.

Autonomous agent: one who is able to make normative judgments based on the balancing of normative arguments according to formal requirements of rationality.

### *Validity*

Normative validity: that a norm ought actually to be applied and followed.

Formal or empirical validity: that certain criteria for membership in a system of norms are met.

Definitive (procedural-definitive) validity: that a norm is the result of a balancing of all relevant arguments.

Objective (substantive-definitive) validity: that any reasonable agent must regard this norm as binding for the norm addressees (bindingness).

### *Types of Normative Speech Act*

(1) Normative judgments or direct normative statements: $\vdash N$

(2) Statements of definitive validity of a norm: $\vdash VAL_{DEF}\ N$

(3) Normative arguments: . . . $O\ VAL_{DEF}\ N$

(4) Normative statements of the validity as an argument: $\vdash VAL_{ARG}\ N$

### *Normative Arguments*

$DF_{NA}$: A normative argument consists of a requirement for validity $O\ VAL\ N_i$ (i being a number 0, 1, . . . which indicates the level of N in a set of requirements for validity of ever higher orders), backed by an infinite set of requirements for validity of higher orders ultimately referring to the same norm $N_i$.

Elementary normative arguments: $VAL_{ARG}N_i$

Relational normative arguments: $VAL_{ARG}(N_i,R_k)$

*Normative Judgements*

Present the direct use of a norm-sentence.

$DF_{AJ}$: Autonomous judgements are normative judgements that result from the balancing of normative arguments.

*Normative Statements*

Are either direct normative statements (normative judgements) or explicit statements of validity of a norm.

Individual statements of definitive validity: $VAL_{DEF(I,A)}N$

Intersubjectively reflected statements of validity: $VAL_{DEF(I,J,A)}N$

Statements of procedural definitive validity: $VAL_{DEF\text{-}PROC}N$

Statements of substantive definitive validity: $VAL_{DEF\text{-}SUBS}N$

*Bindingness (Substantive Definitive Validity)*

$DF_{BIND}$ A norm is binding on an individual norm addressee if it is valid independently of the individual's acceptance of its validity.

*Reasonable Convergence*

$DF_{RC}$ A norm is supported by reasonable convergence if an increasing majority of the agents concerned accept the norm as valid on the basis of a process of intersubjective reflection.

*Balancing, Characteristics*

(1) Openness of the result, that is, there are no criteria sufficient to determine the result of the balancing.
(2) Pro tanto conclusiveness of the normative arguments to be balanced, that is, a normative argument determines the result if there is no counter-argument.
(3) Validity of the competing normative arguments in a situation of conflict, that is, conflicting arguments are valid at the same time and remain arguments demanding a particular result in the case of conflict.
(4) Foundation of a claim of correctness as to the result of the balancing.

*Autonomous Balancing, Characteristics*

(1) The result of the balancing cannot be inferred from already existing norms (openness of balancing), but must be established by autonomous judgement.

(2) Normative arguments are the result of claims that autonomous agents make based on their interests.
(3) Normative arguments include requirements for validity, that is, they demand that a particular norm be accepted as definitively valid.
(4) The structure of requirements for validity implies that normative judgements include a claim to the normative necessity of the established result.

*Basic Justificatory Relation for Autonomous Judgements*

(BJ) If a norm N represents a valid normative argument for a concrete normative consequence R in a particular case C and there is no conflicting norm $N_i$ applicable to this case or all conflicting norms are excluded or overridden in this case, then the norm N', with C as condition and R as normative consequence, is in this case definitively valid.

(BJ.1) If a norm N is valid as an argument for a particular norm N' and there is no norm that is incompatible with it, then N' is definitively valid.

(BJ.2) If a norm N is valid as an argument for a particular norm N' and all the norms $N_i$ that are incompatible with N' are excluded, then N' is definitively valid.

(BJ.3) If a norm N is valid as an argument for a particular norm N' and N receives priority in case of N' over each norm $N_i$ that is incompatible with N in the case of N', then N' is definitively valid.

*Thesis of the Necessary Claim to Normative Necessity*

(NN) Whichever norm, stemming from a balancing of competing normative arguments, the agent states as definitively valid, he must claim that the validity of this norm is required by the stronger argument.

*Factors of Balancing*

$\Delta FM(P_i,N)$: degree of fulfilment of $P_i$ with regard to N

$WR(P_i,P_j)$: the relative weight of $P_i$ against $P_j$

$WR(P_i,P_j,C,N)$: the relative weight of $P_i$ against $P_j$ with regard to N in circumstances C

*Optimality*

$DF_{OPT}$: Optimal results of the balancing of principles are those with the greatest overall value of fulfilment regarding the particular case.

*Autonomy Rights*

Rights regarding the procedures of justifying norms (a priori autonomy rights):

(i) the right to form interest-based claims and normative arguments based on them;
(ii) the right to form normative judgements based on the individual balancing of normative arguments of the agent himself;
(iii) the right to form normative judgements based on intersubjective reflection of competing normative judgements, taking into account the normative judgements of other agents as well, in order to determine which norm should be recognised as collectively binding.

Right to personal autonomy: autonomy rights include the right to live according to one's own interests, life plan or normative convictions.

*Human Rights*

(i) A priori autonomy rights;
(ii) Specific human rights principles to be balanced and exclusionary human rights principles demanding that certain interests or normative positions are not made the object of a balancing;
(iii) Definitive human rights.

*Fundamental Rights:*

(i) Constitutionalised human rights;
(ii) Rights whose legal recognition is a necessary condition of the legitimacy of public authority.

*Legal Validity*

Theses:

(1) The concept of legal validity must be normative in the sense that the legal validity of a norm implies the requirement to apply and follow this norm.
(2) Legal authority must be constructed by means of formal principles.
(3) One cannot exclude the possibility that a legal system includes principles owing to their moral correctness.
(4) Definitively valid legal norms can be identified formally or empirically, as the result of legal procedures of the balancing of normative arguments, but they are established by normative judgements.

*Legal System*

$DF_{LS}$ A legal system is a set of norms that meet the criteria of validity of the system in question or are established as valid on the basis of norms identified by these criteria.

$DF_{LV}$ A norm is legally valid according to a legal system $S_i$ if and only if it meets at least one of the criteria of validity of the system $S_i$.

$DF_{LNA}$ Legal norms are those that law-applying organs ought to apply and follow in their balancing of legal principles and as the results of such balancing.

*Relations between Normative Systems*

(IND1) A legal system $S_1$ is independent of another system $S_2$ if, and in so far as, $S_2$ has no impact on the content of $S_1$.

(IND2) The norms belonging to an independent legal system are defined exclusively by the criteria of this system.

(IND3) A legal system cannot validate or invalidate norms of another legal system that is independent of it.

(DO1) If a legal system $S_1$ can validate a norm in another legal system $S_2$, then $S_1$ dominates $S_2$.

(DO2) If a system $S_1$ completely dominates a system $S_2$ by inferences of validity, then $S_2$ forms part of $S_1$.

(DO3) If a system $S_1$ completely dominates a system $S_2$ by system-transgressing criteria of validity, then $S_2$ is a subsystem but not part of $S_1$.

(SUP) If a system $S_1$ can invalidate any norm in another legal system $S_2$, then $S_1$ is superior to $S_2$.

*Autonomy of a Legal System*

$DF_{AS}$ A legal system is autonomous if it can determine its own content.

## Rules of Argumentation

*General Rules*

(A1) Whoever makes a normative claim must be ready to present a conclusive argument on the question why it is justified making this claim.

(A2) If an autonomous agent has offered a structurally valid normative argument, one who wishes to object to the argument must offer a structurally valid counter-argument.

(A3) The result of the argumentation ought not to depend on the chosen procedure or presentation of arguments.

(A4) Individual autonomy implies that any agent has a right to introduce into the discourse normative arguments as well as those normative judgements that stem from the balancing of such arguments.

(A5) If an autonomous agent claims that a particular norm be accepted as valid and this claim is not defective in formal respects, then other agents must take this claim into account within their own reasoning and must treat it qua normative argument as valid.

(A6) A normative argument for the definitive validity of a norm N must hold that if there should be no counter-argument against it, one must accept that N is definitively valid.

(A7) A normative argument for the definitive validity of a norm N must be realised, with regard to competing arguments, to as great an extent as possible.

(A8) A normative argument must claim that it is possible in theory, without regard to empirical features of the agents concerned, that each reasonable agent accept it as a valid argument.

(A9) An autonomous agent putting forward a normative argument based on an individual interest must acknowledge the normative relevance of individual interests to the argument in general.

(A10) Normative arguments of autonomous agents must be based on coherent conceptions of interests or life plans.

(A11) Autonomous agents may form normative judgements based on their individual balancing of the relevant arguments and claim that other agents ought to accept this judgement.

(A12) Normative judgements of autonomous agents constitute normative arguments in the course of reasoning of other agents with respect to the bindingness of norms.

(A13) Intersubjectively reflected normative judgements based on individual balancing of the relevant arguments, including those following from the normative judgements of autonomous agents, justify claims as to which norm ought to be accepted as definitively valid and hence be applied and followed.

(A14) An autonomous agent cannot determine by his individual normative judgement alone which norms are collectively binding.

(A15) A norm may be claimed to be binding if it is supported by reasonable convergence of autonomous agents and, in addition, a commonly binding norm is needed.

*Inference Rules for Normative Arguments*

(IA1) If $N_i$ is valid as a normative argument and $N_i$ is logically equivalent to $N_j$, then $N_j$ is valid as a normative argument.

$$VAL_{ARG}N_i \,\&\, (N_i = N_j) \text{->} VAL_{ARG}N_j$$

(IA2) If $N_1$ is valid as a normative argument for $R_1$ and the fulfilment of $R_2$ promotes the fulfilment of $R_2$, then $N_1$ is valid as a normative argument for $R_2$.

$$VAL_{ARG}(N_1,R_1) \,\&\, PROM(R_2,R_1) \text{->} VAL_{ARG}(N_1,R_2)$$

(IA3) If $N_1$ constitutes a valid argument and a particular result R promotes the fulfilment of $N_1$, then $N_1$ is a valid argument for R.

$$VAL_{ARG}(N_1) \,\&\, PROM(R,N_1) \text{->} VAL_{ARG}(N_1,R)$$

(IA4) A statement of priority of one argument over another with respect to a particular norm implies a normative judgement that this norm is definitively valid.

$$\mid PRIOR(ARG_{Ni}/ARG_y, N_i) \text{->} \mid O\ VAL_{DEF}N_i$$

(IA5) Within an ideal procedure of normative argument, a normative judgement of the definitive validity of a particular norm implies a normative statement of its definitive validity.

$$\mid O\ VAL_{DEF}N_i \text{->} \mid VAL_{DEF}N_i$$

(IA6) A statement of a definitive requirement of the definitive validity of a norm implies a statement that this norm is definitively valid.

$$\mid VAL_{DEF}\ O\ VAL_{DEF}N_i \text{->} \mid VAL_{DEF}N_i$$

(IA7) A statement that a norm is definitively valid implies a statement of a definitive requirement of the definitive validity of a norm.

$$\mid VAL_{DEF}\ N_i \text{->} \mid VAL_{DEF}\ O\ VAL_{DEF}\ N_i$$

(IA8) A relative normative statement $\mid VAL_{DEF\text{-}PROC}N_i$, stating and accepting the result of a particular justificatory procedure PROC, implies normative judgements $\mid OVAL_{DEF}N_i$ and $\mid N_i$.

$$\mid VAL_{DEF\text{-}PROC}N_i \text{->} \mid OVAL_{DEF}N_i$$

$$\mid VAL_{DEF\text{-}PROC}N_i \text{->} \mid N_i$$

*Requirements of Correct Balancing*

(B1) Solutions that restrict a principle unnecessarily, without any gain for a conflicting principle, are inadmissible.

(B2) The indifference curves must be negatively sloped, that is falling, running from northwest to southeast. They must not be horizontal or vertical.

(B3) The priority among conflicting principles $P_1$, $P_2$ regarding a possible result N in circumstances C is a function of the difference of fulfilment (ΔFM) that the choice of N or ¬N makes to the fulfilment of $P_1$ and $P_2$, and the relative weight (WR) of $P_1$ against $P_2$ in circumstances C regarding N.

(B4) The greater the degree of non-fulfilment of a principle to be justified, the greater the relative weight of a conflicting principle in the particular case must be in order to justify the degree of non-fulfilment of the first principle.

(B5) The value of fulfilment of a principle is positively correlated to the degree of its fulfilment and its relative weight.

(B6) The value of fulfilment of a particular balancing result N is positively correlated to the values of fulfilment of the respective principles in conflict.

(B7) The result of the balancing of principles must present an optimal solution to the particular case.

(B7') One must choose, as a result of the balancing of normative arguments, a solution with the highest value of fulfilment that can be achieved by the particular decision.

(B7") One must give, as result of the balancing of normative arguments, priority to that argument with greater weight (importance) in the concrete case.

(B8) In a conflict of $P_1$ and $P_2$ concerning case C and consequence R, priority must be given to the principle the fulfilment of which achieves the higher value of fulfilment (or that is of greater weight/importance) in the circumstances of case C.

(B9) If $P_1$ receives priority over $P_2$ in case $C_1$ and in case $C_2$ the value of fulfilment of $P_1$ is greater than in $C_1$, then, *ceteris paribus*, $P_1$ receives priority over $P_2$ in $C_2$.

(B10) If $P_1$ receives priority over $P_2$ in case $C_1$ and in case $C_2$ the degree of fulfilment of $P_2$ is smaller than in $C_1$, then, *ceteris paribus*, $P_1$ receives priority over $P_2$ in $C_2$.

(B11) If $P_1$ receives priority over $P_2$ in case $C_1$ and in case $C_2$ the abstract weight of $P_1$ is greater than in $C_1$, then, *ceteris paribus*, $P_1$ receives priority over $P_2$ in $C_2$.

(B12) If $P_1$ and $P_2$ are of equal relative weight in case $C_1$ and in case $C_2$ the abstract weight of $P_1$ is greater or the degree of fulfilment of $P_2$ is smaller than in $C_1$, then, *ceteris paribus*, $P_1$ receives priority over $P_2$ in $C_2$.

*Claims to Correctness of Normative Judgements*

(C1) One who makes a normative judgement based on the balancing of normative arguments must claim the formal correctness of his judgement in accordance with requirements of rationality and its normative correctness in the sense that the stated norm ought to be accepted as definitively valid.

(C2) Normative judgements must claim to be based on a correct balancing.

(C3) The balancing must claim to present a coherent solution to the conflict of the normative arguments it encounters.

(C4) Normative judgements must be guided by the same arguments, that is, one must apply a normative argument to all cases to which it is applicable.

(C5) A normative judgement must follow a normative argument as long as there is no sufficient reason for a contrary judgement.

(C6) One who makes an autonomous judgement must recognise the equal right of other autonomous agents to make such judgements.

(C7) Autonomous judgements must reflect the consent of autonomous agents as the aim of discourse.

(C8) Autonomous judgements can only propose norms as definitively valid that might find the consent of other autonomous agents.

(C9) Normative judgements as to definitively valid norms can only be established on the basis of intersubjective reflection, considering also the normative views of other autonomous agents in order to determine which norm ought to be accepted as collectively binding.

*Rules regarding Legal Validity*

(VL1) If a norm N is valid in a legal system L, then also valid in this system is a requirement to apply N.

$$VAL_{L}N \rightarrow VAL_{L}\ O\ APPL\ N$$

(VL2) If a norm N is definitively valid in the legal system L, then, according to this system, there is a valid normative argument in L for the absolute, non-system-relative validity of the norm N.

$$|VAL_{LDEF}N \rightarrow |VAL_{LARG}\ VAL_{DEF}\ N$$

(VL3) The claim of the legal system L for the absolute, non-system-relative validity of its norms constitutes normative arguments that these norms be recognised as definitively valid.

$$|VAL_{LARG}\ VAL_{DEF}\ N \rightarrow |VAL_{ARG}\ VAL_{DEF}\ N$$

# *Bibliography*


Aarnio, A (1987) *The Rational as the Reasonable* (Dordrecht, Kluwer)
——(1990) 'Taking Rules Seriously' 42 *ARSP-Beiheft* 180
Afonso da Silva, V (2003) *Grundrechte und gesetzgeberische Spielräume* (Baden-Baden, Nomos)
Albert, H (1980) *Traktat über kritische Vernunft*, 4th edn (Tübingen, Mohr)
Alchourrón, C E and Bulygin, E (1971) *Normative Systems* (Vienna, Springer)
Alexy, R (1979) 'Zum Begriff des Rechtsprinzips' 1 *Rechtstheorie-Beiheft* 59
——(1980) 'Die logische Analyse juristischer Entscheidungen' 14 *ARSP-Beiheft* 181
——(1987) 'Rechtssystem und praktische Vernunft' 18 *Rechtstheorie* 405
——(1989a) *Theory of Legal Argumentation* (Oxford, Oxford University Press) (orig *Theorie der juristischen Argumentation* (Frankfurt, Suhrkamp, 1978)
——(1989b) 'Probleme der Diskurstheorie' 43 *Zeitschrift für philosophische Forschung* 81
——(1991) *Theorie der juristischen Argumentation*, 2nd edn (with a new postscript) (Frankfurt, Suhrkamp)
——(1993) *Mauerschützen* (Hamburg, Meiner)
——(1995) 'Diskurstheorie und Menschenrechte' in *Recht, Vernunft, Diskurs* (Frankfurt, Suhrkamp) 127–64
——(1997) 'Grundrechte im demokratischen Verfassungsstaat' in *Justice, Morality and Society, A Tribute to Aleksander Peczenik* (Dordrecht, Kluwer) 27–42
——(1998a) 'Die Institutionalisierung der Menschenrechte im demokratischen Verfassungsstaat' in S Gosepath and G Lohmann (eds), *Philosophie der Menschenrechte* (Frankfurt, Suhrkamp) 244–64
——(1998b), 'Law and Correctness' 51 *Current Legal Problems* 205
——(1999) 'The Institutionalisation of Reason' in L J Wintgens (ed), *The Law in Philosophical Perspectives* (Dordrecht, Kluwer) 23–45
——(2000) 'On the Structure of Legal Principles' 13 *Ratio Juris* 294
——(2002a) *A Theory of Constitutional Rights* (Oxford/New York, Oxford University Press) (orig *Theorie der Grundrechte* (Baden-Baden, Nomos, 1985)
——(2002b) *The Argument from Injustice, A Reply to Legal Positivism* (Oxford, Clarendon Press) (orig *Begriff und Geltung des Rechts* (Freiburg/München, Alber)
——(2003) 'On Balancing and Subsumption: A Structural Comparison' 16 *Ratio Juris* 433
——(2007a) 'An Answer to Joseph Raz' in G Pavlakos (ed), *Law, Rights and Discourse: The Legal Philosophy of Robert Alexy* (Oxford/Portland, Hart) 37–55
——(2007b) 'Thirteen Replies' in G Pavlakos (ed), *Law, Rights and Discourse: The Legal Philosophy of Robert Alexy* (Oxford/Portland, Hart) 333–66
——(2009) 'Ideales Sollen' in L Clérico and J Sieckmann (eds), *Grundrechte, Prinzipien, Argumentation* (Baden-Baden, Nomos) 21–38
——(2010) 'The Dual Nature of Law' 23 *Ratio Juris* 167
Apel, K-O (1973) *Transformation der Philosophie*, vol 2 (Frankfurt, Suhrkamp)
Atienza, M (2006) *El Derecho como argumentación. Concepciones de la argumentación* (Barcelona, Editorial Ariel)
Atienza, M and Ruiz Manero J (1998) *A Theory of Legal Sentences* (Dordrecht/Boston/London, Kluwer)

Atria, F (2001) *On Law and Legal Reasoning* (Oxford/Portland, Hart)
Ávila, H B (2006) *Theorie der Rechtsprinzipien* (Berlin, Duncker & Humblot)
Bäcker, C (2008) *Begründen und Entscheiden. Kritik und Rekonstruktion der Alexyschen Diskurstheorie des Rechts* (Baden-Baden, Nomos)
Barry, B (1990) *Political Argument*, 2nd edn (New York, Harvester/Wheatsheaf)
Baumann, P (2001) *Die Autonomie der Person* (Paderborn, Mentis)
Bayon, J C (1991) *La normatividad del derecho* (Madrid, Centro de Estudios Constitucionales)
Beck, L W (1960) *A Commentary on Kant's Critique of Practical Reason* (Chicago/London, Chicago University Press)
Bernal Pulido, C (2003) *El principio de la proporcionalidad y los derechos fundamentales* (Madrid, Centro de Estudios Políticos y Constitucionales)
—— (2004) 'The Structure and the Limits of Balancing' 97 *ARSP-Beiheft* 79
—— (2006a) 'On Alexy's Weight Formula' in A J Menendez and E O Eriksen (eds), *Arguing Fundamental Rights* (Dordrecht, Springer) 101–10
—— (2006b) 'The Rationality of Balancing' 92 *ARSP* 195
—— (2009) 'Die Fundamentalität der Grundrechte' in L Clérico and J Sieckmann (eds), *Grundrechte, Prinzipien und Argumentation* (Baden-Baden, Nomos) 83–97
Bertea, S (2009) *The Normative Claim of Law* (Oxford/Portland, Hart)
Besson, S (2005) *The Morality of Conflict: Reasonable Disagreement and the Law* (Oxford/Portland, Hart).
Bittner, R (1983) *Moralisches Gebot oder Autonomie?* (Freiburg/München, Alber)
Böckenförde, E-W (1991) *Staat, Verfassung, Demokratie. Studien zur Verfassungstheorie und zum Verfassungsrecht* (Frankfurt, Suhrkamp)
Borowski, M (2006) *Die Glaubens- und Gewissensfreiheit des Grundgesetzes* (Tübingen, Mohr Siebeck)
—— (2007) *Grundrechte als Prinzipien*, 2nd edn (Baden-Baden, Nomos)
Brandom, R B (1994) *Making it Explicit: Reasoning, Representing, and Discursive Commitment* (Cambridge, MA/London, Harvard University Press)
Bratman, M E (2009) 'Intention, Practical Rationality, and Self-Governance' 119 *Ethics* 411
Brink, D (1989) *Moral Realism and the Foundations of Ethics* (Cambridge, Cambridge University Press)
Broome, J (1991) *Weighing Goods* (Oxford/Cambridge, MA, Blackwell)
Brożek, B (2007a) *Rationality and Discourse: Towards a Normative Model of Applying Law* (Warszawa, Oficyna)
—— (2007b) 'The Weight Formula and Argumentation' in G Pavlakos (ed), *Law, Rights and Discourse: The Legal Philosophy of Robert Alexy* (Oxford/Portland, Hart) 319–30
Brugger, W (1999) *Liberalismus, Pluralismus, Kommunitarismus* (Baden-Baden, Nomos)
Buchwald, D (1990) *Der Begriff der rationalen juristischen Begründung* (Baden-Baden, Nomos)
Christensen, R and Fischer-Lescano A (2007) *Das Ganze des Rechts. Vom hierarchischen zum reflexiven Verständnis deutscher und europäischer Grundrechte* (Berlin, Duncker & Humblot)
Clérico, L (2001) *Die Struktur der Verhältnismäßigkeit* (Baden-Baden, Nomos)
Coleman, J L (1982) 'Negative and Positive Positivism' 11 *Journal of Legal Studies* 139
—— (2009) 'Beyond Inclusive Legal Positivism' 22 *Ratio Juris* 359
Corradetti, C (2009) *Relativism and Human Rights: A Theory of Pluralistic Universalism* (Springer, Dordrecht)
Darwall, S (2006) *The Second-Person Standpoint: Morality, Respect and Accountability* (Cambridge, MA/London, Harvard University Press)

Dreier, R (1991) *Recht-Staat-Vernunft* (Frankfurt, Suhrkamp)
Dummett, M (1981) *Frege. Philosophy of Language* (London, Duckworth)
Dworkin, R (1978) *Taking Rights Seriously*, 2nd edn (Cambridge, MA, Harvard University Press)
—— (1985) *A Matter of Principle* (Oxford, Clarendon Press)
—— (1986) *Law's Empire* (London, Fontana Press)
—— (2006) *Justice in Robes* (Cambridge, MA/London, Harvard University Press)
Fox-Decent, E and Criddle E J (2009) 'The Fiduciary Constitution of Human Rights' 15 *Legal Theory* 301
Frege, G (1879) *Begriffsschrift. Eine der arithmetischen nachgebildete Formelsprache des reinen Denkens* (Halle, Verlag von Louis Nebert) (transl in T W Bynum (ed), *G. Frege, Conceptual Notation and Related Articles* (Oxford ,1972))
—— (1891) 'Funktion und Begriff' in *Funktion, Begriff und Bedeutung* (G Patzig (ed), Göttingen, Vandenhoeck) (transl in P Geach and M Black (eds), *Translations from the Philosophical Writings of Gottlob Frege* (Oxford, 1952) 21–41)
Gesang, B (2000) *Kritik des Partikularismus* (Paderborn, Mentis)
Gosepath, S and Lohmann G (eds) (1998) *Philosophie der Menschenrechte* (Frankfurt, Suhrkamp)
Greenberg, M (2004) 'How Facts Make Law' 10 *Legal Theory* 157
Günther, K (1988) *Der Sinn für Angemessenheit* (Frankfurt, Suhrkamp)
Habermas, J (1991) *Erläuterungen zur Diskursethik* (Frankfurt, Suhrkamp)
—— (1996) *Between Facts and Norms* (Harvard, MA, MIT Press) (orig *Faktizität und Geltung*, 4th edn (Frankfurt, Suhrkamp, 1994))
—— (1998) *The Inclusion of the Other* (Harvard, MA, MIT Press) (orig *Die Einbeziehung des Anderen* (Frankfurt, Suhrkamp, 1996))
Hage, J (1996) 'A Theory of Legal Reasoning and a Logic to Match' 4 *Artificial Intelligence and Law* 199 (reprinted in H Prakken and G Sartor (eds), *Logical Models of Legal Argumentation* (Dordrecht/Boston/London, Kluwer, 1997) 43–117)
—— (1997) *Reasoning with Rules: An Essay on Legal Reasoning and Its Underlying Logic* (Dordrecht/Boston/London, Kluwer)
Hansson, S O (2001) *The Structure of Values and Norms* (Cambridge, Cambridge University Press)
Hare, R M (1952) *The Language of Morals* (London/Oxford/New York, Clarendon Press)
—— (1963) *Freedom and Reason* (Oxford, Oxford University Press)
—— (1981) *Moral Thinking* (Oxford, Clarendon Press)
—— (1989) *Essays on Political Morality* (Oxford, Clarendon Press)
Hart, H L A (1958) 'Positivism and the Separation of Law and Morals' 71 *Harvard Law Review* 593
—— (1994) *The Concept of Law* (1961), 2nd edn (Oxford, Clarendon Press)
Heidemann, C (1997) *Die Norm als Tatsache* (Baden-Baden, Nomos)
—— (2005) 'Law's Claim to Correctness' in S Coyle and G Pavlakos (eds), *Jurisprudence or Legal Science* (Oxford/Portland, Hart) 127–46
Höffe, O (1998) 'Transzendentaler Tausch – Eine Legitimationsfigur für Menschenrechte?' in S Gosepath and G Lohmann (eds) *Philosophie der Menschenrechte* (Frankfurt, Suhrkamp) 29–47
Hofmann, E (2007) *Abwägung im Recht. Chancen und Grenzen numerischer Verfahren im Öffentlichen Recht* (Tübingen, Mohr)
Hohfeld, W N (1923) *Fundamental Legal Conceptions as Applied in Legal Reasoning and Other Legal Essays* (New Haven, Yale University Press)

Holländer, P (1993) *Rechtsnorm, Logik und Wahrheitswerte* (Baden-Baden, Nomos)
Honneth, A (2000) *Das Andere der Gerechtigkeit* (Frankfurt, Suhrkamp)
Hurley, S (1989) *Natural Reasons* (New York/Oxford, Oxford University Press)
Iglesias Vila, M (2001) *Facing Judicial Discretion: Legal Knowledge and Right Answer Revisited* (Dordrecht, Kluwer)
Iosa, J F (2011) 'La estructura del conflicto entre autoridad y autonomía' *Analisi e Diritto* 31
Jansen, N (1997) 'Die Abwägung von Grundrechten' 36 *Der Staat* 27
—— (1998a) *Die Struktur der Gerechtigkeit* (Baden-Baden, Nomos)
—— (1998b) 'The Validity of Public Morality' 84 *ARSP* 1
Jestaedt, M (1999) *Grundrechtsentfaltung im Gesetz* (Tübingen, Mohr)
Kain, P (2004) 'Self Legislation in Kant's Moral Philosophy' 83 *Archiv für Geschichte der Philosophie* 257
Kamm, F (2001) 'Conflicts of Rights: Typology, Methodology and Nonconsequentialism' 7 *Legal Theory* 239
—— (2002) 'Rights' in J Coleman and S Shapiro (eds), *Oxford Handbook of Jurisprudence and Philosophy of Law* (Oxford, Oxford University Press)
Kamp, G (2001) *Logik und Deontik* (Paderborn, Mentis)
Kant, I (1996a) 'Groundwork of the Metaphysics of Morals' in *Practical Philosophy: The Cambridge Edition to the Works of Immanuel Kant* (M J Gregor (transl and ed), Cambridge, Cambridge University Press)
—— (1996b) 'Critique of Practical Reason' in *Practical Philosophy: The Cambridge Edition to the Works of Immanuel Kant* (M J Gregor (transl and ed), Cambridge, Cambridge University Press)
Kaufmann Marcel (1997) *Politische Gestaltungsfreiheit als Rechtsprinzip* 8 *Staatswissenschaften und Staatspraxis* 161
Kaufmann, Matthias (1996) *Rechtsphilosophie* (Freiburg/München, Alber)
Kelsen, H (1960) *Reine Rechtslehre*, 2nd edn (Deuticke, Vienna) (transl *The Pure Theory of Law* (Berkeley/Los Angeles, University of California Press, 1967))
Kern, L and Nida-Rümelin, J (1994) *Logik kollektiver Entscheidungen* (Oldenbourg, München, Wien)
Klatt, M (2004) *Theorie der Wortlautgrenze. Semantische Normativität in der juristischen Argumentation* (Baden-Baden, Nomos)
Koch, H-J and Rüssmann, H (1982) *Juristische Begründungslehre* (München, Beck)
Koller, P (2005) 'Zur Theorie des rechtlichen Stufenbaus' in *Hans Kelsen. Staatsrechtslehrer und Rechtstheoretiker des 20. Jahrhunderts* (S Paulson and M Stolleis (eds), Tübingen, Mohr) 106–21
Korsgaard C M (1996) 'The Authority of Reflection' in *The Sources of Normativity* (Cambridge, Cambridge University Press) 90–130
Kramer, M (1998) 'Rights Without Trimmings' in M Kramer, N Simmonds and H Steiner, *A Debate over Rights: Philosophical Enquiries* (Oxford, Oxford University Press) 7–111
(1999) *In Defense of Legal Positivism: Law Without Trimmings* (Oxford/New York, Oxford University Press)
Larenz, K (1983) *Methodenlehre der Rechtswissenschaft*, 5th edn (Berlin/Heidelberg/New York, Springer)
Lindahl, L (1977) *Position and Change* (Dordrecht, Reidel)
MacCormick, N (1977) 'Rights in Legislation' in P M S Hacker and J Raz (eds), *Law, Morality, Society* (Oxford, Clarendon Press) 189–209
—— (1978) *Legal Reasoning and Legal Theory* (Oxford, Clarendon Press)

——(2005) *Rhetorics and the Rule of Law* (Oxford, Oxford University Press)
MacIntyre, A (1985) *After Virtue*, 2nd edn (Notre Dame, University of Notre Dame Press)
Marmor, A (1992) *Interpretation and Legal Theory* (Oxford, Clarendon Press)
——(2001) *Positive Law and Objective Values* (Oxford, Clarendon Press)
Martin, R (1993) *A System of Rights* (Oxford, Clarendon Press)
McDowell, J (1998) *Mind, Value, and Reality* (Cambridge, MA/London, Harvard University Press)
Mele, A R (1995), *Autonomous Agents: From Self-Control to Autonomy* (Oxford, Oxford University Press)
Merkl, A (1931) 'Prolegommena zu einer Theorie des rechtlichen Stufenbaus' in A Verdross (ed), *Festschrift für H. Kelsen* (Vienna, ) 252–94
Moore, M (2004) *Objectivity in Ethics and Law* (Ashgate/Dartmouth, Burlington)
Nagel, T (1991) *Equality and Partiality* (New York/Oxford, Oxford University Press)
——(1995) 'Personal Rights and Public Space' 24 *Philosophy and Public Affairs* 83
Nagl-Docetal, H (2003) 'Autonomie zwischen Selbstbestimmung und Selbstgesetzgebung' in H Pauer-Studer and H Nagl-Docetal (eds), *Freiheit, Gleichheit, Autonomie* (Vienna/Berlin, Oldenbourg/Akademie Verlag) 296–326
Neuner, J (2005) *Die Rechtsfindung contra legem*, 2nd edn (München, Beck)
Nino, C S (1991) *The Ethics of Human Rights* (Oxford, Oxford University Press)
——(1996) *The Constitution of Deliberative Democracy* (New Haven/London, Yale University Press)
Nute, D (1997) 'Apparent Obligation' in D Nute (ed), *Defeasible Deontic Logic* (Dordrecht/Boston/London, Kluwer) 286–315
Paton, H J (1958) *The Categorical Imperative: A Study in Kant's Moral Philosophy*, 3rd edn (London, Hutchinson)
Parfit, D (1984) *Reasons and Persons* (Oxford/New York, Oxford University Press)
——(2006) 'Normativity' in R Shafer-Landau (ed), *Oxford Studies in Metaethics* (Oxford, Clarendon Press) vol 1, 325–80
——(2011) *On What Matters* (Oxford, Oxford University Press)
Patterson, D (1996) *Truth and Law* (Oxford, Oxford University Press)
Patzig, G (1994) 'Philosophische Bemerkungen zum Begriff der Autonomie' in G Patzig, *Gesammelte Schriften I: Grundlagen der Ethik* (Göttingen, Wallstein Verlag) 174–89
Paulson, S L (1990) 'Kelsen on Legal Interpretation' 10 *Legal Studies* 136
——(2006) 'On the Background and Significance of Radbruch's Post-War Papers' 26 *Oxford Journal of Legal Studies* 17
Pavlakos, G (2007) *Our Knowledge of the Law: Objectivity and Practice in Legal Theory* (Oxford/Portland, Hart)
——(2008) 'Non-Individualism, Rights, and Practical Reason' 21 *Ratio Juris* 66
——(2010) 'Law, Normativity and the Model of Norms' in S Bertea and G Pavlakos (eds), *Essays on Normativity in Law and Morality* (Oxford, Hart)
Peczenik, A (1989) *On Law and Reason* (Dordrecht/Boston/London, Kluwer)
Perry, S (2009) 'Beyond the Distinction between Positivism and Non-Positivism' 22 *Ratio Juris* 311
Postema, G J (1996) 'Law's Autonomy and Public Practical Reason' in R P George (ed), *The Autonomy of Law: Essays on Legal Positivism* (Oxford, Clarendon Press)
Prakken, H (1997) *Logical Tools for Modelling Legal Argument: A Study of Defeasible Reasoning in Law* (Dordrecht/Boston/London, Kluwer)
Putnam, H (1995) 'Are Moral and Legal Values Made or Discovered?' 1 *Legal Theory* 5

Raabe, M (1998) *Grundrechte und Erkenntnis* (Baden-Baden, Nomos)
Radbruch, G (2001) *Rechtsphilosophie*, 3rd edn (1932) in G Radbruch, *Rechtsphilosophie, Studienausgabe*, 2nd edn (R Dreier and S L Paulson (eds), Heidelberg, C.F Müller) (transl in Kurt Wilk, *The Legal Philosophies of Lask, Radbruch, and Dabin* (Cambridge, MA, Harvard University Press 1950))
——(2006) 'Statutory Lawlessness and Superstatutory Law' 26 *Oxford Journal of Legal Studies* (orig. 'Gesetzliches Unrecht und übergesetzliches Recht' (1946) *Süddeutsche Juristenzeitung* 105)
Rawls, J (1971) *A Theory of Justice* (Oxford, Oxford University Press)
Rawls, J (1985) 'Justice as Fairness: Political not Metaphysical' 14 *Philosophy and Public Affairs* 223
——(1988) 'The Priority of Right and Ideas of the Good' 17 *Philosophy and Public Affairs* 251
——(1993) *Political Liberalism* (New York/Chichester, Columbia University Press)
——(1995) 'Reply to Habermas' *Journal of Philosophy* 132
Raz, J (1972) 'Legal Principles and the Limits of Law' 81 *Yale Law Journal* 823
——(1979) *The Authority of Law* (Oxford, Clarendon Press)
——(1983) *Theory of a Legal System*, 2nd edn (Oxford, Clarendon Press)
——(1986) *The Morality of Freedom* (Oxford, Clarendon Press)
——(1994) *Ethics in the Public Domain* (Oxford, Clarendon Press)
——(1996) 'Intention in Interpretation' in R P George (ed), *The Autonomy of Law* (Oxford, Oxford University Press) 249–86
——(1999) *Practical Reason and Norms*, 3rd edn (Oxford, Oxford University Press)
——(2007) 'The Argument from Justice, or How Not to Reply to Legal Positivism' in G Pavlakos (ed), *Law, Rights and Discourse: The Legal Philosophy of Robert Alexy* (Oxford/Portland, Hart) 17–35
Reath, A (2006) *Agency and Autonomy in Kant's Moral Theory, Selected Essays* (Oxford, Clarendon Press)
Richards, D A J (1981) 'Rights and Autonomy' 92 *Ethics* 3
Riecken, J (2003) *Verfassungsgerichtsbarkeit in der Demokratie. Grenzen verfassungsgerichtlicher Kontrolle unter besonderer Berücksichtigung von John Hart Elys prozeduraler Theorie der Repräsentationsverstärkung* (Berlin, Duncker & Humblot)
Riehm, T (2006) *Abwägungsentscheidungen in der praktischen Rechtsanwendung. Argumentation – Beweis – Wertung* (München, Beck)
Rivers, J (2006) 'Proportionality and Variable Intensity of Review' 65 *CLJ* 174
——(2007) 'Proportionality, Discretion and the Second Law of Balancing' in G Pavlakos (ed), *Law, Rights and Discourse: The Legal Philosophy of Robert Alexy* (Oxford/Portland, Hart) 189–206
Rodriguez, J (2002) *Lógica de los sistemas jurídicos* (Madrid, Centro de Estudios Políticos y Constitucionales)
Rodriguez-Blanco, V (2004) *Meta-Ethics, Moral Objectivity and Law* (Paderborn, Mentis)
Rorty, R (1993) 'Human Rights, Rationality, and Sentimentality' in S Shute and S Hurley (eds), *On Human Rights: The Oxford Amnesty Lectures* (New York, Basic Books) 111–34
Schneewind, J (1998) *The Invention of Autonomy* (New York, Cambridge University Press)
Schroeder, M (2008) *Being For: Evaluating the Semantic Program of Expressivism* (Oxford, Clarendon Press)
——(2010) *Noncognitivism in Ethics* (London/New York, Routledge)
Searle, J (1995) *The Construction of Social Reality* (New York, The Free Press)

Sen, A and Williams, B (1973) 'Introduction: Utilitarianism and Beyond' in A Sen and B Williams (eds), *Utilitarianism and Beyond* (Cambridge, Cambridge University Press) 1–21
Shafer-Landau, R (2003) *Moral Realism: A Defence* (Oxford, Clarendon Press)
Shapiro, S (2009) 'Was Inclusive Legal Positivism Founded on a Mistake?' 22 *Ratio Juris* 326
Sieckmann, J-R (1990) *Regelmodelle und Prinzipienmodelle des Rechtssystems* (Baden-Baden, Nomos)
——(1992) 'Legal System and Practical Reason' 5 *Ratio Juris* 288
——(1994) 'Semantischer Normbegriff und Normbegründung' 80 *ARSP* 227
——(1995) 'Zur Begründung von Abwägungsurteilen' 26 *Rechtstheorie* 45
——(1997a) 'Richtigkeit und Objektivität im Prinzipienmodell' 83 *ARSP* 14
——(1997b) 'Zur Analyse von Normkonflikten und Normabwägungen' in *Analyomen 2. Proceedings of the 2nd Conference 'Perspectives in Analytical Philosophy'* (Berlin/New York, de Gruyter) vol III, 349–56
——(1998) *Modelle des Eigentumsschutzes* (Baden-Baden, Nomos)
——(2003a) 'On the Tension between Moral Autonomy and Rational Justification' 16 *Ratio Juris* 105
——(2003b) 'Why Non-monotonic Logic is Inadequate to Represent Balancing Arguments' 11 *Artificial Intelligence and Law* 211
——(2004) 'Autonome Abwägung' 90 *ARSP* 66
——(2005) 'Principles as Normative Arguments' in C Dahlman and W Krawietz (eds), *Values, Rights and Duties in Legal and Philosophical Discourse*, 21 *Rechtstheorie Beiheft* 197
——(2007a) 'The Concept of Autonomy' in T Gizbert-Studnicki and J Stelmach (eds), *Law and Legal Cultures in the 21st Century: Diversity and Unity* (Cracow, Oficina/Kluwers) 149–70
——(2007b) 'Human Rights and the Claim to Correctness in the Theory of Robert Alexy' in G Pavlakos (ed), *Law, Rights and Discourse: The Legal Philosophy of Robert Alexy* (Oxford/Portland, Hart) 189–205
——(2009a) *Recht als normatives System* (Baden-Baden, Nomos)
——(2009b) 'Probleme der Prinzipientheorie der Grundrechte' in L Clérico and J Sieckmann (eds), *Grundrechte, Prinzipien und Argumentation. Studien zur Rechtstheorie Robert Alexys* (Baden-Baden, Nomos) 39–66
——(2010a) 'The Theory of Principles: A Framework for Autonomous Reasoning' in M Borowski (ed), *On the Nature of Principles*, 119 *ARSP-Beiheft* 49
——(2010b) 'Balancing, Optimisation, and Alexy's "Weight Formula"' in J Sieckmann (ed), *Legal Reasoning: The Methods of Balancing*, 124 *ARSP-Beiheft* 103
——(2011) 'Prinzipien, ideales Sollen und normative Argumente' 97 *ARSP* 178
Simmonds, N E (1998) 'Rights at the Cutting Edge' in M Kramer, N E Simmonds and H Steiner, *A Debate over Rights* (Oxford, Oxford University Press) 113–232
Slote, M (1989) *Beyond Optimizing* (Cambridge, MA/London, Harvard University Press)
Somek, A (2006) *Rechtliches Wissen* (Frankfurt, Suhrkamp)
Soper, Ph (1996) 'Law's Normative Claims' in R P George (ed), *The Autonomy of Law* (Oxford, Oxford University Press) 215–47
Spaak, T (2007) *Guidance and Constraint: The Action-Guiding Capacity of Theories of Legal Reasoning* (Uppsala, Iustus Förlag)
Spector, H (1994) *Autonomy and Rights* (Oxford, Oxford University Press)
Stavropoulos, N (1996) *Objectivity in Law* (Oxford, Clarendon Press)
——(2009) 'The Relevance of Coercion: Some Preliminaries' 22 *Ratio Juris* 339

Steiner, H (1994) *An Essay on Rights* (Oxford/Cambridge, MA, Blackwell)
—— (1998) 'Working Rights' in M Kramer, N E Simmonds and H Steiner, *A Debate Over Rights* (Oxford, Oxford University Press) 233–301
Stemmer, P (2008) *Normativität. Eine ontologische Untersuchung* (Berlin/New York, de Gruyter)
Stück, H (1998) 'Subsumtion und Abwägung' 84 *ARSP* 405
Stuhlmann-Laeisz, R (1983) *Das Sein-Sollen-Problem* (Stuttgart/Bad Cannstatt, Frommann-holzboog)
Székessy, L (2003) *Gerechtigkeit und inklusiver Rechtspositivismus* (Berlin, Duncker & Humblot)
Thomson, J J (2008) *Normativity* (Chicago/La Salle, Open Court)
Trapp, R (1988) *'Nicht-klassischer' Utilitarismus. Eine Theorie der Gerechtigkeit* (Frankfurt, Klostermann)
Tugendhat, E (1993) *Vorlesungen über Ethik* (Frankfurt, Suhrkamp)
Tugendhat, E (1998) 'Die Kontroverse um die Menschenrechte' in S Gosepath and G Lohmann (eds), *Philosophie der Menschenrechte* (Frankfurt, Suhrkamp) 48–61
Tuori, K (2002) *Critical Legal Positivism* (Ashgate, Burlington)
Waluchow, W (1994) *Inclusive Legal Positivism* (Oxford, Clarendon Press)
Walzer, M (1994) *Thick and Thin: Moral Arguments at Home and Abroad* (Notre Dame/Indiana, University of Notre Dame Press)
Wang, P-H (2003) *Defeasibility in der juristischen Begründung* (Baden-Baden, Nomos)
—— (2010) 'Principles as Ideal Ought: Semantic Considerations on the Logical Structure of Principles' in J Sieckmann (ed), *Legal Reasoning: The Methods of Balancing*, 124 *ARSP-Beiheft* 29
Watkins-Bienz, R M (2004) *Die Hart-Dworkin Debatte. Ein Beitrag zu den internationalen Kontroversen der Gegenwart* (Berlin, Duncker & Humblot)
Wedgwood, R (2007) *The Nature of Normativity* (Oxford, Clarendon Press)
Weinberger, O (1996) *Alternative Handlungstheorie* (Wien, Böhlau)
Wellman, C (1995) *Real Rights* (New York/Oxford, Oxford University Press)
—— (1997) *An Approach to Rights* (Dordrecht, Kluwer)
Wildt, A (1982) *Autonomie und Anerkennung. Hegels Moralitätskritik im Lichte seiner Fichte-Rezeption* (Stuttgart, Klett-Cotta)
Williams, B (1973) 'A Critique of Utilitarianism' in J J C Smart and B Williams (eds), *Utilitarianism For and Against* (Cambridge, Cambridge University Press)
Wimsatt, W C (2006) 'Inconsistencies, Optimization and Satisficing: Steps towards a Philosophy for Limited Beings, Comment on Russell Hardin' in C Engel and L Daston (eds), *Is there Value in Inconsistency?* (Baden-Baden, Nomos) 201–20
Wolff, R P (1998) *In Defense of Anarchism* (Berkeley, University of California Press)
Wood, A (2008) *Kantian Ethics* (Cambridge, Cambridge University Press)
Wright, G H von (1963) *Norm and Action* (London/New York, Routledge & Kegan Paul)
Zoglauer, T (1998) *Normkonflikte – zur Logik und Rationalität ethischen Argumentierens* (Stuttgart/Bad Cannstatt, Frommann-holzboog)
Zuleta, H R (2008) *Normas y justificación. Una investigación lógica* (Barcelona, Marcial Pons)

# Index

www.ingramcontent.com/pod-product-compliance
Ingram Content Group UK Ltd.
Pitfield, Milton Keynes, MK11 3LW, UK
UKHW020832290926
15470UKWH00009B/1859/J

9 781849 463461